STUDIES IN AMERICAN HISTORY

XI

John Gilbert Winant

HE WALKED ALONE

ALONE

A BIOGRAPHY OF JOHN GILBERT WINANT

BY

BERNARD BELLUSH

The City College
The City University of New York

FOREWORD

BY

ALLAN NEVINS

1968

MOUTON

THE HAGUE · PARIS

Printed in the Netherlands by Mouton & Co., Printers, The Hague

For Gerry and Debbi

FOREWORD

by

Allan Nevins

A Letter to John G. Winant

My dear Chief — for you were my Chief for a time in the American Embassy in London, as you were Chief to others there, and to numerous men and women at different times in the Social Security Administration, in the International Labor Office, and in the staff-rooms of the United Nations Economic and Social Council. It was always more than a pleasure to work under your gentle sway; it was an inspiration.

It is good to know that at last we have in this book about your career a study that is competent, penetrating, honest in the exacting meaning that you would give the word, and appreciative. You always puzzled us a little, not merely because you were too shyly unassuming and tongue-tied to explain yourself, but because there seemed so great a disproportion between your abilities, hopes, and aspirations, and your achievements. We never doubted that you were one of the great idealists of your time, and that you had half-hidden qualities of spiritual leadership that you would eventually use in shaping measures and activities of large practical scope. You never did, although you occupied offices, as suggested above, in which you found or created valuable opportunities.

You were not without ambition; you even thought once or twice that the Presidency might come within your reach, and in 1944 you expected, with good warrant, that you might be named for Vice-President. You did not lack courage, as you showed when you grappled with the hard political bosses of New Hampshire. (Do you remember the time Lord Halifax, the British Foreign Minister, came into your Embassy office, where I happened to be sitting, to ask if you could not act to get the American press to suppress news of anti-British riots in India in the interests of Anglo-American amity, and how decisively you rejected the absurd proposal and put him in his place?) You were capable of making important friendships; with Woodrow Wilson, for example; with Franklin D. Roosevelt (and still more, Eleanor Roosevelt); and with Winston Churchill.

You could never make an electrifying speech, but, like Ernest Bevin, you could say a few stumbling words so plainly from the heart that they gave a large audience a sense of trust and liking. As a writer, you were never polished, original, or forceful, and your one attempt at a large important book in your reminiscent *Grosvenor Square* struck you yourself as a failure. Yet your devotion to two great aims — a larger and kindlier democracy at home in America, and a stronger spirit of international concord in the world, was so impressive, and your elevation of spirit was so marked, that we kept hoping that you would grasp larger opportunities, and use them with a more practical acumen than you had previously proved yourself to possess. Why did you disappoint us, and yourself? The answer to this question is, of course, complex, and only a careful reading of this book can provide clues to it.

Perhaps, some of it is suggested in familiar images of John Bunyan. His Pilgrim, by high aims and hard labor, avoiding the Slough of Despond and the Valley of Humiliation, did admirably until he came to a fearsome place called Doubting Castle, owned by a Giant Despair whose consort was named Diffidence. We cannot read this volume, so fully researched and well-written, without feeling that you, from your early days of student failure at Princeton to your mature days in Washington, London, and Geneva, suffered from disabling perplexities and self-mistrust until at last you found yourself a bankrupt in health, money, and political power, shut into Doubting Castle with Giant Despair and Diffidence, finding your only way out by the terrible path of suicide. Is this true, O Chief?

Or was it that, like Hamlet, you found that the times were hopelessly out of joint — that, as one of the best idealists and most truly humane men of your age, you were laboring in an environment that could offer you nothing but hopelessly cruel frustrations? Why, then, did you not summon a more iron fortitude? Could you not have added still more splendid chapters to those you had already written? Reading this record, we believe that you might have added new chapters of importance and heartening quality. Alas! — Why not? Or would you have been broken as your revered leader Woodrow Wilson was broken? But here we find one of the great values of this book. In its study of the times, of American character and leadership, and of the failure of many a gallant hope and effort, it repeatedly leaves us exclaiming, Alas! Why?

Huntington Library
San Marino, California
December 19, 1967

TABLE OF CONTENTS

INTRODUCTION

Less than three miles from John G. Winant's home on Pleasant Street in Concord, stood the gleaming, gold-domed State House of New Hampshire. In the opposite direction, nearby, nestled at the base of the rolling foothills of the White Mountains, were the sprawling buildings of St. Paul's Episcopal preparatory school.

During the early decades of the twentieth century Winant's father, seeking to emulate wealthier friends and business associates, sent his four sons to St. Paul's. Three of them absorbed the conservative culture and goals of more affluent classmates; John Gilbert, the eldest, chose, instead, to become an ardent exponent of progressive reform movements. St. Paul's School remained for him, at least in his memories, the one place which fulfilled his yearnings for peace and happiness. There he felt wanted and understood; there he was welcome; there he found refuge. When his collegiate world crashed around him, he returned to St. Paul's to teach and mature his tremendous gift — to inspire, to stimulate, to challenge, to mold character.

St. Paul's lay in the heart of Concord's variegated Ward Seven and the voters in this Ward began the schoolmaster's public career by electing him as a Republican to the largest House of Representatives in the nation, and then to one of the smallest Senates. From Concord he journeyed to Paris in 1917 to enlist in the Air Service. By 1920, he was back at St. Paul's with a beautiful bride, and then soon again in the State Legislature. In 1924 the voters of New Hampshire sent Gil Winant to the State House as the youngest Governor in the nation. Twice more, Granite State citizens elected Winant as their Chief Executive during the most tragic domestic crisis in the nation's history. From Ward Seven, the three-time Governor moved on as a reformer for laboring men and women throughout the world, heading the International Labor Organization in Geneva, Switzerland. Less than two years after a second world holocaust enveloped mankind, Winant returned briefly to renew himself among friends in

Ward Seven, on the way to his new diplomatic post in London.

This history teacher never really left the soft, green hills of New Hampshire which rolled gently away from the tall windows of his Pleasant Street mansion. He never escaped St. Paul's, for his thoughts constantly turned to happier days as student and schoolmaster. And, after years of service in London left him physically exhausted and mentally despondent, as a lonely, brooding and harassed man he returned to Ward Seven in Concord to take his own life.

SOME COMMENTS ON ACKNOWLEDGEMENTS AND SOURCES

Many individuals, from all walks of life, and from many countries, have furnished the writer with invaluable information and insights. Whether they were charwomen at the American Embassy in London, three Prime Ministers of Great Britain, a President of the United States, or taxi cab drivers and shopkeepers in Concord, New Hampshire, they gave freely of their time and recollections. Many are identified later, along with their relationship to Winant. To all of them, including those not cited, go profound appreciation for an enriching scholarly and human experience.

The writer hopes that others will not be affronted when he singles out a limited number for special mention. The Winant family was at all times helpful. Maurine Mulliner, a colleague and personal friend of Winant, proved a constant tower of strength, an invaluable source, and a wise counsellor. The late Robert Perkins Bass, venerable patron saint of an earlier New Hampshire progressivism, and his close friend and associate, John R. McLane, were crucial for the political and social history of their state. Orol Mear's lifetime devotion to Winant, as a member of the household staff since the early 1930's, enabled her to contribute vivid and meaningful recollections. Carol R. Lubin supplied vital letters and background of the International Labor Organization.

Allan Nevins, mentor to a generation of American historians, first convinced the writer to assume the task of independent biographer. Subsequent research among archives, and memorable meetings with involved personalities of the twentieth century, facilitated not only a kaleidoscopic view of American progressivism, but a reliving of the fascinating years of the New Deal at home, as well as the tragic era of World War II abroad.

Herman Kahn, former Director of the Franklin D. Roosevelt Library at Hyde Park, New York, now at the National Archives, was, as always, a gracious, helpful, and knowing colleague. The Historical Division staff at the State Department proved, at all times, cooperative. In contrast, its counterpart in the Army of the United States insisted that the writer undergo fingerprinting in advance of research. This he refused to do, for he deemed it an affront to responsible scholars. The Washington Office of the International Labor Organization of the United Nations made available its confidential records of private meetings of the Governing Body, and of its Emergency Committee, for the period of Winant's involvement. Professor Fred Israel kindly shared his notes of the Breckinridge Long Diary prior to publication. I am indebted to Robert P. Bass, Jr., for granting me access to his father's papers at Dartmouth College.

Warmest appreciation is extended to Allan Nevins, and to those close friends who read the manuscript at different stages and saved the writer from many mistakes — Fred Israel, a warm-hearted and strengthening colleague at City College; poetess Suzanne Henig of the State University of New York at New Paltz; and Denise Rathbun with her incisive editorial criticisms. And then there is an extremely knowledgeable, but unknown, Reader. The remaining errors are, of course, the writer's alone.

The greatest debt is due Jewel Bellush, an endlessly stimulating colleague for the last two decades. With her interdisciplinary background in American history and political science, she catalyzed the writer to ever greater challenges in the ebb and flow of this work. Gerry and Debbi Bellush never stopped rooting from the sidelines, and are now thoroughly indoctrinated in proof reading, and in the need for footnotes and index.

Grateful appreciation is extended the American Philosophical Society, and The City College Research Fund, for their multiple grants which helped sustain the writer during sabbatical and research leaves. The Baker Library at Dartmouth College served as a scholarly haven each summer, while the History Department and library of the University of California at Berkeley were tremendously helpful during a sabbatical leave in 1959-60.

More work can, and must, be done by psychologists, political scientists, and other social scientists. Winant's governorship, for example, merits fuller development as a case study of a state's reponse to social, political, as well as economic ills and crises.

To avoid repeating the many secondary works already cited in footnotes, the reader is referred in the bibliographical section to the primary sources located in archives, or supplied by family and friends of Winant, along with the relationship of some of the individuals interviewed.

BERNARD BELLUSH

Utrecht, The Netherlands
May 1, 1967

CHAPTER I

"TALL, SENSITIVE, WITH PIERCING EYES"

St. Paul's School was located in Concord, New Hampshire's capital city. Without woolen and cotton mills, Concord had developed slowly and, in contrast to other industrialized New England communities, retained an "English stock free from the influx of foreign mill workers".[1] Only when the State Legislature was in session during the first few months of odd-numbered years did a placid Concord suddenly assume the air of a bustling community.

But the school was isolated from even this peaceful outside world, the expanse of school property lying within a great bend of the peaceful Turkey River which meandered lazily through the surrounding countryside and then paused, momentarily, in a lovely pond on the campus. Some sixty years after its pre-Civil War founding, close to one hundred buildings of varied sizes and uses were spread out on an attractive campus. For almost nine months of every year, long stretches of forest and undergrowth, and lovely tree-shaded paths, echoed to the voices of over 300 boys and developing young men who came from all parts of the nation to prepare for college. The bulk of students, however, represented four states in the Middle Atlantic and New England regions.[2]

Two large, unprepossessing T-shaped dormitories which dominated a segment of the campus housed most of the students. From their classes, playing fields, or nearby library, they would cross the campus at various times of the day to return to their quarters. Most of them slept in simple, unadorned cubicles seven by four feet, furnished with a dresser, a wooden chair and a narrow iron bed. Primarily the children of prosperous entrepreneurs or professionals, their living facilities could not be deemed luxurious.

When Frederick Winant's sons first came to St. Paul's, the institu-

[1] Arthur S. Pier, *St. Paul's School, 1855-1934* (New York, Charles Scribner's Sons, 1934), p. 361.
[2] T. S. Matthews, *Name and Address* (New York, Simon and Schuster, 1960), p. 146; St. Paul's School, *The Annual Report of the Rector to the Corporation of the School* (Concord, N.H., November, 1917), p. 17.

tion, like most preparatory schools of the time, lacked much in the way of high scholastic standards and human relationships. Its intellectual climate was as Spartan as its dormitories. Winant later recalled that he had first found the institution a "home of old world intrigue and what idealism there was might be described as ingrown. There were exceptions, ... but by and large manners counted for more than morals, and personal charm was rated far above intellectual attainments and justice gave way to baser considerations."[3] Though the school would improve under the rectorship of Dr. Samuel S. Drury, several years were to elapse before he would take over, and still more time before he could make his influence felt.

Less than 300 years earlier, Dutch ancestors of John Gilbert — who would be called Gil by his closest friends — first settled in the new world. The family name finally became Winant after some half dozen variations. In 1758, Pieter Winantse was buried on Staten Island in New York harbor at the age of ninety-six. Seventy-three years later Cornelius Winant was born, his direct descendant and grandfather of John Gilbert.[4]

In the late eighteenth century, some Scotch-English Gilberts crossed the ocean and settled in the village of Ridgefield in western Connecticut. On the eve of the Civil War one of their descendants, John Adams Gilbert, moved to New York City in search of marriage, greater excitement, and enlarged business opportunities. By November 1864, Jeanette Laura was born to prospering Gilbert and his wife, now the owners of a wholesale hardware establishment. Within seven months, Cornelius Winant, a successful builder of sailing vessels in Brooklyn, announced the birth of a son, Frederick. Twenty-one years later, climaxing a two-year courtship, handsome Frederick married attractive Jeanette Laura.

[3]   John G. Winant to S. S. Drury, written between April 19 and May 1, 1921. This is part of a letter written to the Rector, Dr. Drury, who was considering an offer to become Rector of Trinity Church in New York, to which he had been elected April 18. Dr. Drury rejected the offer on May 1, 1921. Also, Roger W. Drury, *Drury and St. Paul's* (Boston, Little, Brown and Co., 1964), pp. 59-62.
[4]   Bleecker Bangs, *Our Ancestors* (Brooklyn, N.Y., Kings County Journal, 1896), pp. 94-111; *The New York Genealogical and Biographical Record* (New York, New York Genealogical and Biographical Society, 1879), X, 24; Charles W. Lenz and William T. Davis, *Staten Island and Its People. A History, 1609-1929* (New York, Lewis Historical Publishing Co., Inc., 1933), p. 204. Also, interviews with Frederick Winant, Jr., on December 8, 1959, June 15, 1960, and telephone conversation on March 3, 1962; Frederick Winant, Jr., to author, August 2, 1960, March 7 and July 26, 1962.

Jeanette Winant was a forceful and, at times, domineering individual who yearned for the life and amenities of more affluent members of the urban middle class. Shy, reserved and conformist in thinking and behavior, Frederick had dropped out of Columbia College to form a real estate brokerage firm. But not until he was admitted to partnership with Douglas Robinson did he succeed financially. Thereafter, Mr. Winant devoted himself to fulfilling his wife's material desires and the needs of a burgeoning family.

The Winants had four sons. John Gilbert, the eldest, was born February 23, 1889, in a rented brownstone house on New York City's fashionable East Sixty-ninth Street, between Fifth and Madison Avenues. Cornelius became the youngest after his birth in mid-June 1895.[5]

Throughout their childhood years, the Winant boys were a closely knit group. After school hours, they usually played together in the quiet residential area fronting the family brownstone at 103 East Seventy-first Street, which Mr. Winant had purchased in 1899. At other times, the four boisterous brothers rushed off to nearby Central Park and clambered over rocks or played baseball in the springtime and football in the autumn.

Their home was a typically comfortable five-level brownstone crammed in between similar houses. Guests walked up a flight of stairs from the outside street level to a first floor hall from which could be observed a seldom used parlor on the left with a dining room in the rear. A small "l" served as the pantry, and a dumbwaiter brought up food from the basement kitchen. The second story contained a master bedroom and an every-day living room. The floor above was crowded with two large bedrooms, Gil and Clinton sharing the front one, Cornelius and Frederick the rear. The housekeeper was assigned a small room on the same level. The top floor had a large front room for unused furniture, clothes — and visiting guests — while two rear bedrooms housed maids, when employed. Much of the time Mr. Winant could afford a sleep-in servant.

As she reared the children in the milieu of politically conservative, upper middle class, protestant values and prejudices, the mother spent a little more than she should and showered her "darlings" with love and interest. As her first born, Gil was the "light" of her life and she indulged him over the years, neglecting to instill in him the need

[5]   The other sons were Clinton D., born 1890, and Frederick, Jr., 1892.

for disciplined devotion to academic studies or to any single task at hand. As a result, he acquired an unfortunate trait of generally doing only what he felt like. Mr. Winant, meanwhile, seemed unable, or preferred not, to stand up to his wife in most key decisions involving his children's development. He was increasingly portrayed by Mrs. Winant as the cause for her frequent headaches and being "so unkind I could not live with him". On one occasion she agreed to a temporary reconciliation, returning from residence in Concord where Gil was teaching, because she did not want the other children to live alone in their home in New York City with their father. Within days, however, she lamented, "I should never have left Gil".[6]

Shy and retiring like his father, Gil attended the Craigie Private Day School and then St. Bernard's in New York. From the start he had most difficulty with mathematics, science and foreign languages, subjects which required the greatest diligence and discipline of un-interrupted concentration. Even subjects he enjoyed became un-palatable, at times, because of the stultifying teaching methods. On the other hand, he could relax and be totally absorbed in reading for enjoyment. He was deeply influenced by biographies of Abraham Lincoln and, above all, by the writings of Charles Dickens which recorded the destructive impact of the Industrial Revolution upon growing children. Winant recalled, years later, how he recoiled at Dickens' description of the inhuman treatment accorded employees by industrial and commercial managers.[7]

Regardless of the children's educational commitments, and much before the end of the spring semester, mid-May signalled the departure of Mrs. Winant and her sons for extended summer vacations on Long Island, Connecticut, or Europe. Eventually, Mr. Winant purchased attractive hilltop acreage in South Salem, New York. This property, which remained a family possession through World War I, was topped by a ninety-foot water tower, frequently used by visitors and summer residents as a navigational aid to help them through the region's maze of back roads. From the pillared porch of their com-

---

[6] Interviews with Frederick Winant, Jr., December 8, 1959 and June 15, 1960. Handwritten comments by Mrs. Frederick Winant, Sr., on envelopes of letters sent her by John G. Winant postmarked August 9, 1916, October 30, 1916, and on other envelopes, lament her unhappy marriage. After the children had gone to college, there were frequent separations, finally culminating in divorce. Subsequent footnote references to John Gilbert Winant will be noted as JGW.
[7] Memo by Maurine Mulliner of JGW conversation, dated April 14, 1940.

fortable, three-story farmhouse, the Winants could look far out over the surrounding countryside.[8]

During these summer vacations, Mrs. Winant usually brought along a tutor to help Gil with the class work he had not mastered the previous year. When liberated by the teacher, young Winant and his brothers dashed off to play ball, climb trees, jump into haystacks, wander through the countryside, or watch the farm hands work the land. Once, as a tall, thin twelve-year-old, bubbling with ideas and planning ahead, Gil promoted a combined chicken-dog show, the profits to be used to purchase uniforms for the local band. Although his primary interest was his prize chickens, he included dogs in the exhibition because their owners had more money to spend. The band played during the all-day show and Gilbert's chickens won all the prizes. The total profit of this venture was $1.29.[9]

By the beginning of October, the Winant clan was back at the New York brownstone where the brothers delighted in sliding down the steep, curving balustrade at a dangerous speed, fortunate to land upright on the bottom level. For a few years, their shouts and laughter filled the house. However, quiet gradually enveloped the home as, one by one, the boys left for boarding school and then college. Thereafter, only on school holidays did life return to the Winant residence.

The earliest books the Winant boys remember seeing around the house were by Louisa May Alcott. Finally rebelling against being forced to read them, Gil, backed by his brothers, convinced his parents to purchase some manly, exciting works. Reading became more popular in the Winant household after the shelves were stocked with George A. Henty's adventure and war novels, including *Among Malay Pirates, Bonnie Prince Charlie, Redskin and Cowboy, With Cortez in Mexico,* and *With the Allies to Pekin.* Eventually, the boys graduated to Charles Dickens and other literary classics.

Too rarely involved in key decisions concerning his children, Mr. Winant displayed carelessness in the selection of a boarding school for his two oldest boys in 1904. After registering them for a preparatory academy in upstate New York and sending their trunks ahead in early September, Presbyterian Winant suddenly learned, to his horror, it was a Catholic school. In desperation, he turned to his

---

[8] "Where Are They Now? Henry Agard Wallace", *The New Yorker*, XXXVI, No. 26 (August 13, 1960), 62. This property was subsequently owned by the late Vice President Henry A. Wallace.
[9] Memo by Maurine Mulliner of JGW conversation, April 14, 1940.

business colleague, Douglas Robinson, at which time the baffled parent first learned of his partner's association with St. Paul's school as an alumnus and trustee. A speedy exchange of communications with the school's rector facilitated the hasty enrollment of Gil and brother Clinton.[10]

St. Paul's did not train its boys for general participation in business, professional or social life. Although the school's motto was "Let us learn here and now, the kind of knowledge that will stand us in good stead in the hereafter", the institute sought to prepare students for Harvard, Princeton and Yale entrance examinations. Learning often meant memorizing minute, isolated facts; this moved a visiting educator to comment that despite some evidence of a search for knowledge, this objective remained absent in most classes. He also noted that a significant percentage of examination failures were due to the fact that a large proportion of boys had not learned habits of application or industry. The discussion of ideas faltered in most classrooms, as did self-guidance, insuring poor retention of the material taught. Given the masters' generally autocratic and hostile manner and their dominance of the classroom, the poor results were scarcely surprising.[11]

These unfortunate school characteristics accentuated the weaknesses which Gil brought with him to St. Paul's as a Fourth Former in 1904. Instead of graduating in June 1907, failing grades forced him to spend an additional year at the institution, constantly under pressure to attain passing marks or to prepare for makeup examinations. The one subject which seemed to pose little difficulty was history.[12] He was slightly amused when the visiting Episcopal Archdeacon of Brooklyn urged him to consider entering the ministry. The struggling student quickly ruled out this suggestion as beyond his competency. He nervously anticipated failure in most tests, often with the remark

---

[10] Frederick Winant, Jr., to author, August 2, 1960, June 16, 1963, and interviews with F. Winant, Jr., December 8, 1959 and June 15, 1960. Also, Raymond S. Spencer to author, August 6, 1960.

[11] *Annual Report*, St. Paul's, 1916, pp. 49-50; Drury, *Drury and St. Paul's*, p. 63.

[12] JGW to Jeanette L. Winant, postmarked November 21, 1907; February 19, March 10, 23, 24, 28, 31, 1908. In the author's possession are duplicate records of every examination mark given Winant as well as his monthly ratings during his years at St. Paul's. As the Rector's secretary informed the author in 1960, ". . . I would hazard a guess that Mr. Winant was not a good student". Raymond P. Spencer to author, August 2, 1960.

that "Exams start tomorrow and am afraid I shall not do very well in them".[13]

Aware of Gil's academic difficulties, but not the explanation for them, the father likewise remained ignorant of other characteristics in his son's developing personality — an extreme sensitivity toward, and intense interest in, his fellow human beings in and outside of the classroom. Goaded on by reports from some of Gil's classmates and from his younger son, Clinton, who had graduated from St. Paul's the previous June, the father insisted that his oldest son could apply himself if he wished. In a momentary stance of independence, he wrote Rector Henry Ferguson that it would be best for Gil to leave school if he failed his forthcoming examinations in February 1908. Only then might he realize that he had to apply himself seriously for the Princeton entrance examinations with the aid of a tutor.[14]

Shortly after the February marks were posted, Gil's smallish scrawl informed his parents that he had failed three of six examinations. ". . . My head was so muddled by the time exams came from craming [sic], getting to bed to [sic] late at night and not taking enough exercise that I made a mess of my exams and did not do justice to myself. In fact I did not pass my geometry the one thing I have passed every time this year. . . ." However, he didn't feel too badly, for he had only narrowly failed two of the tests.[15]

In the face of his projected decision, the elder Winant was soon confronted with a pleading offspring who felt that the honor of the institution, in addition to his future career, depended upon his remaining at St. Paul's for the spring semester. Gil played an unique role for a St. Paul's student, and subsequently would as an alumnus. As Captain of the Halcyon intramural crew during his senior year, tradition automatically elevated him to the status of elder statesman of his graduating class. In addition, his understanding, dedication and devotion to fellow students, as well as to the Rector, would be rewarded with the School Medal for outstanding service. When student unrest developed in the Sixth Form, more than a year after Gil's graduation, the Rector would suggest to a somewhat incredulous new mathematics instructor that they await Winant's return from

[13] JGW to J. L. Winant, postmarked October 4 and December 13, 1907.
[14] Interview with Ernest M. Hopkins, July 6, 1953; Frederick Winant, Sr., to Henry Ferguson, January 11, 1908. St. Paul's School files.
[15] JGW to J. L. Winant, postmarked February 19, 1908; duplicate of grade records in author's possession.

Princeton for the annual Thanksgiving reunion. The headmaster confidently expected this "Old Boy" to solve the problem. Fifty-one
years later, this same mathematics instructor recalled how student
disaffection disappeared after young Winant had spoken with Sixth
Form leaders. The Rector had been correct; Gil might have difficulty
with academic courses but he could counsel wisely and effectively.[16]
Dr. Ferguson had early recognized that, despite Gil's shyness among
large groups, this tall, sensitive youth with piercing eyes had unique
qualities of leadership, and related extremely well with small numbers
of students and parents. As a result, young Winant was periodically
absent from classes he could ill afford to miss, at the behest of the
Rector, who invited him to escort visiting parents around the
campus.[17]

Gil also argued that his presence as captain and stroke of the
Halcyon intramural crew would insure victory on Racing Day when
competing crews would be cheered on by fellow students and visiting
parents. Besides, he still hoped to graduate in June. In a subsequent
letter to the Rector, Mr. Winant sadly acknowledged that he had "as
much backbone as a cup of custard" when, against his better judgment, he relented and permitted Gilbert to remain at St. Paul's.[18]

Gil failed four of five examinations immediately before the Easter
vacation. He even bungled the English test for which he had "never
worked harder", and for which he had probably done "more work
than anybody in the class".[19] Aware that he must pass in order to
graduate, Gilbert remained at St. Paul's for the first of his two-week
Easter vacation strenuously preparing for makeup examinations. His
efforts bore fruit in two tests, for he received "80" in plane geometry
and "78" in physics.[20]

[16]   Interview with Clarence E. Rexford, July 7, 1960, the mathematics instructor
involved.
[17]   H. Ferguson to F. Winant, Sr., May 7 and October 24, 1907. St. Paul's
School files. Interview with Frederick Winant, Jr., December 8, 1959. Frederick
entered St. Paul's in September 1907, and was a fellow student of his older
brother for a full academic year before the latter graduated in June 1908.
Gilbert's Sixth Form records indicate that he was absent from at least 46 classes
and late 75 times.
[18]   Frederick Winant, Sr., to Henry Ferguson, March 4, 1908. St. Paul's School
files.
[19]   JGW to J. L. Winant, postmarked March 23, 1908. He received 50 in plane
geometry, 44 in trigonometry, 21 in physics, and 42 in English. Duplicate of grade
records in author's possession.
[20]   Ibid., postmarked March 31, 1908. Duplicate of grade records in author's
records in author's possession.

With spring in evidence, one of the largest Race Day crowds of parents and cheering students, including Gil's mother, but not his father, assembled along the tree-lined shores of Long Pond. A close contest developed along much of the mile and a half straightaway during the major race between the Winant-led Halcyons and the Shattucks. As the finish line drew near, however, the Shattuck crew pulled steadily ahead to victory.

This defeat, crowning his persistent academic setbacks, underscored Gil's awareness that he could not learn easily and his oft-stated belief that failure would plague him every step of the way.[21] Throughout his life, there would be an undercurrent of insecurity or sense of failure, for he remained dissatisfied with, or uncertain about, his achievements as teacher, legislator, administrative executive or diplomat.

Gil managed to receive his diploma at graduation in June, 1908, and with it went the esteemed School Medal "for distinguished excellence in the performance of school duties." Though he loved St. Paul's, it left him ill-prepared for Princeton's entrance examinations. An unhappy Winant spent the following year studying with tutors.[22]

[21]   *Ibid.*, postmarked March 18, 1908; July 28, 1915.
[22]   Alumni Association of St. Paul's School, *Alumni Horae*, XXVII, No. 3 (Autumn, 1947), 79; Raymond P. Spencer to author, August 2, 1960. Duplicate grade records in author's possession. Also, JGW to J. L. Winant, postmarked July 20, 1908, and May 18, 1909.

CHAPTER II

"A RARE GIFT FOR INFLUENCING BOYS"

On Thanksgiving Day in 1909, an enterprising freshman entered the Engineering Library at Princeton to return a text he had recently borrowed. In the corner of a dimly lit room, he discovered a lone figure huddled over a pile of disordered books, an unhappy Winant, frustrated by an unresolved drafting problem.[1] This typified days at Princeton, where Gilbert labored unproductively with many courses. Restless and fearful as always when confronted with impending examinations, he would frequently steal away from studies and converse with friends in campus snack bars, or escape to history books and biographies of Abraham Lincoln.

During his freshman year he became embroiled in campus politics in support of his college's president, Woodrow Wilson. Some students had come to Princeton to study with such challenging professors as Wilson in political science, Alexander T. Ormond in philosophy, Samuel Ross Winans in Greek literature and Sanskrit, Andrew Fleming West in Latin, or Jesse Benedict Carter in Indo-Germanic philosophy. Many others, however, majored in football during fall semesters, drank beer during "bull" sessions and crammed before examinations. Prior to Professor Wilson's appointment to the presidency in 1902, a large part of each class displayed little effort and a minimum of scholarship.

In the process of converting Princeton from a small, parochial college into a modern institution of higher learning, Woodrow Wilson raised academic standards and initiated a preceptorial program which sought to introduce undergraduates to a more mature and independent method of study. In addition, he proposed abolishing the cherished eating clubs which, years before, had taken the place of fraternities, and replace them with common dining halls in residential

<hr>

[1] Interview with DeWitt C. Jones, December 16, 1959, who was Vice President of the Class of 1913; JGW to Jeanette L. Winant, postmarked November 18, 1909.

quadrangles. He also came into conflict with former President Grover Cleveland, and a small but potent nucleus among trustees, alumni and students, when he insisted that the proposed graduate school be located in the heart of the undergraduate campus.[2]

Living at the home of the Assistant Rector of Princeton's Episcopal Church, Gil became entangled in bitter arguments over these proposals. The Episcopal churchman violently opposed the college president's plans, while Gilbert remained equally as vehement in his support of them. The exchanges became so heated that he finally found it convenient to move to other quarters.[3]

While his involvement with this hotly debated issue did serve Gilbert well by crystalizing his liberal philosophy, it had a negative effect on his already faltering studies.

Nor did news from home leave him with much peace of mind. With all four Winant boys away, the brownstone on East Seventy-first Street became silent. Lonely without her children, and with few, if any, outside activities to occupy her, Mrs. Winant became increasingly embittered by marital disputes. Letters remained her primary contact with maturing sons whose interests and horizons steadily expanded beyond the family circle. Gil, however, became so disturbed by his mother's expressions of loneliness that he offered to leave college to join her at home and become a real estate broker like his father, even though the business world had never attracted him, because he couldn't bear to think of her "being all alone and not having any fun".[4]

At the end of his freshman year, Princeton dropped Gilbert from the Civil Engineering Program but readmitted him the following September as a candidate for the Bachelor of Science degree.[5]

Winant made little imprint upon most members of his Class of 1913. Some could recall a shy, retiring but perceptive personality. Others, like the world famed neurologist, Wilder G. Penfield, who according to his own words remained "a rather uncouth Westerner with scarcely any friends at all", recalled the occasion when Gil quickly

[2] Hardin Craig, *Woodrow Wilson at Princeton* (Norman, Oklahoma, University of Oklahoma Press, 1960), pp. 123, 128-29, 135-39, 144-46.
[3] Interview with Dr. Spenser Douglas, December 16, 1959. Douglas was a classmate of, though not close to, JGW.
[4] JGW to J. L. Winant, postmarked October 1909. Rest of postmark undecipherable.
[5] Howard W. Stepp to author, October 29, 1959.

hushed up a friend who sought to tease the budding surgeon about coming from a little known prep school.[6]

At the end of his sophomore year, Princeton dropped Gil for inferior grades. When he failed makeup examinations, the school denied him readmission. Appalled at the thought of entering an alien business world, Gilbert reached out to St. Paul's, the one place where he had been understood, where he had played a meaningful role. But there had been changes at the Concord school: Dr. Ferguson had been succeeded by Dr. Samuel S. Drury as Rector.

During his last winter at St. Paul's, Winant had heard the visiting Reverend Drury offer a Sunday sermon in the Chapel and later address the Missionary Society on his work in the Philippines. This well-built, eloquent personality who spoke with a low, vibrant voice so impressed Dr. Ferguson that he influenced the trustees to offer Drury the vice-Rectorship, with the right of succession to Rector. Drury accepted the appointment in April 1910, and little more than a year later became the headmaster.[7]

Dr. Ferguson's successor had been alerted to this alumnus. In fact, during the Thanksgiving reunion in 1910, Dr. Drury had had a long chat with him. When, therefore, young Winant suddenly appealed to Drury, in September 1911, insisting that he could not return to Princeton, the Rector eased the crisis by inviting him to join the St. Paul's staff — and a discouraged twenty-two-year-old Winant soon set out for Concord, the scene of happier days.

The embarrassed alumnus received a warm, understanding welcome from Dr. Drury, who placed him in charge of six boys in the Farm Building. Mornings he studied for February examinations at Princeton, afternoons he helped coach the Old Hundred's football team. In exchange, he received "board, lodging, light, heat, washing, etc., free". For the first time since entering Princeton, he regained a sense of belonging, a sense of purpose.[8]

During the ensuing months, Winant became totally absorbed with the students. The happiness and excitement he had almost forgotten

[6] Interviews with DeWitt C. Jones and Dr. Spenser Douglas, December 16, 1959; Wilder G. Penfield to author, May 25, 1962.
[7] Thirteen years later, Winant reminded Drury that "A boy at school has little to do with selecting a headmaster and I was no exception to the rule although as much as I could do I did to persuade Dr. Ferguson that you were his rightful successior [sic]." JGW to S. S. Drury, undated letter. Dr. Drury's son advises this must have been written between April 19 and May 1, 1921.
[8] JGW to J. L. Winant, postmarked October 12, 1911.

slowly bubbled to the surface as he tapped the hidden pleasures of working with youngsters who came to respect and admire him. He quickly demonstrated an ability to work closely and effectively with young people, to listen patiently to their fears and aspirations and to quietly offer meaningful advice. Dr. Drury planned for the day when the Old Boy would return as a full fledged master.

Gil solved one of his major problems — he had found a career which appealed to his deepest inner desire: to serve. Equally important, in Drury he had a warm, understanding friend who would strengthen him during critical years ahead. Winant always thought that the Rector possessed something of "Washington's aloofness and much of Lincoln's kindliness".[9] As one contemporary colleague put it, the idealistic headmaster would, one day, walk into heaven holding aloft a white flag and leading the alumni of St. Paul's behind him.[10]

After Gil reentered Princeton in February 1912, his class work during the spring semester enabled him to return in September with high hopes of graduating the following June. Winant, however, remained happier conversing with friends, reading Dickens and John Ruskin, and then throwing himself into the presidential campaign of 1912. Gil's rearing by upper middle class oriented parents, and a pronounced family diet of conservative Republicanism prior to each election, had been more than amply balanced by his extensive involvement with the works of Dickens and Ruskin. One of the pioneers in the social gospel and Christian Socialist movements in Britain, John Ruskin had inspired a number of clergymen and other Americans in the late nineteenth century to take an active role in the labor movement, promote the eight-hour day, labor for cooperative factories and stores and, infrequently, advocate the public ownership of the means of production.

At the same time, Ruskin's romantic preachments, which found in war certain positive contributions to the public good, prepared Winant for an early choice in the 1912 campaign. For some time he had been attracted by the vibrant and virile leadership exuded by Theodore Roosevelt, who had linked war and imperialism with moral righteousness and idealism. This attraction became all the greater when the former President launched his New Nationalism in support of the positive state, which Winant concluded would go far towards

[9] Undated letter from JGW to S. S. Drury. Dr. Drury's son advises that this was written between April 19 and May 1, 1921.
[10] Interview with Charles C. Monie, July 7, 1960, a retired master of St. Paul's.

eradicating some of the worst ills and inequities underscored by
Dickens and Ruskin. Roosevelt, he would insist, was one of "our
truest Americans and one of the few really great men of this century...".[11] Embracing the Bull Moose progressivism of Roosevelt,
rather than the New Freedom of Woodrow Wilson, Gil spent many
days preparing for the arrival of his candidate to address a student
campus rally — hiring a band, organizing a welcoming committee
headed by a football hero, and issuing releases to the college and
local press. By the time Roosevelt finally arrived at the outskirts of
Princeton, three hours behind schedule, only Gil, his brother Frederick and the band were still waiting. Even the welcoming committee
had dispersed to the campus, where the candidate eventually addressed a large, though not overly friendly, assemblage of students
from the steps of a dormitory.[12]

By election day, Gil had fallen so far behind in his school work
that he shortly withdrew from Princeton for the last time.[13] Once
more he turned to St. Paul's. This time he fell back upon an earlier
offer from Dr. Drury to return, after graduation, as a schoolmaster
and personal assistant. Aware that Gil had "a great and rare gift of
influencing boys along the very highest paths", the Rector had previously suggested a two-year mastership.[14] Informing the headmaster of his decision to leave Princeton, Winant blamed Latin for
preventing him from graduating and explained that he had "taken
nearly all the courses that I care particularly about and think the
best thing for me to do just now is to go to some place where I can
read and study by myself, and would like at the same time to be
doing something that might be helpful to other people. I know no
place where I could combine these things so well as at school. Besides I have insomnia again. Last year I was able to throw it off up
there; but here it constantly bothers me."

Gil yearned for St. Paul's where he might pursue "... a life with
an aim, and some definite work to be done in the attaining of it....
In regard to money I would like to get neither more nor less than I

[11]   Merle Curti, *The Growth of American Thought* (New York, Harper & Bros.,
1943), pp. 630, 670-71; JGW to J. L. Winant, January 21, 1919.
[12]   Interview with Frederick Winant, Jr., December 8, 1959.
[13]   Howard W. Stepp to author, October 29, 1959. Shortly after Winant was
first elected Governor of New Hampshire in November 1924, Princeton's Board
of Trustees awarded Winant an honorary degree of Master of Arts. In January
1943, Princeton gave Ambassador Winant an honorary LL.D.
[14]   Samuel S. Drury to JGW, March 9, 1912.

would be worth in whatever capacity you chose to use me. . . . What sort of teacher I would make you probably know better than I do."[15] Drury welcomed him back with open arms.

A disconsolate Winant remained at St. Paul's during commencement ceremonies at Princeton the following June, when the large 1913 Class Cup made the rounds of the 280 graduating students at a special campus ceremony.[16]

Two months after his return to St. Paul's, in the spring of 1913, the new master was reappointed at an annual salary of 800 dollars. The following year passed happily and all too quickly for Gilbert. His classroom became his kingdom, and students responded to his intense loyalty. He befriended youngsters, particularly the homesick, and instilled in many of them a love for the institution which knit them to St. Paul's. Decades later, many "returned" as trustees or officers of the alumni association.[17]

In class, he frequently related past events to experiments unfolding under Woodrow Wilson's New Freedom. For these offspring of affluence Winant sometimes painted a disconcerting picture of laboring men, women and children suffering, in an unregulated economy, from long hours in debilitating working conditions. While refusing to advocate any specific social reform doctrine in the classroom, he nevertheless underscored the responsibility of St. Paul's students to comprehend the plight of the underprivileged.[18] His portrayal of a young, virile nation maturing under Jeffersonian democracy remained one of the highlights of an otherwise average course in American history. Only when he approached the Civil War, however, did his classes truly sparkle as he gave life and meaning to

---

[15] Undated letter from JGW to Samuel S. Drury, found in the "John G. Winant" folder at St. Paul's School, immediately following Dr. Drury's March 9, 1912 letter to JGW. Since Winant made his decision to leave Princeton in January 1913, it seems logical to place the time around the latter date.

[16] *Twenty-Fifth Year Record of the Class of 1913* (Princeton University, 1938[?], n.p.), pp. 7-9. Some of the other members of the Class of 1913 who where subsequently awarded the Cup were Dr. Wilder G. Penfield, Roger W. Straus, Robert McLean, Professor Charles W. Hendel, Ferdinand Eberstadt, Alan T. Waterman, John Farr Simmons, and Courtney Johnson.

[17] JGW to J. L. Winant, April 14, 1913; St. Paul's *Alumni Horae*, 1920-1957; T. S. Matthews, *Name and Address*, p. 156. Interview with Geoffrey S. Smith, December 11, 1959. Mr. Smith was a former student of Winant's and a trustee at St. Paul's. Winant's *Letter from Grosvenor Square*, a partial account of his stewardship as Ambassador to Great Britain, is dedicated "To Geoffrey Story Smith".

[18] Interview with Geoffry S. Smith, December 11, 1959.

Abraham Lincoln. His students encountered Lincoln's human qualities — his patience, his understanding, and his devotion as a public
servant — as excerpts from the Emancipation Proclamation and from
his addresses sailed effortlessly across the room. The students generally concluded that Abe Lincoln from Illinois, whom fate destined for
a tragic end, endured as the moving force behind this schoolmaster.[19]

Gaunt, awkward, and usually in need of a haircut, Winant lectured
to his students, and, in the style of his own teachers, rarely invited
discussion. Pacing up and down in front of the class with long, slow,
steady strides, he conveyed great intensity, often painfully searching
for the next word. He would ram his big hands into the pockets of
his unpressed trousers, sometimes swaying from side to side, "with
a look of distress on his face as if his belly hurt him". On occasion, he
retreated into a corner of the room where two bookcases formed a
right angle and seemed to be climbing up the shelves on his elbows.
While most classrooms reverberated from the thunder of masters
vying with each other in shouting their lessons home, Winant's subdued voice at times verged on a whisper. One visiting educator described him as a "little depleted in energy", and suggested that he
"increase his surplus of vitality", and follow his students with appropriate questions when a pupil hesitated "or went astray in his
thinking".[20] An alumnus recalled that, in spite of the schoolmaster's
shy stammerings, he was an incredibly inspiring teacher, conveying
a burning conviction that the United States was a "wonderful country, the most gloriously hopeful experiment man had ever made".[21]

It followed naturally, then, that being ambitious, and feeling
the need for a more dramatic outlet for his restless energies, twenty-
five-year-old Winant determined to emulate his hero, Abe Lincoln. Dr.
Drury sympathized with his young friend and encouraged his involvement in local politics.

Traditionally Republican Ward Seven, which encompassed St.
Paul's and the homes of workers from nearby railroad yards, biennially sent three delegates to the Lower House of the State Legislature. Committed to seek one of these posts in the September 1914
primaries, the history teacher spent an increasing number of evenings
canvassing the neighborhood. When his father learned of his son's

[19] *Ibid.*
[20] T. S. Matthews, *Name and Address*, p. 156; Confidential undated report by
Professor M. V. O'Shea to Dr. Drury in 1916. Found in the 1916 file of the
Rector at St. Paul's School.
[21] T. S. Matthews, *Name and Address*, p. 156.

decision he exploded in opposition. Still smarting from Gilbert's failure to graduate from Princeton, just as he himself had not graduated from Columbia College, the elder Winant deemed his son too immature and lamented a temperament which appeared to lead him hastily and wildly into strange paths. Perceiving in young Winant one destined for high public service, Dr. Drury sought to calm the disturbed parent by pointing out that Gil's teaching schedule had been revised to facilitate his serving as a legislator. The Rector explained to Mr. Winant the significance of his son's unique personality; "his quiet, strong principles, tempered by deep sympathies", had enabled him to carry out personal measures which no one else at St. Paul's could effect. "I regard him as one of the most valuable assets that the school has ... and I shall make every effort to retain him." The State of New Hampshire would benefit from the dedicated and knowledgeable services of young Winant, for the community was badly in need of farsighted legislation.[22]

But Dr. Drury failed, in this instance, to move a suddenly determined parent. Rarely having seen his father so distressed in the past, and not wishing to exacerbate the already strained relations between his parents, Gilbert reluctantly withdrew from the political race — for that year.[23]

The following summer, while attending classes at Harvard, young Winant suffered another, more crushing disappointment. Happy with increasing responsibilities at St. Paul's, he wrote his mother in mid-July, "I have heard that I was to be made the head of the history department...; but have not been told so by the Rector, although I hope it is true. Know for a fact that I am to have all the college entrance history, next year, which coupled with the fact that I do more work in that department than any other man might seem to justify that hope." [24] Within days he received a note in which Dr. Drury sought to indicate, as gently as possible, that he could never expect the headship of the Department. It should have been apparent to the young master that without a college degree his academic career would always be stunted, but he was unable to view the facts realistically. The Rector's letter revived the latent despondency and deep feelings of insecurity which had plagued him since early child-

[22] Frederick Winant, Sr., to Samuel S. Drury, April 8, 1914, St. Paul's files; Samuel S. Drury to Frederick Winant, Sr., April 23, 1914, St. Paul's files.
[23] JGW to S. S. Drury, August 28, 1914.
[24] JGW to J. L. Winant, July 19, 1915.

hood. This stunning blow revived his fear that he would be "hammering until the grave without any more than hearing the echo ring back, never knowing the joy of achievement which is justly, the reward of only real success".[25]

Recalling the pride which had overwhelmed the mother of New Hampshire's Episcopal Bishop when she had visited her son soon after his appointment, a brooding Winant sadly lamented:

It does seem, Mum, that you could live on as long as Methuselah before I could even do anything like that for you. One of the sadest [sic] things I ever read was a short quotation which I found in one of Hugh Black's sermons, The Shut Door. "It is the bitterest element", says Lord Morley, "in the vast irony of human life that the time-worn eyes to which a son's success would have brought the purest gladness are so often closed forever before success has come". It was Abraham Lincoln who said: "That all he was, all he ever hoped to be, he owed to his mother." Certainly, I could say the same, Mum; but I have got to be somebody first, and it seems an awful long row to hoe.[26]

Ironically, all that Winant was by this time — as well as two of his three brothers — and all that he would continue to be the rest of his life, he owed, not only to his innate personality but also to his mother's rearing — insecure, unsure, a failure as a disciplined student, as well as unrealistically ambitious in the academic world.

Healed by time, a more subdued Winant returned to St.Paul's in September. Although his responsibilities included evening supervision of twenty students in The Farm Building, he often absented himself because of involvement in Republican politics. Like most St. Paul's boys who admired him, these Fourth Form students cooperated during his unofficial absences. These evenings away from the campus usually found the schoolmaster once more ringing doorbells and becoming familiar with workers from the nearby railroad yards, with the butchers, the truck drivers and the maintenance men who served St. Paul's.[27]

The evenings the history teacher remained in The Farm were often spent with students crammed into already crowded rooms. He had an apartment which contained a study, bedroom and private bath. Books lined the walls of all three rooms; toppled over chairs; stood in perilous columns in corners and on the bed. He constantly purchased

[25] Ibid., July 28, 1915.
[26] Ibid.
[27] Interviews with C. E. Rexford, July 7, 1960; and with Geoffrey S. Smith, December 11, 1959.

new ones and read them with painstaking marginal notes. When a student called, he would sit on a pile of books, or Winant did.[28]

The conversations could go on for hours; they might discuss issues raised in class or personal matters of vital concern. Not infrequently, the master belatedly realized that the clock on the mantle had approached midnight and that the boys should have been asleep long before. There are those who still insist that a stronger personal link with students, and greater familiarity with their thinking, insured that this instructor would have greater impact upon many of them than the Rector.[29]

The study of history remained a passion with Winant. William Roscoe Thayer's two-volume work on John Hay, which had just reached its tenth printing, impressed him as being as good as any book of its kind he had ever read, especially those chapters dealing with Abraham Lincoln and Theodore Roosevelt. At this time, he was working on "half a dozen things — Treaty of Ghent, the Single Term, Lincoln [sic] First Inaugural, Jackson Valley Campaign of 1861-1862." He had also begun a short monograph on the House of Representatives of 1820 and the Senate of 1850. In his "spare time" he had been looking into the lives of Robert Morris, William Loundes and Meshech Weare, an eighteenth-century New Hampshire man, supplemental to his teaching, library work, a correspondence business course, and "desultory reading of the Law". Young Winant understated the situation when he concluded that "All these things with the care of the boys have kept your young 'hopeful' pretty busy. Would do better if I would stick to a few things but can't seem to manage it...."[30] By leading an overly busy and active life he attempted to crowd out the insecurity and uncertainty he mistakenly associated with an otherwise empty existence.

The change in organization and leadership of student affairs epitomized Winant's contributions to St. Paul's. As a student, and then teacher, he had been disturbed by the dominant role played by two secret societies over student campus affairs. After numerous proddings, he finally convinced the Rector to send six students to Kent School for a long weekend to observe its Student Council and the

[28] *Ibid.*; T. S. Matthews, *Name and Address*, p. 156.
[29] Interview with Geoffrey S. Smith, December 11, 1959; T. S. Matthews, *Name and Address*, pp. 151, 156-57.
[30] William R. Thayer, *The Life and Letters of John Hay*, 2 vols. (Boston, Houghton Mifflin, 1915). JGW to J. L. Winant, December 2, 1915. Records do not disclose completion of any of these projects.

school's self-help system. After the delegation reported back to St. Paul's student body, Fifth Formers in the secret societies heatedly debated the issue for weeks. Immediately prior to their summer vacation, they agreed, by majority vote, to abandon their secret organizations and forfeit their traditional prerogatives through adoption of a new constitution establishing a Boys' Council. Sixth Form students would henceforth elect the officers and a majority of Council members, who would meet frequently with the Rector to discuss matters which could be handled by boys themselves.

The development of democratic self-management among St. Paul's students took a tremendous stride forward with the creation of the Boys' Council. Alumni recalled that Winant had insured development of democratic thinking among the Fifth Formers, who voted through this fundamental change in 1917.[31] The attainment of a more democratic and responsible student government on the St. Paul's campus was a projection of the future when Winant would seek to expand political and economic democracy for the citizens of his state, of the nation, and of the world.

[31] Interview with C. E. Rexford, July 7, 1960; S. S. Drury to JGW, November 24, 1917; St. Paul's School, *The Annual Report of the Rector* ... (Concord, N.H., November 1917), p. 20; interview with Geoffrey S. Smith, December 11, 1959. Smith, a member of the Fifth Form in June 1917, was on the committee which investigated the student governing body at Kent School. He was a Trustee of St. Paul's in 1947, when Winant died. Also, Drury, *Drury and St. Paul's*, pp. 63-65; John Richards, "John Gilbert Winant, 1904-08", *Alumni Horae*, XXVII, No. 3 (Autumn, 1947), 79.

CHAPTER III

"TO BE USEFUL TO MY FELLOWMAN"

Since his return to St. Paul's as a schoolmaster, young Winant had
pursued his political interests through active involvement in state
and local elections.[1] Impelled by inner drives which made him feel
deeply about the problems of his fellow man; influenced by the
writings of Dickens and John Ruskin and by the examples of Lincoln
and Theodore Roosevelt; and strengthened in his determination to
serve by the encouragement of Dr. Drury; it seemed quite natural
for Winant to enter politics.

His attachment to the Republican Party came from his parents and
social milieu, yet he had exhibited independence when casting his
first presidential ballot for Roosevelt in 1912. He endorsed those who
recognized the need for social change in order to cope with an in-
dustrializing society.

The tall schoolmaster had never forgotten Charles Dickens' powerful description of workers' hovels and the debilitating effect of factory
work. In all likelihood, he had never read Friederich Engel's *The
Condition of the Working Class in England in 1844*, or Karl Marx's
Das Kapital. But this was unnecessary to insure his revolt against
the meaner manifestations of his parents' society. Throughout his
life he remained influenced by one of the most vigorous and incisive
critics of the uglier stages of capitalism — wealthy, aristocratic Ruskin, who finally drove himself mad thinking too much of these
problems. Winant's yearning to aid the less fortunate would insure
him a lifetime of restlessness.

By the eve of America's involvement in the First World War, the
industrial revolution had long since pockmarked many of the rolling
hills and valleys of New Hampshire. But aside from the brief progressive administration of Governor Robert Perkins Bass, 1911-1912,
social and economic developments had been ignored by too many

---

[1] Edward J. Gallagher to author, August 14, 1960. Mr. Gallagher was publisher
of the *Concord Patriot*, candidate for Mayor of Concord in 1913, and subsequently Mayor of Laconia, N.H.

lawmakers. Fearful of change and tradition-bound to conservative thinking, rural legislators generally looked askance at those like Winant who sought to move the state into the twentieth century.

Many a tradition, however, was shattered during the 1916 presidential race when Granite State citizens also selected a new Governor and Legislature. Long before the G.O.P. National Convention, competing forces within the Republican Party lined up delegates for favorite sons and national leaders, including Supreme Court Justice Charles Evans Hughes, and the unquenchable Theodore Roosevelt. After the latter failed to secure significant Republican support, he disdainfully rejected the Progressive nomination of the Bull Moose convention. The New Hampshire delegation to the collapsing Progressive gathering then reluctantly endorsed Hughes. This signaled the disappearance of the Progressive Republican movement as a potent force in New Hampshire until 1924. Hughes was nominated on a platform that carefully muted its criticism of Wilson's progressive legislation, and which was broad enough to satisfy many of the party's insurgents. In foreign affairs, it called for "a straight and honest" neutrality, while commending the President's general conduct in this field.

A week after the regular Republican convention nominated Hughes, Democrats went through the motions of ratifying Wilson's renomination and a platform developed primarily by the President. It defended his domestic and foreign policies, favored preparedness measures, condemned those hyphenated groups and organizations which Wilson felt promoted the interests of a foreign power and praised the Chief Executive who had "kept us out of war".

As the campaign launched into high gear with first Hughes, and then Wilson, criss-crossing the nation in search of votes, war with Mexico appeared uncomfortably imminent. State militias, including New Hampshire's, mobilized in response to border raids by Pancho Villa's insurgents. Disturbed by front page headlines detailing wholesale bloodletting on Europe's battle fields, increasing numbers of peace-minded Progressives veered toward Wilson in reaction to Theodore Roosevelt's warmongering statements and Hughes's condemnation of the President's "softness" toward Mexico and the violation of American sea rights.[2]

___

[2] George E. Mowry, *The California Progressives* (Berkeley, University of California, 1951), pp. 274-77.

In December 1915, the G.O.P. leadership of Concord's Ward Seven had finally designated the schoolmaster as one of three regular district nominees for the State's Lower House. Without protest, this time, from his father, young Winant pursued a personal primary campaign, devoid of national issues. He diligently canvassed Republicans, often to the detriment of classroom preparation.[3] His campaign literature consisted of a brief, mimeographed announcement indicating familiarity with Edmund Burke and John Stuart Mill when he idealistically promised to follow the dictates of his own conscience:

... it becomes my duty to make known to you my understanding of the job that I seek at your hands and can only hold under your favor.

Insofar as I am able I shall be governed by the will of the people whom I hope to represent and at all times will follow the dictates of my own conscience.

If elected to office it will be my endeavor to represent you to the best of my ability. I can honestly say that I have no greater ambition in life than to be useful to my fellowman.[4]

A variegated, outlying region which hugged the western edge of Concord, Ward Seven comprised a rather diverse group of railroad shop laborers, farmers and the staff at St. Paul's. Except for the Boston and Maine Railroad repair shops, the State's capital had few features of an industrial city, and as the families of these workers remained the largest single bloc in Ward Seven, any aspiring local candidate had to secure much of their support to insure victory. It was unusual for a member of St. Paul's faculty to ring doorbells in the car shop district, but meeting constituents face to face remained this candidate's most potent weapon, especially since four candidates competed for the three G.O.P. nominations. The most untalented platform speaker imaginable, Winant insured sheer agony for those who heard his choppy, uneven phrases, interspersed with long pauses as he groped for the next word. And yet, though he sorely tried the patience of his most sympathetic listeners, he rarely lost his audience. Instead, he seemed to mesmerize them with his obvious inner struggle. At meetings, he resolutely stood his ground, straining for the next phrase and refusing to surrender the podium until he completed his remarks with a wringing wet shirt and a fatigued audience.

Winant's personal warmth proved helpful in converting voters to

---

[3] JGW to Jeanette L. Winant, postmarked August 18, 1916; interview with Geoffrey S. Smith, December 11, 1959.
[4] Copy in author's possession.

his cause – his awkward yet animated hand shaking, his ability to make people feel important and his evident desire to serve them. These traits proved more effective than his opponent's oratorical skills, for he ran ahead of his more experienced adversaries in the September primaries.[5] A week later, Republicans swept the Maine elections, which normally foreshadowed a national G.O.P. victory in November.

During the weeks preceding the elections, Winant visited most Ward Seven voters, leaving behind a small printed throwaway featuring the photograph of a handsome, determined young man in a high starched collar. Although organized labor remained suspect in the eyes of many community leaders, particularly in Republican New Hampshire, the schoolmaster insisted that his campaign literature bear the imprint of the union label – a gesture particularly appreciated by workers in the Boston and Maine repair shops. With the exception of his party's gubernatorial candidate, Winant led the lengthy G.O.P. slate including his party's presidential candidate in his ward by as much as ten percent.[6]

Results in the race for the State's Lower House, however, did not warrant comment in Concord's newspapers, for reporters sought to verify, and then interpret, the amazing returns of the presidential contest. Not only had Democratic papers in the East conceded Wilson's defeat by midnight of election day, but little more than 24 hours after the polls closed, the *Concord Evening Monitor* still claimed the nation for Hughes, along with the state by a 500-vote plurality. The following day, however, Republican newspapers reluctantly reported that President Wilson had "temporarily" forged ahead in New Hampshire by a scant 54 votes, with Democrats claiming California and victory. Not until four days after election did this Republican journal finally yield the state and the nation to Wilson, after California had definitely gone into the Democratic column by just over 4,000 votes.[7]

Wilson's New Freedom and Roosevelt's warmongering had in-

[5] *Concord Evening Monitor*, September 6, 1916; Harlan C. Pearson, *Biographical Sketches of the Governor, Councillors and Members of the Senate and House of Representatives of the New Hampshire Legislature for 1917* (Concord, N.H., A. Chester Clark, 1917), p. 32. Winant received 189 votes to 173 for his two closest opponents, and 171 for the loser.
[6] State of New Hampshire, *Manual for the General Court, 1917* (Manchester, N.H., John B. Clark Co., n.d.), pp. 372, 405.
[7] *Concord Evening Monitor*, November 8-16, 1916; *The American Year Book 1916* (New York, D. Appleton and Co., 1917), p. 170.

fluenced many a New Hampshire Bull Mooser to split his ticket, converting a 7,000 G.O.P. gubernatorial plurality into a 56-vote margin for the Democratic presidential incumbent. Wilson captured the electoral college by a mere 23-vote majority, with California providing thirteen, and New Hampshire four, of these votes. Only two states had gone for Wilson east of the Mississippi and north of the Mason-Dixon Line.[8]

By the beginning of the year, the spotlight in New Hampshire focused on the new State Legislature and Governor. Composed of 404 Representatives and 24 Senators, the General Court remained overwhelmingly Republican.[9]

One of the most unusual lawmaking bodies in the nation, the General Court boasted the largest Lower House and one of the smallest Senates. The authors of New Hampshire's State Constitution, adopted in 1783, believed they were expressing the democratic viewpoint when they provided for an immense monster known as the Lower House of the General Court. Naively concluding that great numbers would make it extremely difficult, if not impossible, for any single pressure group to control or corrupt a majority of lawmakers, the founding fathers of the Granite State insured that one of the least populated states would have the largest, if not most inefficient, lawmaking group in the nation. For while it may be educational for most individuals to serve in government, in fact, the absence of 100 to 150 Representatives from many legislative sessions made quorums difficult and the Lower House was so unwieldy in size that most of its work had to be done by a handful of committees, lessening the number involved in general floor debate. Many who had something to say would hesitate to address a body of 400; to call the roll required not less than 35 minutes.[10] Most lawmakers rarely participated in committee consideration of bills, while a comparatively small number had more work than they could properly handle, for they were consistently delayed by having to drag along "their more or less supine,

[8] *Manual for the General Court, 1917,* p. 354.
[9] *New Hampshire Manual 1917,* XV, 187, 486-91. While the State Senate contained 16 Republicans to 8 Democrats, the figures for the House apparently identified 239 Republicans, 159 Democrats, 2 Progressive Republicans, 2 Independents and 2 vacancies. The Governor's, or Executive, Council was composed of 4 Republicans and 1 Democrat.
[10] A perceptive analysis of the New Hampshire Legislature is found in an unpublished master's thesis written for Dartmouth College in 1914 by the yet unknown political science student, Leonard D. White, "A Study of the New Hampshire Legislature of 1913".

sluggish, or uninterested colleagues". Too much dead wood characterized the Legislature.[11]

The presence of this large, passive base tended to facilitate control by a small clique of able, well-financed leaders,[12] and, particularly, enabled the Boston and Maine Railroad to rule effectively over this vast assemblage for years.

By 1890, spokesmen for the Boston and Maine Railroad had become the most powerful economic and political force in the state. Initially, their carefully designed strategy was to reach into the Democratic Party but, during the Bryan campaign in 1896, they transferred their primary "loyalty", leadership, funds, lobbyists and lawyers to the Republican cause.[13] But to insure low taxes, and to curtail attempts to regulate its activities, the railroad leaders contrived to work closely with both parties.

Looking through the towering windows to the left of the Speaker's podium, lawmakers could observe an uninterrupted expanse of the Capital grounds, and the famed Eagle Hotel. In the Boston and Maine's "throne room" at this hostelry, lobbyists once lined the pockets of willing lawmakers and dispensed free railroad passes to legislators, editors, newsmen, clergymen, Republicans, Democrats and Prohibitionists, among others. The railroad also advertised extensively in the state's newspapers.[14]

The town caucus method of selecting political candidates and delegates to statewide nominating conventions facilitated railroad-industry domination. Generally controlling a majority of the Governor's Council, an archaic institution devised to limit the power of colonial governors, the Boston and Maine held veto power over gubernatorial appointments to regulatory agencies.[15] From 1895 to 1906, the Granite State Legislature achieved little without first con-

[11]   *Ibid.*, pp. 87-88.
[12]   The original article on the election of Representatives and the ratio of representation was first amended in 1877, and then a new article was inserted in 1942 — Constitution of the State of New Hampshire, Part Second, Article 9.
[13]   William L. Dunfey, "A Short History of the Democratic Party in New Hampshire", unpublished master's thesis for the University of New Hampshire, 1954, pp. 50-56.
[14]   Leon Burr Richardson, *William E. Chandler, Republican* (New York, Dodd Mead & Co., 1940), pp. 430-31; interview with Robert Perkins Bass, June 14, 1951.
[15]   Dunfey, "Democratic Party in N.H.", pp. 57-148; Ernest E. Morrill, "The Functions and Efficiency of an Executive Council in an American Commonwealth, with Special Reference to New Hampshire", a master's thesis written for Dartmouth College in 1912, is a study of the historical background and role of the Executive Council.

sulting the legal counsel or lobbyists for the Boston and Maine. Despite the dispersal of power among separate branches of government, despite bicameralism, despite the division of executive authority between the Governor and the Governor's Council, and despite "independent" regulatory agencies, the Boston and Maine alone, at the turn of the century, efficiently tied all these fragmented parts together.

More than a century before, the factory system had come to New Hampshire with the construction of the Amoskeag Mills in Manchester in 1810. This mill, which had been steadily expanding since its founding, became the world's largest cotton textile manufacturing plant by the middle of the century, and part of the State's key industry. Other textile plants mushroomed in Nashua, Dover, and in lesser known factory towns.[16] By the late nineteenth century, textile mills dotted the countryside. These unattractive brick or wood factory structures straddled the state's swift flowing streams which soon became clogged and polluted with industrial refuse. The mills recruited thousands of laborers from nearby villages and outlying farms. Women, children and men generally suffered from depressed wages and long hours of labor in the midst of unwholesome working conditions.[17] This type of industrial exploitation had ruined the health of generations of British workers; it would do the same to many Granite State residents. While bringing economic development and enterprise to the rolling hills of New Hampshire, the industrial revolution also brought slum ghettos to expanding mill towns.[18]

After completion of the railroads between Montreal and New England in the 1850's, and following the end of the Civil War, tremendous numbers of French-speaking Canadian Catholics migrated across the American border. Encouraged by worsening economic conditions in Canada, by glowing letters of American opportunities from recently removed relatives, and by the activities of Amoskeag

[16] James D. Squires, *The Granite State of the United States* (New York, The American Historical Co., 1956), I, 288-95; Works Progress Administration, *New Hampshire, A Guide to the Granite State* (Boston, Houghton Mifflin Co., 1938), pp. 53-55.

[17] By 1860, non-agricultural workers in New Hampshire labored on the average of eleven hours daily, six days a week. Factory wages for adult men were perhaps as high as $8 a week. Forty years later the average wage of working people had increased about two dollars weekly. Squires, *The Granite State*, I, 288; II, 489.

[18] From a population of 3,235 in 1840, Manchester increased by 70,000 by 1910. State of New Hampshire, *Manual for the General Court, 1921* (Concord, N.H., n.p., n.d.), pp. 347-48. Hereafter cited as *N.H. Manual, 1921*.

Mill agents, hundreds of thousands from the Quebec area streamed into New England after 1865.[19] By the twentieth century they constituted one-third of Manchester's population, and the largest single bloc in Nashua on the Massachusetts border.[20] Rarely welcome in the Yankee, Protestant-dominated Republican Party which sought to protect the "purity" of its Scotch-English ancestors, French Canadians generally turned to the Democratic Party as the haven for minority groups. The leadership of the Democracy saw in these immigrants the hope for future control of State politics.[21] The textile industry and the railroad had controlled the state for such a long time that most people accepted it as something "which must be endured because it could not be cured".[22]

Shortly before the turn of the century, St. Louis-born novelist Winston Churchill returned to his ancestral village of Cornish in western New Hampshire. There he wrote *The Crisis, The Crossing,* and *Coniston,* which painted a realistic picture of life and politics under the domination of a railroad. In his search for material, the author permitted flattered neighbors to elect him to the State Legislature in 1902 and again in 1904. With the publication of *Coniston* in 1906, Churchill, one of the most widely read authors in America, became involved in a furious statewide campaign. That summer a small nucleus of civic-minded citizens, who called themselves Lincoln Republicans, rebelled against the railroad dictatorship and induced Churchill to belatedly enter the contest for the Republican gubernatorial nomination. In a whirlwind campaign of some six weeks in search of committed delegates, the author belabored the theme of railroad domination.[23]

[19] Squires, *The Granite State,* II, 478-80. By 1906, 78,000 French Canadians had settled in New Hampshire.
[20] Works Progress Administration, *New Hampshire,* p. 76; *N.H. Manual, 1921,* p. 348.
[21] Dunfey, "Democratic Party in N.H.", pp. 92-94, 124-33.
[22] William H. Child, *History of the Town of Cornish, New Hampshire* (Concord, N.H., Rumford Press, 1911), I, 306; Richardson, *Chandler,* pp. 623-40. Also, interviews with John R. McLane, December 5, 1950, and R. P. Bass, June 14, 1951.
[23] Warren Irving Titus, "Winston Churchill, American: A Critical Biography", Unpublished doctoral dissertation for New York University, 1957, p. 1; William E. Chandler, *The Churchill Reform Movement* (Concord, N.H., Rumford Printing Co., 1906), pp. 1-19. These Lincoln Republicans campaigned for: prohibition of free passes on railroads; direct election of Railroad Commissioners; correct and modernized valuation of railroad property for taxation purposes; a corrupt practices act and publicity for campaign contributions; registration of lobbyists and publication of their fees; a primary election law; establishment of a State Tax

Churchill and his supporters came close to making political history. These political neophytes almost executed the political coup of the new century when they barely failed to capture the gubernatorial nomination.[24] The cumulative impact of Churchill's statewide campaign, and the hairbreadth victory of the G.O.P. railroad choice for Governor at the November polls, clearly indicated to the Boston and Maine that it could no longer ruthlessly control the legislative decision-making process. Before long, some of the basic principles of the Lincoln Republicans would become law.[25]

Devoted to conservation and popular democracy, and actuated by a profound sense of noblesse oblige, handsome, thirty-one-year-old Robert Perkins Bass had returned from Chicago to his wealthy family homestead in Peterborough to fight the railroad and support Winston Churchill. Successful in gaining election to the Legislature, Bass pushed through legislation prohibiting the issuance of free railroad passes to State employees and overcame opposition of the conservative Republican leadership to save the state some $100,000 in questionable or needless expenditures. As a member of the State Senate in 1909, he led a successful revolt against blatant lobbying by Boston and Maine agents. The ensuing legislation provided for more equitable taxation of railroads and a direct primary system.[26]

Taking advantage of New Hampshire's first primary contest the following year, the revived Lincoln Republicans insured the nomination and then election of Bass as Governor. Before he concluded his term as Chief Executive, the Peterborough patrician brought the Granite State into the twentieth century with enlightened social welfare and regulatory legislation. Being that rare idealist in politics, Bass was the only G.O.P. governor to stand by Theodore Roosevelt's drive for the presidency as a Bull Mooser. As a result of retaliation by Republican state leaders, Bass was denied the opportunity to serve

Commission; stringent enforcement of the liquor laws and of existing anti-gambling laws.

[24] Titus, "Winston Churchill", pp. 229-45; interviews with John R. McLane, December 5, 1950, and with R. P. Bass, June 14, 1951. For Churchill's autobiographical novel dealing with the 1906 campaign for delegates to the nominating convention, read *Mr. Crewe's Career*.

[25] The G.O.P. gubernatorial condidate won by a mere 2,800-vote plurality which lacked the necessary constitutional majority. The election was thrown into the Republican-dominated legislature which selected the GOP nominee as winner.

[26] Jerome G. Beatty, "The Rescue of New Hampshire", *Collier's*, XLVII, No. 7 (May 6, 1911), 22, 31; Chapters 46, 66, 126 and 153, Laws of N.H., 1909; interview with R. P. Bass, June 14, 1951.

his constituency as a United States Senator — a marked loss to the
nation. Historians, however, must record that Bass pulled New
Hampshire into the mainstream of progress and laid the groundwork
for future advances under another progressive, Winant of St. Paul's.

With close to one-half of the 404 Representatives elected to New
Hampshire's Lower House in November 1916 born prior to 1867,
many before the Civil War, and in the face of an increasingly urban-
ized and industrialized nation, little progressive legislation could be
expected from the overwhelming number of lawmakers who had
spent their lives in rural isolation, or in small, farm-dominated communities. These thrifty, rural-oriented legislators had little appreciation of the needs of working men and women and normally followed
the negative dictates of conservative spokesmen for the Amoskeag
textile interests, the shoe manufacturers, the lumber operators and
other industries.[27]

On January 3, 1917, young Winant joined his fellow Representatives
on the upper floor of the gold-domed Capitol Building. From one of
the semi-circular, pewlike wooden benches, he observed Corinthian
columns rising along the walls, and electric lighting which cast a
steady glow across the room. Facing him from behind the Speaker's
stand were oil portraits of George Washington, who visited New
Hampshire in 1789; native son John P. Hale who had been a United
States Senator, presidential nominee of the Free Soil Party in 1852
and Minister to Spain; Daniel Webster, born and schooled in New
Hampshire; and Franklin Pierce, a Governor of the Granite State
who became a Senator and then the fourteenth President of the
United States. Winant apparently made a mental note to remedy at
least one inadequacy — the absence of a portrait of Abraham Lincoln.
In dire need of dedicated lawmakers who could readily assume the
arduous, time consuming burden of legislative committee assignments,
Republican House Speaker Arthur P. Morrill acted promptly when
he learned of Winant's eager willingness to serve, and appointed him

[27]   White, "A Study of the New Hampshire Legislature of 1913", p. 21; *Concord
Evening Monitor*, January 1, 1917; and Pearson, *Biographical Sketches of the
... N.H. Legislature for 1917*, pp. 12-63. Farmers included the Governor and
79 Representatives. There were also 22 lumbermen, 26 professionals, 5 clergymen, 19 real estate managers, 18 mill operators, 56 merchants, 21 manufacturers
and 45 skilled craftsmen. The remainder were distributed among clerks, shoe
makers, mill hands, hotel keepers, foremen, stable keepers, undertakers, bakers
and one school teacher.

to the important Committee of the Revision of the Statutes. The Speaker subsequently came to regret this decision for he afforded the progressive schoolmaster an opportunity to become increasingly well known throughout the State and to successfully challenge him for the Republican gubernatorial nomination.[28]

Winant had not really surveyed the slums or sweatshops which scourged Manchester and Nashua, nor could he yet count any factory workers or spokesmen of organized labor as close friends. He did not seem aware of the developing martyrdom of West Coast labor leader Thomas J. Mooney, whose trial in San Francisco for a purported "Preparedness Day" bombing began the very day the General Court convened in the Granite State. But those who knew Winant well were not surprised when the young Concord legislator grasped the initiative in proposing social welfare legislation. Before long, many Republicans and Democrats, and the few ineffective spokesmen of organized labor, became aware of this freshman lawmaker who enunciated an outspoken sensitivity to depressed living standards and lamentable working conditions.

Unlike traditionally silent freshmen lawmakers, Winant tended to emulate State Senator Franklin D. Roosevelt's vigorous first term in Albany in 1911.[29] The schoolmaster advanced some of the most controversial proposals, urging the State to keep abreast of changing patterns in American society and protect the well-being of its citizenry. He would not be satisfied with the "safe, sane" character of the Governor's inaugural address.[30] The young teacher introduced a bill to limit the labor of women and children to 48 hours weekly.[31] He also proposed legislation to regulate the assignment of wages, to increase respect for our national anthem and to establish a legislative drafting and reference bureau.[32] The last proposal stemmed from an exchange of correspondence with Professor Joseph P. Chamberlain of the Legislative Drafting Research Fund at Columbia University,

[28]   *Concord Evening Monitor*, January 3, 1917. Of 34 standing committees, this was one of six which shouldered the bulk of the session's work. White, "A Study of the New Hampshire Legislature of 1913", pp. 27-43.

[29]   Henry F. Pringle, *Alfred E. Smith, A Critical Study* (New York, Macy-Masius, 1927), pp. 139-43.

[30]   *Journal of the House of Representatives, January Session, 1917* (Concord, N.H., n.p., n.d.), pp. 41-52. Hereafter cited as *Journal of the House, 1917*.

[31]   *Concord Evening Monitor*, January 4, 1917; *Journal of the House, 1917*, p. 104.

[32]   *Journal of the House, 1917*, p. 105. House Bills 252, 253, 254.

the start of a lengthy, fruitful solicitation of suggestions for the revision of many New Hampshire laws.

Winant embarrassed many lawmakers when he reported out the proposal to extend suffrage to women. Overriding his pleas during a heated debate which raged for almost three hours, a fifty-three vote majority decreed that the time had not yet come to give the ballot to the opposite sex.[33]

When the House Labor Committee held public hearings on Winant's proposal to reduce the hours of labor for working women and minors to 48 from 55, he came well prepared with witnesses, reports and communications. From Professor Chamberlain of Columbia University, he had acquired a working knowledge of the background of such proposals. From California, Progressive Republican Governor Hiram Johnson, recently elected to the United States Senate, wrote him at length about a 48-hour law which had worked well on the Coast.[34] Winant's supporting witnesses included spokesmen for the New Hampshire Federation of Labor, the Cigar Makers Union, the textile workers, the telephone operators, a lawyer, a doctor and the wife of a well known liberal Republican. While one witness called attention to the high death rate from tuberculosis among working children in Manchester, a second characterized the textile manufacturers of the state as "human spiders engaged in sucking the life blood out of the little buds of the garden of New Hampshire." After the doctor insisted that passage of this proposal would be of inestimable aid to the health and welfare of future generations, the author of the bill warned that strenuous pressure would be placed on the committee by those who were against it. He had already been informed by fellow lawmakers that the order had come down from certain corporations to "put the screws on Winant".[35]

Lobbyists for textile manufacturers opposed the bill insisting that

---

[33] *Journal of the House, 1917,* pp. 470-72; *Concord Evening Monitor,* March 7 and 8, 1917. A month earlier the Senate had rejected a similar proposal, 16 to 7. The House vote was 205 to 152.

[34] Minutes of the hearing by the House Labor Committee on February 20, 1917. Found in Drawer 22 of the Winant Collection at the Franklin D. Roosevelt Library in Hyde Park, N.Y.; *Concord Evening Monitor,* February 21, 1917.

[35] *Ibid.;* in 1931, the Governor's office disclosed that during the previous fifteen year period, the death rate from tuberculosis had been reduced by 76 per cent in the cities and 41 per cent in rural communities. Approximately 3,000 state residents had been saved from death by tuberculosis alone during this period. "A Proclamation for Christmas Seals", by Governor John G. Winant, 1931. Winant Collection, Drawer 8.

their clients would be forced out of the state if the proposal passed, criticized unfavorable climatic and freight conditions in New Hampshire, and underscored unfair southern competition in the form of long hours of labor and lower salaries.[36] These industrial spokesmen easily swayed the Committee's rural-minded majority.

When Representatives ignored Winant's 48-hour proposal, he threw his support to the 52-hour amendment of the Governor's bill for a reduction from 55 to 54 hours. In the ensuing debate the opposition again conceded "expediency" in their reasoning, that enactment of the amendment would cause New Hampshire mills to move South. Despite Winant's personal appeal from the floor, no more than 75 members of the House supported the 52-hour amendment by voice vote, whereas the 54-hour proposal was overwhelmingly adopted.[37] The lobbyists for the Amoskeag textile mills had done their work well.

Before the conclusion of the session, the lawmakers searched their souls once more in the process of voting upon another Winant proposal which cut across party lines — the abolition of capital punishment. Refusing to accept rejection by a majority of the Judiciary Committee as final, he requested and secured a special order from the House permitting consideration of his proposal. After a lengthy debate evoked by Winant's supporting remarks, party unity split as the teacher went down to defeat by a vote of 190 to 142.[38]

Throughout this session, the youthful Concord lawmaker exhibited increasing mastery of legislative initiative and parliamentary procedure, along with a stubborn, unyielding trait. Neither apathy nor outright hostility on the part of party leaders dissuaded him from pressing for social welfare goals. Only a world at war could do that. Early in the legislative session, as relations with Germany worsened, Winant's mind frequently wandered far afield to Europe. His youngest brother, Cornelius, had joined the French Foreign Legion fighting in the Balkans. On February 1, the young lawmaker sat in a crowded

[36] Minutes of the hearing by the House Labor Committee on February 20, 1917. Found in Drawer 20 of Winant Collection. Also, *Concord Evening Monitor*, February 21, 1917.
[37] *Journal of the House, 1917*, pp. 98, 100, 628, 630, 722, 725, 726, 929; *Concord Evening Monitor*, April 3, 1917. This became Chapter 196, Laws of N.H., 1917. A copy of Winant's 1917 proposal for the 48-hour measure was found in his library table in November 1947, after his suicide.
[38] *Journal of the House, 1917*, pp. 130, 403, 559; *Concord Evening Monitor*, March 20, 1917.

Representatives Hall to hear former President William Howard Taft urge a joint session of the Legislature to support military preparedness, especially in view of Germany's newly announced policy of unlimited submarine warfare. With diplomatic relations severed two days later, a Democratic President received the wholehearted endorsement of the Concord lawmaker and his fellow colleagues by special resolution.[39]

Two weeks after Woodrow Wilson signed the resolution decreeing a state of hostilities between the United States and the German Empire, the curtain fell on the legislative session in Concord. While Republican spokesmen contended that this had been a memorable Legislature, Winant lamented the Granite State's retreat in the face of fundamental changes sweeping the nation.[40] He did not emerge from the legislative spotlight as a statewide leader, yet his vigorous espousal of women's suffrage, the 48-hour law for women and children, and the abolition of capital punishment stamped him as an advanced liberal, a man the surviving remnants of Lincoln Republicans might view as a potential ally.

---

[39] *Concord Evening Monitor*, February 1, 3, 6, 1917.
[40] *Ibid.*, April 20, 1917.

CHAPTER IV

"THE FLYING PART OF IT IS GREAT"

Untroubled by pacifist leanings or the "plague on both your houses" attitude afflicting many Progressives prior to April 1917, Gil Winant had been deeply stirred by President Wilson's idealistic pleas, and by Theodore Roosevelt's appeals for American involvement in the European conflict. He was, in addition, psychologically knitted to Abraham Lincoln, who had led the country through an earlier war crisis, and to his three brothers already in uniform. Restless, urgently requiring a sense of dramatic involvement to prove himself, he sought to join the air service.

Failing to secure immediate appointment to the flying corps during a visit to Washington, Winant set out for Europe. Obtaining passage on the first available French steamer in July 1917, he departed from Staten Island, where some of his Dutch ancestors lay buried.[1]

The nine-day journey across the Atlantic proved uneventful and extremely boring to one who was restless and uncomfortable without purposeful action and constant movement, unable to relax or sit quiet. Disembarking at Bordeaux and boarding a Paris-bound train were welcome respites. The peaceful countryside unfolded its beauty as the train sped northward to the French capital. Finally accepted by the American Air Service, Winant headed for a French flying school near Tours, "in a wonderful little valley that follows along the Loire. On one side there are some fine old chateaux and on the other bank green pastures with a background of trees. At sunrise from the upper ether it is very lovely."[2]

Gil Winant faced the imposing hurdle of a rigorous training program before he could receive his wings, evincing pleasure at starting at the bottom because "the flying part of it is great." Frequently, however, during the long hours of study and practice training under French instructors, he expressed fear of being assigned to an aviation

[1] JGW to Jeanette L. Winant, July 23, 1917.
[2] *Ibid.*, postmarked or dated August 8, 12, 20, and September 11, 1917.

camp as an instructor. He insisted that he had come "here to fight and would be heartbroken if they didn't give me a fair chance at the front".[3]

It is difficult to imagine a flier in 1918 having *any* chance considering the infant stage of airplane development, the crude landing fields, the death traps called planes, inadequate instruments and primitive weather information. Somewhat typical was the manner in which Winant selected an airfield for an emergency landing on one of his return flights from Paris — he "just happened to see a row of hangers with a good field to land in not far off and so decided to come down. . . ".[4] To be forced to fly blind because of a sudden change in weather could mean death or serious injury. With planes not immune from ordinary rifle fire, pilots who survived the war years could justly claim charmed lives.[5]

Winant made slow progress, but managed to avoid the two crashes which meant "washout" from the Air Service. By mid-October, he moved to an advanced training camp near Issoudun, where he practiced with rounded, wing-clipped Bleriot "penguins". Toward the end of the year he amazed his fellow students, who had never seen him either land or take off smoothly, by soloing and passing his final tests. To celebrate this victory, the newly commissioned First Lieutenant hurried to Paris and the famed Opera House to listen to a brilliant performance of "Carmen".[6]

Letters from home meant much to him, though his father tended to devote an inordinate amount of space to lamenting the sharp drop of his stock holdings, particularly railroad issues.[7] More hopeful news came from St. Paul's students and alumni. The deepest loyalty, sometimes bordering on idolatry, shone through these letters; typical was one Sixth Former who sent lengthy, descriptive accounts of campus developments. "I'd give anything to see you and talk to you. I could talk steadily with you for 24 hours at a shot right now. Gee, I'd like

[3] *Ibid.,* September 12, 1917.
[4] Interviews with Arthur J. Coyle, March 13 and 19, 1952; JGW to J. L. Winant, April 22, 1918.
[5] Gorrell, "History of the Air Service", unpublished and unnumbered pages, Vol. El, NA Record Group 120, File Box Number 232, File folders of Aero Squadron Numbers 1 and 8, in the Records of the AEF, National Archives, Washington, D.C. (hereafter cited as Gorrell, "History of the Air Service"); JGW to J. L. Winant, March 1, 1918.
[6] JGW to J. L. Winant, September 17, 21, October 3, 6, 25, 30, 1917, and January 1, April 17, 1918.
[7] Frederick Winant, Sr. to JGW, November 16 and December 12, 1917.

to hear you laugh and kid me. I get so darn homesick for you sometimes I could cry as I used to in your room in the Tower". The student
noted that when Dr. Drury spoke about the masters who had gone
off to war, he fell into the habit of referring to Winant "as a sort
of deity".[8]

An alumnus at Harvard recalled the pictures and scraps of writing
of Abe Lincoln and "how we used to talk about him. Ever since, I've
always sort of connected you up with Lincoln and felt that you must
treat the neighbors around the school the way he treated his old
neighbors who saw him off at Springfield." [9]

Dr. Drury missed the strength of his young friend, especially when
attending wartime meetings of the new Boys' Council. As he sat on
the edge of the sofa at council meetings, he often recalled how a
patient Winant would "placate and sometimes pour on oil and often
by a glance of the eye admonish me to hold my tongue. Oh, for
silence. Oh, for the Christian grace of reticence." [10]

On the last day of January 1918, Lieutenant Winant reported for
active duty to the Commanding Officer of the U.S. First Aero
Squadron stationed outside the tiny village of Amanty. In contrast
to most branches of the armed forces, the work of this air observation
squadron was essentially an individual affair. The pilot and observer,
isolated in their plane relied exclusively on their own resourceful-
ness. In ground units, the soldier normally had friends and comrades
nearby, ready to lend a helping hand. Even among fighter pilots,
the leader had his patrol at his back, insuring moral and material
support. The story of an observation squadron remained almost
entirely that of its individual flyers.[11]

Billeted in the unprepossessing village tavern, Winant found everyone and everything welcome in this ancient structure including the
cow, the chickens and other odd pets. On cold, damp nights, a
roaring fireplace made the interior pleasantly comfortable with wood
supplied by the tavernkeeper, at a modest price.

For six days of each week, French instructors conducted classes

[8] Geoffrey S. Smith to JGW, 1917. Undated otherwise.
[9] Jim King to JGW, February 2, 1918.
[10] S. S. Drury to JGW, November 24 and December 13, 1917.
[11] The bulk of information concerning the First and Eighth Aero Squadrons was
secured from Winant's letters to his mother, tape recorded interviews with Arthur
J. Coyle on March 13 and 19, 1952, and from unpublished manuscripts and
material found in the Records of the AEF, National Archives, Washington, D.C.
Most helpful at the National Archives was Gorrell's "History of the Air Service".

in radio, machine gunnery, and ground liaison work. On Sundays, the shy Lieutenant from St. Paul's usually wandered off by himself across the peaceful countryside, stopping at an attractive site to eat his picnic lunch. On one of these walks he unexpectedly stepped back five centuries when he came upon the birthplace of Joan of Arc. A beautiful chapel stood over the spot where she had "caught her vision". Deeply moved, the history teacher pondered the fact that the Maid of Orleans was only nineteen years old when burned at the stake. Unlike himself, she had accomplished "a great deal in a short time. Her character and humble origin have made her life an inspiration to the common people of France not unlike Lincoln with us and yet their work was very different." [12] How he yearned to play a vital role!

One evening, while resting comfortably in the Amanty tavern glancing at a recent issue of *The Concord Patriot,* fellow officer Arthur J. Coyle suddenly stopped at his bedside. Recognizing the paper, the latter inquired why Winant read his mail. It was only then that these two flyers first learned that they not only subscribed to the same paper, but came from the same city. From that moment, a life-long friendship began between these contrasting personalities. Despite their apparent closeness and frequent meetings in France, Coyle seldom heard Gil speak of himself or divulge his innermost feelings, a pattern Winant would maintain throughout his life.[13] Short, vigorous and effervescent, youthful Coyle had left school in his early teens because of poverty in his Concord home. Immediately prior to America's involvement in the war and before he had reached voting age, he joined the few Army flyers stationed at Mineola, Long Island, and eventually the First Aero Squadron when it reached Amanty.[14]

A hard working soldier, devoted to flying and his plane, Winant usually labored alongside his mechanics on engines and guns. Whether helpful is difficult to determine, for he was not mechanically inclined. Somewhat typical had been his experience with the family car shortly before leaving for France. Returning home with two flat, beribboned front tires, the shaken driver had explained to his somewhat incredulous father that since he did not know how to change the first

[12] JGW to J. L. Winant, January 31, 1918.
[13] Interviews with Coyle, March 13 and 19, 1952.
[14] *Ibid.*

flat tire, he just kept driving in low gear even after he had gotten a second blowout.[15]

His expensive uniforms constantly disclosing wrinkles and grease and oil stains, Winant was the worst-dressed pilot in the outfit. Too serious to enjoy off-duty hours with fellow pilots imbibing beer or wine, let alone stronger liquors, he found it difficult to relax at Squadron parties or to "raise hell" during visits to the French capital. None of his fellow officers ever doubted that he remained sober in Paris. Instead of heading for the nearest bar and its attractive occupants, Winant visited the Opera House, ate at well-known restaurants, and meandered through the Louvre — alone, in the company of a brother, or with his friend, Tommy Hitchcock. Yet he made an effort to live up to the ideals of humanity and concern for his fellow man. Quite often he called it a night by helping inebriated comrades back to the hotel or airdrome. When the Squadron's Supply Officer turned out to be an alcoholic, he assumed much of that individual's pencil work.[16]

By the time the First Aero Squadron moved on to Ourches-sur-Meuse, southeast of St. Mihiel in April 1918, to begin operations over the front lines, the German Supreme Command seemed confident of victory. The new Bolshevik Government in Russia had withdrawn from the war, enabling the Central Powers to transfer a steady flow of divisions to the Western Front. Beginning in March, the Germans made a number of critical breakthroughs, and not until July did the tide begin to ebb. Ironically, these debilitating German offensives eventually achieved for the Allies what the latter's efforts had failed to insure the previous three years.

In May, shortly before the First Division undertook a general front line assault, ground force headquarters requested the photographing of enemy gas projectors immediately behind the front lines. Such a mission required the pilot to fly within 1,500 feet of enemy troops, in range of every weapon. Enemy pursuit planes could then swoop in for the kill. The pilot and observer on such photographic missions were fortunate to return. When Flight Commander Coyle requested volunteers, observer Culbert and Pilot Walter Barneby stepped forward. Orphaned since childhood, the reckless, boastful Barneby had little respect for fellow pilots who did not trumpet about female

[15] Interview with Frederick Winant Jr., December 8, 1959.
[16] Interviews with Coyle, March 13 and 19, 1952; JGW to J. L. Winant, January 1, February 18, 25, March 22, April 17 and November 20, 1918.

conquests, and he inevitably directed sharp barbs at Winant. Absent when Barneby volunteered, Winant went directly to Coyle as soon as he returned to quarters. Apparently determined to prove to Barneby that he was just as good a man, he insisted that he should be given the assignment instead. Coyle asked: "What have you done that you've got to go out and get killed." Gil replied coolly: "I think I'm a little better prepared to die than the boy that is going out." Coyle reluctantly acceded to his request.[17]

The plane took off in pre-dawn darkness from an unlighted airport which usually serviced only daytime flying. Few colleagues expected to see his Spad again and, theoretically, they shouldn't have. When the plane finally returned, bouncing along the runway in a routinely rough Winant landing, Coyle observed a portion of shrapnel lodged in a wing spar, the cowl pierced and a piece of the propellor missing. No one at that airdrome had seen a plane return safely in that condition. The mission accomplished, Coyle delivered the photographs to First Division Headquarters.[18]

In June, after the Spads were replaced with Sampson airplanes, the Squadron moved on to Saints, not distant from the Second Battle of the Marne. Coyle, meanwhile, had become Commanding Officer while Winant had been made a Flight Commander. In late May, German General Ludendorff had sought to break across the Marne and envelop Paris. After an initial startling success, enemy troops reached the Marne on May 30; halted by a wall of men set up by French General Pétain, by the appearance of Americans on the battle line, and by the counter-attack of the U.S. Second Division at Chateau Thierry. By the second week of June, Germans could no longer pursue their advance in this sector; the scales of war having finally tilted. From this point, German strength fell continuously and morale declined precipitously, while that of the Allies increased with Americans pouring across the Atlantic.

As dusk was about to descend on July 12, Coyle received a telephone call from the commanding general in the immediate front

[17]   Interview with Coyle, March 13, 1952.
[18]   *Ibid.*; description of mission and achievements also contained in letter recommending a decoration for Lt. Winant, written by Lt. Arthur J. Coyle as Commanding Officer of the 1st Aero Squadron and addressed to the Chief of the Air Service, 1st Army Corps, A.E.F. Although undated, this recommendation was written between May 8, 1918, when Coyle was made Company Commander, and October 26, 1918, when he was transferred out. Lt. Barneby was killed exactly one week after Winant's mission, and Winant's observer likewise died in action shortly thereafter.

lines. He wanted urgent verification of statements by German prisoners that the enemy was using the cover of night to concentrate immense quantities of arms and manpower for a projected attack on either side of Reims, to break down the eastern buttress of the Marne salient. Despite Coyle's retort that his airdrome lacked lights with which to guide the pilot back to base, the General insisted that the flight be made. Coyle reluctantly gathered his men about him and, after relaying the orders, asked for volunteers. Minutes later Winant and an observer were skimming the treetops behind enemy lines. In the gathering darkness, they noted tremendous concentrations of German manpower, armaments and emblazoned trains moving steadily toward the front. Back at the darkening airdrome officers and enlisted personnel hurriedly lined up every available truck and vehicle and directed their light beams onto the landing strip, while gasoline flares were dispersed along its entire length. Fortunately, Winant managed to feel his way back over the airdrome where he found the eery ground darkness broken by thin streams of lights and flickering flares outlining the runway. He came in slowly for an unexpected safe landing, but with the usual big bounce. Moments after he alighted from the cockpit, a thick ground fog enveloped the landing field.[19]

The Germans began their last powerful effort on July 15 with a two-pronged offensive around Reims. The attack east of Reims faltered because of French artillery and machine guns, while to the west the Germans managed to cross the Marne for a momentary success. Having failed to achieve the surprise which marked their earlier offensives, the attack petered out on the 16th. Two days later, Allied forces, including Americans, began a series of counter-offensives which would not cease until the November armistice. Casualties in the First Aero Squadron markedly increased because of heavy German concentration of fighter aircraft with superior firepower. Coyle's exhausted pilots flew endless missions from daybreak to nightfall. Tension became so great that even Winant sought relaxation, one evening, in the form of warm sixty-cent champagne. That night he became terribly ill.[20]

In early August, with the Germans on the defensive, Winant as-

---

[19] Gorrell, "History of the Air Service", unnumbered pages; interview with Coyle, March 13, 1952.
[20] Liddell Hart, *A History of the World War 1914-1918* (Boston, Little, Brown and Company, 1935), pp. 531-40; interview with Coyle, March 13, 1952.

sumed command of the Eighth Aero Squadron (Observation). The new company commander brought some fifty officers and 160 enlisted personnel to Amanty where he conducted a final period of intensive training. On the last day of August, the Squadron moved to Ourches-sur-Meuse to become the second unit to reach the front lines with Liberty planes. Within days, the outfit engaged in decisive military action on the St. Mihiel salient, southeast of Verdun, in support of the American First Division.[21] Shortly after midnight of September 12, 3,000 pieces of artillery opened up on the salient with such a blast that buildings on the airdrome trembled as if shaken by an earthquake. In the process of erasing the salient, members of Winant's outfit remained continuously in the air during daylight hours.[22]

By the beginning of October, Allied forces broke through the Hindenburg Line on the Western Front, while major successes in Salonika finally forced the war-weary Bulgarians to sign an armistice. Toward the end of the month, Austria sued for peace, Turkey surrendered, and finally in Marshal Foch's railway carriage in the Forest of Compiègne, north of Paris, German representatives accepted dictated terms on November 11.

When the war ended, the 8th Aero Squadron had been actively engaged for two and one-half months. During this brief period, its members logged 900 hours of flying with only one forced landing. But in the final analysis, casualties included eight officers killed, three injured and six "missing in action." As Captain Winant noted, "All that was given us to do we did to the limit of our ability."[23]

Within four months after the Russian Bolsheviks had overthrown the Kerensky regime, their representatives finally signed a peace treaty at Brest-Litovsk. When ratification was referred to the All-Russian Congress of Soviets in March 1918, President Wilson ap-

---

[21] "Report on operations against the St. Mihiel Salient", submitted by 1st Lt. John G. Winant to the Commanding General, 1st Division, December 10, 1918. Vol. E1, NA Record Group 120, File Box Number 232, File folders of Aero Squadron Numbers 1 and 8. National Archives, Washington, D.C.
[22] Major General C. P. Summeral to JGW, September 15, 1918. A photographic reproduction of this letter was found, along with a listing of the complement of the 8th Aero Squadron, in Rector Drury's files at St. Paul's School.
[23] "Report on operations against the St. Mihiel Salient", submitted by JGW, December 10, 1918. The insignia of the Squadron, which Winant created, was an eagle with widespread wings, whose talons grasped the upper ring of a cracked Liberty Bell. Near the top of the bell was the inscription, "In God We Trust".

pealed to the Russian people to reject the German demands, promising full, though not immediate, assistance in their "attempt to free themselves forever from autocratic government" and to assist them in their becoming "masters of their own life".[24] Impressed with President Wilson's letter to the Russian people, Winant nevertheless felt that the negative attitude of the Allies toward Russia since the November Revolution had made many doubt Allied disinterested adherence to democratic ideals. On the other hand, the support given the Russian Revolution by the Central Powers, "although purely selfish and to no good ends", had placed them "in a better position" than our friends. The President alone, he felt, had "stood out firmly for the right as God has given us as a people to see the right and I hope he may hold fast to his position whatever the price may be".[25]

Winant looked forward to his return to the "North Country" where he would get a "shack" of his own in which his mother could join him and make up for all the time lost during the war years. In the meantime, he became increasingly impatient because he "never was much of a hand at standing still". If only they would give him special leave to go to England to study at Oxford or Cambridge, then he would be much happier.[26]

When Theodore Roosevelt passed away quietly in Oyster Bay with the sounds of military victory still ringing in his ears, Winant felt he had been torn from his best friend. Like many others, the schoolmaster blindly worshipped the former President who had played a sad and destructive role during the war years by stimulating wartime hysteria: he had damned conscientious objectors and constitutional Socialist candidates; he had condoned mob action, "fed the spirit that expressed itself in lynchings, amateur witch hunts, intolerance of every kind.... He disgraced not just his own but his nation's reputation." Winant, however, felt that the nation had lost its "truest American and one of the few really great men of this country...."[27]

Toward the end of January, Winant labored strenuously as post commander of the Sazeray Airdrome in addition to directing his old outfit. Although, at times, his job seemed overwhelming, he reached the important conclusion that he liked "organization work". Not until

[24] *The New York Times,* March 4, 5 and 12, 1918.
[25] JGW to J. L. Winant, April 10, 1918.
[26] *Ibid.,* January 13 and 21, 1919.
[27] *Ibid.,* January 21, 1919; John M. Blum, *The Republican Roosevelt* (Cambridge, Harvard University, 1954), pp. 157-58.

April 1919, however, did he finally return to the States to receive his honorable discharge at Mitchell Field on Long Island.[28]

On the eve of Armistice, Dr. Drury finally permitted himself the luxury of planning for Winant's return to St. Paul's. Mindful of the great sequences of the war, of the wartime role of his young friend, and his tremendous impact on the campus, the rector urged him to return to New Hampshire to combine life at the school with a political career in the state. He offered Winant his mastership, carefully noting that "during the next few years positions of real scope and initiative other than heads of departments..." would be developed.[29]

Not until February did the Captain find peace of mind to reply. Although he had constantly looked forward to returning to St. Paul's, his work as a pilot and commanding officer had inspired him to gaze far beyond the confines of the school and to yearn for a career in politics. While delighted to return to the campus for a few years, he no longer looked on teaching as his permanent career.

[28] JGW to J. L. Winant, January 25, 1919; Gorrell, "History of the Air Service", unnumbered page. Winant's honorable discharge certificate is at the F. D. Roosevelt Library in Hyde Park.
[29] S. S. Drury to JGW, November 7, 1918.

CHAPTER V

"AN ALTERNATIVE TO CONSERVATISM"

In April 1919, Captain Winant returned to a considerably altered country. Woodrow Wilson no longer headed a united nation. Big industry, generally grown bigger and tired of according organized labor a partnership in the community, developed "American" plans to isolate unions and other "discordant elements". Extensive cultivation of western marginal land to feed the war-hungry of Europe, followed by postwar rejuvenation of foreign agriculture, would soon lead to a strangling farm depression at home. Many Americans were responding to German defeat and Soviet success with hysteria which frequently denied constitutional freedoms as Democratic Attorney General A. Mitchell Palmer, and lesser counterparts throughout the nation incited crusades against Communists, Socialists and other dissidents.

In New Hampshire, the Amoskeag textile mills, the Boston and Maine Railroad and the utilities continued to exert significant influence through the G.O.P. and the conservative new Senator in Washington, George H. Moses. Despite Wilson's Granite State victories in 1912 and 1916, New Hampshire Democrats remained ineffective in statewide politics. Since the turn of the century, the Republican majority in the State Senate ranged from 22 in 1900 to 8 in 1916, and in the Lower House, 253 to 80. Farmers remained the backbone of the G.O.P., though farm units dropped almost one-third. By 1920, urban centers claimed over 50 per cent of the State's population, with some 50,000 living in Manchester alone. Except for the previous two presidential elections, only one of the ten New Hampshire counties ever voted for a Democratic presidential candidate since 1896. A repetitive uniformity of Republican total votes characterized virtually all counties, particularly the dominant rural ones.[1] While Democrats did better in urban centers, the French Canadians

---

[1] *Statistical Abstract of the United States* (Washington, D.C., Department of Commerce, 1921), p. 141; Edgar E. Robinson, *The Presidential Vote, 1896-1932* (Palo Alto, Stanford University, 1934), p. 59.

and Irish within the Democracy rarely united because of their inability to compromise and apportion candidates. The labor vote remained insignificant, even though New Hampshire was the third most industrialized state in proportion to population. A multitude of relatively small and difficult-to-organize business establishments diffused potential labor strength.[2]

Recalling Dr. Drury's insistence that he was "destined to bless and empower the community in which [he] may live",[3] thirty-year-old Winant appraised the task ahead. His strong base in Concord must be revived, along with a statewide organization of Republican liberals. Not only did he yearn for marriage and children, but he realized that being a family man would help his political career.

As a student at St. Paul's, young Winant had first met Mrs. Archibald D. Russell, a wealthy socialite, when she visited the rector to discuss her son's status in school. Impressed by her charming personality and wide interests, he portrayed her as "one of the kindest and nicest women" he had ever met.[4] At Princeton, he often dined at the Russell retreat near the University, sometimes disconcerted by the giggly personalities and awkward speech mannerisms of two young daughters. In 1917, on the eve of his departure for the Air Service, he again met Mrs. Russell and her daughter, Constance. By this time an attractive young lady, Miss Russell spent the evening with Gil on a window bench stuffing anti-capital punishment pamphlets into envelopes, while the mother engaged the two in conversation. At the time Winant was engaged to a New Yorker, and Miss Russell committed to a young man soon to be killed in the war. Neither displayed more than casual interest in the other.[5]

During the intervening war years, Constance Rivington Russell blossomed into a beautiful young woman, touched by the deaths of her betrothed and her mother. Winant's girl, meanwhile, had married another Army officer. Invited to the Russell estate shortly after his return from the war, Gil was unexpectedly drawn to the beauty and gentleness of Constance. His visits became frequent as a courtship bloomed through the summer of 1919.[6] Descended from Scotch-

---

[2] Paul Davis, et al. (eds.), Presidential Nominating Politics in 1952, The Northeast (Baltimore, The Johns Hopkins Press, 1954), II, 28.
[3] S. S. Drury to JGW, July 11, 1917.
[4] JGW to Jeanette L. Winant, February 28, 1908.
[5] Memo of conversation between Mrs. John G. Winant and Miss Maurine Mulliner, October 7, 1948. Copy in author's possession.
[6] Interview with Frederick Winant, Jr., December 8, 1959.

English ancestors, Miss Russell had attended exclusive private schools and frequented Princeton, Bar Harbor, Southampton and Europe. Her grandfather, Percy Rivington Pyne, had been president of the National City Bank of New York, while her father, a trustee of Princeton University, had recently retired as one of the leading realtors in New York. The product of extremely conservative economic and political thinking, Miss Russell knew little, and cared less, about the grimmer aspects of an industrialized society.

Constance and Gilbert represented two contrasting ways of life. One pursued the path of an active socialite in bright city circles and exclusive summer colonies, the other a quiet existence in the North Country where hard winters came early and stayed late. One accepted the conservative thinking of American society, while the other labored with middle-class progressive ideology. One preferred parties, theatre-going and dog shows, while the other, with a social welfare bent, plunged into politics. One led an ordered life of mealtimes and social engagements, while the other thought little of schedules or regular working hours. Not least important was the fundamental contrast in financial resources. Upon the death of her mother, young Constance immediately inherited a minimum annual income of some $15,000, while the schoolmaster had virtually no capital he could call his own, or that this father could bequeath him.[7]

Despite the intense courtship, Winant did not lose sight of his other objectives. After a warm reunion with Dr. Drury in New York, he became Second Vice-Rector at St. Paul's.[8] He then sought out Robert Perkins Bass, the former Progressive Governor who had pulled the Granite State into the twentieth century. During the war years, Bass had worked with the United States Shipping Board and with Felix Frankfurter in the War Labor Policies Board. Winant found him in New York revising the famed protocol which Supreme Court Justice Louis D. Brandeis had developed years before to bring industrial peace to the garment industry. Impressed with Winant's background, missionary zeal and willingness to assume responsibility,

[7] When Gilbert and Constance were first engaged, she learned that he did not have enough money with which to come down to New York to see her. At that moment, she sent him $2,000, the first of a series of such grants. Memo of conversation between Mrs. John G. Winant and Maurine Mulliner, October 7, 1948. Also, interview with Frederick Winant, Jr., December 8, 1959, who contends that Gilbert was given $100,000 by Mr. Russell shortly before he died.
[8] S. S. Drury to JGW, August 9, 19 and September 4, 1919. This was the position of Administrative Assistant to Dr. Drury.

Bass endorsed the younger man's desire to re-enter politics, under-scoring the advantages of a small state where a dedicated individual could become well known to much of the electorate. He would have to start anew at the bottom of the ladder, especially since he had migrated from urban New York to a rural-oriented state where friend-ships were generally born, not made.[9] Winant apparently left this conference in high spirits for his objectives had been endorsed, and he had favorably impressed the titular head of liberal Republicanism in New Hampshire. From that moment, Bass followed the teacher's career with increasing interest, and within three years planned a new political coup, with the schoolmaster as his protege.

In September, Winant returned to St. Paul's and quickly fell into the familiar pattern of teaching and molding student character. As Second Vice-Rector, he assumed a number of time-consuming ad-ministrative responsibilities, particularly the Boys' Council. Shortly thereafter, he proposed marriage to Constance Russell and then sought her father's approval. When Archibald D. Russell solicited Dr. Drury's reactions to "Gilbert Wynant" [sic], the Rector replied that during the ten years he had known Gilbert it was apparent from the start that "by reason of his complete selflessness and astonishing ability patiently to take another's point of view", he affected men and boys in a unique way. Drury had become increasingly dependent upon his younger aide, because "he was one of the great and deep influences in this place. . . . In Gilbert we have a man who is a born leader; an unswerving idealist; a man of unquestioned courage and complete virility and yet with all the tenderness of a saint." [10]

In the midst of planning for a Christmas vacation wedding, Mr. Russell suddenly took ill and died at his home during the last week in November. The marriage ceremony took place before a small gathering, conducted by Dr. Drury at New York's Episcopal Church of the Incarnation on December 20. Unattended and without ushers, the bride was given in marriage by her brother, and Frederick

[9] Interviews with Robert Perkins Bass on November 28, 1950 and June 14, 1951.
[10] S. S. Drury to Archibald D. Russell, undated. Copy of letter was submitted to author by Roger W. Drury, son of Dr. Drury, who advised the author that this letter was written "about mid-1919". This was prior to October 24, 1919, the date of Mr. Russell's reply to Dr. Drury thanking the latter for writing him such "noble sentiments" about "Gilbert Wynant" [sic]. Archibald D. Russell to S. S. Drury, October 24, 1919.

Winant, Jr., was best man.[11] After spending their honeymoon in Cuba, the newlyweds returned to St. Paul's in early January, taking up temporary residence in the Rector's house. With the Drurys away on sabbatical leave, the personality of the Acting Rector did not permit Gilbert to assume a "vital place in the administration of affairs." Winant avoided conflict by devoting himself to his normal responsibilities, and by renewing contacts with former constituents and the local G.O.P. organization. Republican leaders noted that the schoolmaster had augmented his availability with an impressive war record and recent marriage.[12] With the presidential race only months away, New Hampshire's Senator George H. Moses opened national campaign headquarters for General Leonard Wood, a former Roosevelt Roughrider. Others seeking the Republican presidential nomination included wealthy Governor Frank Lowden of Illinois and Senator Warren G. Harding of Ohio.[13]

Toward the end of January 1920, Winant announced his candidacy as an unpledged alternate delegate to the Republican National Convention, but his campaign was restricted to a few news releases.[14] In early March, some 15,000 registered Republicans braved huge snowdrifts to easily elect the "regular" slate of delegates. Although Winant polled less than half that cast for the victors, he profited in the long run from newspaper publicity which stamped him as an independent, unbeholden to the conservative party leadership. Equally significant, Concord gave him more votes than the incumbent Governor elected as an organization delegate.[15]

The reactionary Senate cabal of the G.O.P., once more in control of the Upper House, selected handsome Warren G. Harding of Ohio as the party's standard bearer, but were forced to accept New England's puritan, Calvin Coolidge, as his running mate. In a world of revolution and social unrest, those who dominated middle class America yearned for such respectable "leadership". Democrats went through the motions of nominating Ohio's Governor James Cox and youthful Franklin D. Roosevelt, who would be overwhelmed by con-

---

[11] JGW to S. S. Drury, November 29, 1919; S. S. Drury to Rev. Dr. Silver, December 15, 1919; *The New York Times*, November 29, 1919 and December 21, 1919.
[12] JGW to S. S. Drury, April 3, 1920. Rector's files at St. Paul's School.
[13] *Concord Evening Monitor*, January 8 and 10, 1920.
[14] *Ibid.*, January 27, 1920.
[15] *Ibid.*, March 10, 13 and 29, 1920.

servatives yearning for "normalcy" and by liberals and progressives alienated by the repression of civil liberties under the Wilson administration.[16]

In New Hampshire, the conservative incumbent, George H. Moses, ran again for the United States Senate seat. An ardent opponent of Wilson's New Freedom and woman suffrage, Moses headed Samuel Gomper's blacklist after supporting the anti-strike clause in the Esch-Cummins Transportation Act. While never a popular idol, he had years earlier learned enough from the quixotic Senator William E. Chandler to become a master at the game of politics. Since his tour of duty as Minister to Greece under the Taft Administration, he had developed a personal political machine structured on the building blocks of every town and hamlet in the state. Making the high tariff his major campaign issue in a purported effort to protect the shrinking textile industry, Moses insured himself extensive financial support from big business throughout the nation. Although he had defeated his Democratic opponent by only 1,100 votes two years earlier, Moses had increased his personal following since then by meticulous attention to correspondence and requests from constituents.[17]

In July 1920, Winant submitted his nomination petitions as the G.O.P. organization candidate for the State Senatorial designation in the sprawling 9th District. Preponderantly rural and Republican, this area encompassed two wards in Concord and thirteen villages and hamlets stretching westward within a radius of 25 miles. The primary campaign in Winant's district went unnoticed as newspapers dealt with such developments as Tennessee becoming the 36th State to ratify the Susan B. Anthony Amendment to the Constitution, insuring suffrage rights for women. From the security of his front porch in Marion, Ohio, Harding indicted the League of Nations as a failure, while in Boston, Coolidge solemnly proclaimed the people weary of White House "vagaries", and endorsed the desire to have the nation go "back to normalcy". Throughout Europe, unrest, conflict or civil war seemed a general pattern.[18] On primary day in September, Winant

---

[16]   John Garraty, *Henry Cabot Lodge* (New York, Alfred A. Knopf, 1953), pp. 357-94; William Allen White, *A Puritan in Babylon* (New York, Macmillan Company, 1938), p. 166.
[17]   *Concord Evening Monitor*, March 24 and April 20, 1920; Merrill A. Symonds, "George Higgins Moses of New Hampshire — The Man and the Era", pp. 41-78. An unpublished doctoral dissertation completed in 1955 for Clark University.
[18]   *Concord Evening Monitor*, August 18, 26 and 28, 1920.

swamped his leading opponent by just under four to one, capturing every town and ward.[19]

From the first election returns in November, it was evident that the Republicans had captured the Presidency and Congress. The G.O.P. landslide began in New England and rolled south and west across the nation. Except for Kentucky and Tennessee, the border states went Republican for the first time since 1872. The Republican tidal wave even engulfed New York's popular Governor Al Smith.[20] New Hampshire gave Harding an amazing plurality which climbed above 32,000. Running far behind the ticket was Senator Moses, though with a comfortable plurality. In the Ninth Senatorial District, Winant ran far ahead of the entire Republican ticket, his 4,351 votes topping Harding's total by 256 and Moses' by more than 500.[21]

The 1920 election signified a turning point for Winant as well as for Moses and New Hampshire. Each man, henceforth, would seek to guide the Granite State along his uncompromising way of thinking. The former Ambassador distrusted the motives of all European nations, and as one of the vociferous irreconcilables, opposed ratification of the Versailles Treaty. He campaigned against the League of Nations even while he expressed the hope that "America would become the moral leader of the world...". One of the most florid orators in Washington, as he helped Lodge lead the assault in the Senate, he portrayed Wilson the dupe of Clemenceau, Lloyd George and Orlando.[22]

In the Ninth Senatorial District, Winant spoke frequently of his war experiences and supported the League of Nations as an endeavor that would prevent future conflicts. His observations abroad had strengthened his determination to press for social welfare legislation to eradicate the inequities in an industrial society. In Winant, Republicans had an alternative to cynical conservatism and outright reaction.

---

[19] *Ibid.*, August 13, 16 and September 10, 1920; State of New Hampshire, *Manual for the General Court* (Concord, Department of State of New Hampshire, n.d.), p. 174. Hereafter cited as *N.H. Manual.*
[20] *Concord Evening Monitor*, November 4, 1920.
[21] *Ibid.*, November 3 to 10, 1920; *N.H. Manual*, pp. 261-62, 286. The Democrats were crushed in the Legislature.
[22] Symonds, "George H. Moses of New Hampshire", pp. 44-57; *Manchester Union*, March 14, 1919.

CHAPTER VI

"PROGRESSIVE INSURGENCY
IN THE NINETEEN-TWENTIES"

The reaction and retrogression which encompassed New Hampshire threw a determined State Senator Winant into the limelight as a progressive spokesman. Unable to resist time-consuming assignments in the Upper House, he devoted the bulk of the fifteen-week legislative session to committee work and floor debate.[1] New Hampshire's population had barely increased during the previous decade, compared to the nation's overall rise of 15 percent. Public school enrollments had declined, while in the nation they had risen five percent. Even industry's spokesmen conceded that the State's Workmen's Compensation Law had become the most inadequate in the nation, while the Sunday law, providing for one day of rest in seven for workers, had broken down entirely.[2]

Pinpointing 103 New Hampshire towns without resident physicians, and underscoring a state infant mortality rate of 87 per thousand, compared with New York's 71, Winant successfully battled the State Medical Association to secure legislative endorsement of the federally proposed Sheppard-Towner Bill. This law would have enabled the state to receive matching grants from Washington and direct subsidies with which to employ public health nurses and establish health clinics and classes in rural areas.[3]

[1] New Hampshire, *Journal of the Honorable Senate, January Session, 1921,* n.p., n.d., pp. 15-16, 52-53, 85, 89, 93, 198-99, 225, 258-59, 391-92, and *passim.* Hereafter cited as *Senate Journal, 1921.* Also, interview with Mrs. John G. Winant, May 19, 1959.

[2] Samuel Crowther, *What We Earn and What We Owe* (Concord, N.H., Commission for the Promotion of Wealth and Income of the People of New Hampshire, 1939 or 1940), p. 57; State Planning and Development Commission of New Hampshire, *State Planning in New Hampshire* (Concord, N.H., n.p., 1935), pp. 31-34, 81-84; U.S. Department of Commerce, *Fifteenth Census of the United States; 1930* (Washington, D.C., Government Printing Office, 1932), pp. 153-72; John B. Andrews to JGW, January 5, 1921; Sulloway Mills to JGW, February 18, 1921; McElwain Company to JGW, March 2, 1921; American Woolen Company to JGW, March 3, 1921.

[3] *Senate Journal, 1921,* pp. 52, 85, 93; *Manchester Union,* January 21, 1923; *Concord Evening Monitor,* March 7, 1923; JGW to John B. Andrews, March 16, 1923; Laws of New Hampshire, Chapter 151, 1921.

Lamenting the absence of an official portrait of Abe Lincoln, Winant pushed through both Houses a Concurrent Resolution providing for the execution of an oil likeness of the martyred President, with funds secured from pennies, nickels and dimes donated by school children.[4] He was less successful, however, in his renewed efforts to create a Legislative Drafting and Reference Bureau, and to enact a 48-hour work law for women and children. Insisting that a modern, streamlined legislative body required professional assistance in the formulation of legislation, and a library for factual information, Winant managed to secure approval in the Upper House. The absence of progressive leadership stymied his proposal in the Lower House.[5] When an overwhelming majority of the House of Representatives rejected a 48-hour working law for women and minors, Winant conceded the hopelessness of pressing for similar legislation in the more conservative Senate.[6]

Winant could have been much more aggressive in his espousal of social welfare legislation, but he found himself virtually alone in the Upper House. Not only did the Senate traditionally represent the more conservative elements in the state, but the Republican sweep of 1920 had accentuated that body's reactionary tendencies. To be effective, he would have had to be part of a functioning progressive caucus. Although barren of social progress, this legislative session remained a memorable one for Winant both professionally and personally. He became increasingly familiar with political leaders and opinion makers throughout the state, and Mrs. Winant gave birth on January 3 to their first child, a daughter. Of great personal significance was the success of his wartime comrade, Arthur Coyle, in striking an unusually lucrative oil well in Texas. As the major investor of the small New Hampshire group which sustained Coyle's work in the oil fields, Winant suddenly became a wealthy man. Economically independent for the first time in his life, he submitted his resignation to Dr. Drury so that he might devote himself to a political career and business investments.[7] Contemplating his friend's departure, Drury

---

[4] *Senate Journal, 1921*, pp. 198-99; *House Journal, 1921*, pp. 465, 651.

[5] *Senate Journal, 1921*, pp. 53, 225, 245, 253; JGW to Vermont Legislative Drafting and Reference Bureau, November 16, 1920; *House Journal, 1921*, pp. 617-18, 625, 670.

[6] *Concord Evening Monitor*, March 2, 1921; *House Journal, 1921*, pp. 346-50; Dunfey, "Democratic Party in N.H.", p. 79.

[7] *Concord Evening Monitor*, January 18, 1921. His business investments will be discussed in Chapter 8.

could only lament that "Winant's influence in the school had been too fine to be defined".[8]

Within two years of the 1920 elections, continued Republican stress on the sanctity of corporate profit and business leadership insured a political upheaval in New Hampshire. Not only had organized labor suffered severe setbacks during strikes commencing in 1919, but industrial leaders generally responded to a brief but critical depression two years later by slashing wages and increasing hours of labor. Through "American" plans, company unions, and controlled communication channels, employers sought to crush a comparatively weak trade union movement. Pleading southern competition and depressed economic conditions, New England textile manufacturers insisted that survival required reduction of their labor overhead. Early in January 1922, these mill owners suddenly announced a second wage reduction of twenty percent and an increase in the industry-wide work week from 48 to 54 hours.[9]

The 16,000 infuriated Amoskeag textile workers, who received half the payroll of industrial Manchester, and whose real wages and per capita income would not rise during the 1920's, exploded with a bitter strike which dragged on for nine months. While managers of textile concerns rejected arbitration pleas from the Commissioner of Labor and from civic and religious spokesmen, and at the same time secured injunctions against picketing and other strike measures, a nationwide strike of railroad repair shopmen further exacerbated the trying situation. For the duration of these disputes, workers were up against press and G.O.P. subservience to railroad and industrial management.[10]

Retiring from the State Senate because of a traditional alternation

---

[8]   St. Paul's School, *Annual Report of the Rector,* December 1921, p. 23.
[9]   *Concord Evening Monitor,* January 17 and February 2, 1922.
[10] Selig Perlman and Philip Taft, "Labor Movements", in John R. Commons and Associates, *History of Labor in the United States, 1896-1932* (New York, Macmillan Co., 1935), IV, 511-14; *Concord Evening Monitor,* January 17, February 24, April 1, 7, 10, 21, June 5, 8, 10, 22, September 2, October 15, November 1, 3 and 27, 1922; William Savacool to Robert Perkins Bass, March 27, 1922; Bass to W. P. Straw, May 8, 1922; W. P. Straw to Bass, May 15, 1922; Bass to Ordway Tead, June 14, 1922; Rev. Herbert A. Jump to Bass, June 29, 1922; "Report by Labor Commissioner on the Controversy between the Cotton Manufacturers and Textile Workers at Manchester, N.H.", Commissioner John S. B. Davie, July 18, 1922; Felix Frankfurter and Nathan Green, *The Labor Injunction* (New York, Macmillan Co., 1930), pp. 253-63.

of Republican candidates in the Ninth District between the eastern and western sectors, Winant won renomination for a seat in the Lower House in September 1922, again leading the G.O.P. slate in his Concord ward. Observant pollsters, however, should have been alerted to a possible upset in November when the respective state-wide primary tallies indicated a forty percent loss for Republicans and a fifty percent increase for Democrats over the last electoral contest.[11]

Former Governor Robert Perkins Bass, who had been disowned by organization leaders because of his support of Roosevelt's Bull Moose candidacy in 1912, successfully sought election to the State's Lower House from historic Peterborough.[12] After committing delegates at the State G.O.P. Convention to a legislative inquiry into the proposed 48-hour-work law for women and children, Bass and Winant organized a progressive caucus for the forthcoming legislative session. The Democrats, meanwhile, endorsed a 48-hour labor law and condemned Republicans in Washington and Concord for supporting railroad and textile management. At Dartmouth College, Senator George H. Moses, ever oblivious to the present, urged students to face up to what he deemed was the great danger confronting the nation at that moment — the powerful influence exerted by labor unions.[13]

On election day 1922, New Hampshire Republicans sustained a disastrous setback with the election of Fred Brown, the first popularly elected Democratic governor in 68 years, the loss of the Lower House of the Legislature and of one of the two Congressional seats as laboring men and women went to the polls to protest their economic plight.[14] Even Winant barely managed to run ahead of the leading Democrat in his ward, a reminder that he had been silent too long on the immediate strike issues.[15] Elsewhere in the nation,

---

[11] N.H. Manual, 1921, p. 172; N.H. Manual, 1923, p. 108.
[12] "List of Voters, Streets, etc., Fall 1922", Bass Papers.
[13] Concord Evening Monitor, September 27, 28, October 14, 1922; Bass to Windsor L. Goodnow, October 5, 1922; Bass to O. L. Frisbee, November 14, 1922; Bass to Felix Frankfurter, December 4, 1922.
[14] Concord Evening Monitor, November 8 and 9, 1922; N.H. Manual, 1923, pp. 212, 255-64; Dunfey, "Democratic Party in N.H.", p. 80.
[15] N.H. Manual, 1921, pp. 256, 286, 294-95; N.H. Manual, 1923, pp. 227, 256. The Senate remained under Republican control though with a Democratic gain of five seats.

Democrats and Progressives made remarkable recoveries from the 1920 Republican landslide.[16]

Three weeks after election, the disastrous textile strike ended. While management spokesmen agreed to retain the previous level of wages, they forced workers to accept a 54-hour week and denied strike leaders their jobs. Amoskeag's autocratic management brought impoverishment to tens of thousands of homes and tremendous losses to the state's economy. When the American economy verged on utter collapse in the 1930's, the immense, sprawling textile company closed its doors forever.[17]

Meeting secretly with Winant and other progressive legislators during the 1923 legislative session, Bass displayed a devotion and competency which frightened conservative Republican leaders. Repudiating a convention commitment, the G.O.P. State Chairman not only lobbied against the 48-hour-work measure but directed most of his rural-minded legislators to reject the proposal for a legislative inquiry. After Bass compiled a "Brandeis brief" in its defense, and Winant assumed floor leadership in its behalf, twenty-eight G.O.P. legislators joined a Democratic majority for victory in the Lower House. The Senate, however, rejected the proposal by a 12 to 10 vote.[18] Having learned to work closely with Democratic progressives, party lines would eventually become a tenuous reality for Winant, especially by 1933 when he found little difficulty helping a national Democratic administration insure the success of the New Deal. His knowledge of New Hampshire politics and awareness of the need for strong

[16]   U.S. Congress, *Official Congressional Directory, 68th Congress, 1st Session, December 1923* (Washington, Government Printing Office, 1923), pp. 129, 131; *Concord Evening Monitor,* November 8 to 10, 1922; Kenneth C. MacKay, *The Progressive Movement of 1924* (New York, Columbia University, 1947), pp. 60-67; and James H. Shideler, "The Neo-Progressives: Reform Politics in the United States, 1920-1925", unpublished Ph. D. dissertation, University of California, Berkeley, 1945, p. 110.

[17]   Manchester's diversified economy is in a healthier state today, for the bulk of its workers are no longer dependent on the whim or stability of a major employer.

[18]   *Senate Journal, 1923,* pp. 16, 85-88 and 315; *House Journal, 1923,* pp. 118-22 and 222-30; Dunfey, "Democratic Party in N.H.", pp. 87-88; Bass to F. A. Musgrove, March 19, 1923; *Concord Evening Monitor,* January 9 and 19, February 14 and 15, April 7, 1923. On March 1, 1923, the *Evening Monitor* became the *Concord Daily Monitor and New Hampshire Patriot.* The new publisher-editor, James M. Langley, secured much of the funds for this purchase from John G. Winant.

leadership had been greatly expanded. Bass, meanwhile, had observed Winant in action and liked what he saw.

Despite the victory of New Hampshire Democrats in 1922, conservatism continued to reign supreme. Republican standpatters in the Senate and in the Executive Council, and the jostling for partisan advantage for the forthcoming elections in 1924, precluded enlightened legislation or appointments to regulatory bodies.

Anxious to alter the steady retreat of his state, former Governor Bass began, late in 1921, to plan for a progressive resurgence. Centering his public activities around a forum on affairs of current interest — the New Hampshire Civic Association which he created — he brought back many Bull Moosers into politics. By the summer of 1923, the Civic Association alarmed opinion makers as well as Old Guard Republicans who correctly suspected political motives behind its activities.[19] With Winant as the candidate, Bass realized that it would require perhaps years of careful organizing and planning before he could hope to wrest control of the governorship from conservative hands.[20]

An attractive personality with an outstanding war record, a beautiful wife, and now two children — John, Jr., arrived in February 1922 — high political aspirations, indefatigability and amazing success with Texas oil insured a most available candidate. Conservative journals would be hard-pressed to challenge Winant, except for his advocacy of the 48-hour-work proposal. But the more the opposition emphasized this issue for rural folk, the more would Republican workingmen and women turn to him. Winant's major handicap remained his halting speeches, which would have insured political oblivion in more sophisticated, urban-oriented states.

Following a series of secret meetings involving former Bull Moose leaders and interested progressives, Bass pushed on with his plans. A full year in advance of the September 1924 primaries, Winant announced his candidacy for the Republican gubernatorial nomina-

---

[19] *Manchester Union*, January 10, 1922 and May 10, 1923; Bass to J. R. McLane, January 26, 1922; Bass to "Committee of 12", January 28, 1922; Bass to R. E. Faulkner, February 21, 1922. Also interview with John R. McLane, June 13, 1951. McLane had been Winant's legal counsel since 1921, and a close friend of Bass.

[20] Bass to JGW, September 9, 1922; Mark Sullivan to Bass, March 21, 1923; Bass to M. Sullivan, March 26, 1923; Bass to JGW, June 18, 1923; Bass to J. R. McLane, June 25, 1923; Bass to F. A. Musgrove, July 5, 1923. Also, interviews with J. R. McLane, June 13, 1951, and with Robert P. Bass, June 14, 1951.

tion. These insurgents hoped to make a respectable showing in this first endeavor and win two years later when Bass would oppose Moses for the Senate seat. Not one of those participating in these secret conclaves believed victory within their grasp in 1924. They realized that over the years Moses had carefully constructed an extremely effective personal organization. In addition, he would leisurely handpick Frank Knox as his gubernatorial nominee, one of the best known citizens in New Hampshire and the publisher of its only statewide newspaper, the *Manchester Union*.[21]

For the next twelve months Winant journeyed up and down and across the state, strengthened by supporters in small and large communities, catalyzed into action by Bass, and the latter's personal executive secretary, H. Styles Bridges. Gaunt, serious, with jutting features that made his eye sockets look very deep, Winant displayed a warm-hearted, reticent personality which worked to best advantage in person-to-person encounters. The extended hands of voters were quickly grasped and vigorously pumped as he conveyed a burning desire to meet and serve them.[22]

Except for a rare occasion when words flowed easily, speaking before large groups remained his greatest personal trial. And yet his impact on listeners continued substantial and unique. A curious psychological phenomenon generally enveloped an audience, converting unsuspecting listeners to allies in his struggle for words. Many seconds might tick by in hushed halls, a seeming eternity, before he uttered the next word. Famed for their reserved, reticent nature, rural voters tended to sympathize with this young man. He may have been born in New York, but he looked and sounded like one of them. The stark contrast with glib, polished orators endeared him to these taciturn North Country folk.[23]

Granite Staters recall another strange phenomenon. As this tall

[21] Bass to S. A. Lovejoy, A. Putnam, F. T. Wadleigh, F. A. Musgrove, and C. E. Clough, all dated August 21, 1923; Bass to JGW, August 27 and September 12, 1923; Bass to J. R. McLane, September 15, 1923; Bass to Mrs. J. W. Remick and to Mrs. J. R. McLane, September 21, 1923. Also, undated six-page memorandum by Bass found in "W" folder of 1925 series of Bass Papers. Interviews with J. R. McLane, June 13, 1951, and with R. P. Bass, June 14, 1951.
[22] Interviews with J. R. McLane, June 13, 1951; and with R. P. Bass, June 14, 1951.
[23] Interview with Robert Jackson, January 27, 1961. Former State Chairman of the New Hampshire Democratic Party, and Secretary of the Democratic National Committee, Jackson had been active in state politics since the first decade of the century.

man with rumpled clothing spoke softly of a deep-rooted determination to serve the people, a lock of hair persistently fell over his forehead. Some thought another Abe Lincoln had come back to New Hampshire.

Day after day, in towns, villages and hamlets, veteran insurgents and progressive recruits took him into the streets to meet friends and neighbors. He spoke of the need for a 48-hour law to protect women and children in factories, of his belief in international cooperation to prevent the scourge of another war, and of his desire to help the poor and the suffering. He manifested a spirituality which went beyond progressivism, but which included it.[24]

As Winant persisted in his canvassing, often in the company of his attractive wife, Bass kept personal secretaries at work writing hundreds of letters to friends and contacts. The former Governor characterized the progressive choice as "so genuine and sincere, that all those who know him well, have a great respect for him whether they agree with his political views or not".[25]

Doubting that the insurgent candidate would make a "creditable showing", an overconfident Frank Knox did not begin a vigorous campaign until the last days of the contest. By that time, Winant had shaken the hands of thousands of voters and indicted his opponent for straddling the key issues of the day. In addition, he struck home when he underscored the theme that only a progressive Republican could cut into the votes which working class districts had cast for Democrat Fred Brown in the previous gubernatorial race. With the Democratic incumbent running for re-election, Winant pointed out that a candidate like conservative Knox could not possibly win in November.[26] Attempting to blunt his opponent's mushrooming support, Knox — who had originally been brought into the Granite State by Bass in 1912 to publish a Bull Moose newspaper — went over to the attack and immediately blundered. Hoping to destroy his opponent through headlines in his *Manchester Union*, Knox sought to

[24] Interviews with J. R. McLane, June 13, 1951; with R. P. Bass, June 14, 1951; and with New Hampshire residents from all walks of life since 1951.
[25] Bass to J. L. Dame, October 5, 1923; Bass to J. W. Barker, November 1, 1923.
[26] George H. Lobdell, Jr., "A Biography of Frank Knox", unpublished doctoral dissertation, University of Illinois, 1954, pp. 6, 152, 192, 199-202; *Concord Evening Monitor*, October 28, 1916; Knox to James Langley, January 8, 1923 [*sic*], Winant Coll. The date should read 1924 for Winant had not announced his candidacy until September 1923. Also, *Boston Herald*, December 24, 1923; *Concord Daily Monitor*, June 19, 27, July 3, 16 and 25, 1924.

lump Winant with Senator Robert M. LaFollette's independent drive for the presidency. Predicting endorsement of Winant's candidacy by LaFollette forces in New Hampshire, Knox denounced the Wisconsin Senator as an enemy of "American institutions" because of the latter's "pro-German, ultra-pacific attitude" during World War I. Through guilt by association, the newspaper publisher sought to destroy Winant.[27]

Hasty telephone calls by Bass resulted in speedy refutations from friendly labor spokesmen, who then reminded the public of Knox's earlier support of Bull Moose insurgents and his subsequent hostility toward progressive legislation and the trade union movement. Winant himself retorted that to couple his own name with LaFollette seemed "disloyal and unwarranted both to the President and to the Republican Party". He rejected the extremes of reaction and of LaFollette's "radicalism", insisting both retarded true progress.[28]

Winant's repudiation of the LaFollette movement demonstrated a timely knack for practical politics, with idealism held in abeyance for another day. Bass's recollections of the 1912 fiasco, when he had supported the Bull Moose candidacy of Theodore Roosevelt, were undoubtedly influential as he spent many a long evening with Winant detailing the setbacks inflicted upon New Hampshire Republican progressives during the decade which followed. In the process, they both agreed that progressive success in the Granite State must lay through the G.O.P., not outside of it.[29]

If his conscience bothered him following his cavalier denunciation of LaFollette, Winant might have eased it by pointing to certain of the Senator's campaign demands which he could not endorse in 1924 — government ownership of railroads and water power resources and the limitation of judicial review. On the other hand, he approved LaFollette's plea for the abolition of injunctions in labor disputes, freedom for farmers and labor to organize and bargain collectively, ratification of the child labor amendment and the denunciation of corruption in government. These issues were much more meaningful

---

[27] *Manchester Union*, August 11, 1924.
[28] *Ibid.*, August 14, 1924; carbon copy of letter by labor leader John L. Barry "To the editor of the Union", undated, found in 1924 folder "B", Bass Papers. Also in folder are preliminary drafts with handwritten corrections which appear to be made by Bass. Also, undated address by Winant during 1924 campaign, found in Drawer 22, Winant Coll.
[29] Interview with R. P. Bass, June 14, 1951.

to Winant, than the nebulous, catch-all statements which poured out of the dull Republican Convention which nominated Calvin Coolidge, and the Democratic free-for-all which finally compromised on John W. Davis. But G.O.P. insurgency in rockribbed Republican New Hampshire had to be "respectable", if it sought victory. Thereafter, Knox soft-pedalled the LaFollette-Winant issue.

Strengthened by Bass and assisted by a devoted young following, a ready supply of funds which facilitated extensive mailings and newspaper advertisements, and a series of fortuitous defections among some key standpatters, Winant handshook his way to an astounding 2,600 plurality out of a total Republican primary vote of just under 40,000.[30]

The ensuing gubernatorial contest proved far less dramatic. Having lost the top post to a progressive insurgent, standpat Republicans generally sat out, or sought to sabotage, the campaign. Although Knox's newspaper at first congratulated Winant on his remarkable victory, subsequent issues concentrated on the three ring national battle. Still smarting from the defeat, the Manchester publisher contacted the Democratic State Chairman on more than one occasion urging him to attack Winant for excessive campaign expenditures.[31] The burden of campaigning for the G.O.P. victor fell upon the tired shoulders of insurgents.

With hardly a difference between the party platforms, both candidates proclaimed their progressive inclinations. Short and squat, Governor Brown had once been a professional baseball player. Often found at his labors with his sleeves rolled up and a quid of tobacco in his jaw, this far from loquacious individual usually sought the retreat of his private office in the State House where he could

---

[30] "Statement of Receipts and Expenditures", submitted to the Secretary of State by John S. Childs, Treasurer of the Winant Campaign Committee, September 2, 1924. Winant Coll. Members of the Winant family contributed over $8,500 to the campaign fund, while Bass donated $1,000, exclusive of the services of his secretarial staff. Also, J. R. McLane to H. Styles Bridges, July 25, 1924; *Manchester Union*, August 11, 14, 18, 25, 1924, and other issues; JGW to J. S. Childs, August 29, 1924; *Concord Daily Monitor*, September 3-11, 1924. The total vote was 20,727 for Winant and 18,092 for Knox. Also, H. Laughlin to JGW, September 3, 1924; O. Echols to JGW, September 7, 1924; L. Garrison to JGW, September 16, 1924.

[31] Undated memorandum of 1924 campaign, dictated by Bass and found in "W" folder of 1925 series, Bass Papers; interview with Robert Jackson, January 27, 1961.

"chaw" without concealment, spit freely and curse Republican obstructionism.[32]

With the return of comparative prosperity, increased farm prices and the absence of labor-management disputes, the overwhelming citizenry resumed their normal habits and voted to "keep cool with Coolidge". Had Harding lived, the exposures of corruption in his administration might have made the race much closer. But Democratic lethargy, a conservative nominee in Davis, and a vibrant old warrior in LaFollette helped insure another disastrous defeat for the Democrats on the national scene. President Coolidge ran up a phenomenal plurality of 41,000 in New Hampshire, helped immeasurably by 9,000 votes which apparently defected from the Democratic to the LaFollette candidacy. Governor Brown apparently picked up much of the LaFollette vote to run at least 9,000 ballots ahead of his ticket, but could not overcome the strong support given his progressive Republican opponent in both rural and urban areas. Though Winant trailed the party ticket, he achieved a significant victory over a popular Democratic incumbent and in spite of a generally immobile G.O.P. organization.[33] The voters evicted the lone Democrat in the five man Executive Council and returned overwhelming G.O.P. majorities in both houses of the State Legislature.[34]

In an era of reaction against idealism and reform, when political spokesmen of big business subverted the regulatory structure of the nation and nationalism and mass hatreds engulfed the land, a thirty-five-year-old progressive and a former Bull Moose Governor executed a phenomenally successful insurgency in Republican New Hampshire. Senator Moses could never understand Winant's popularity, refusing to concede the potential strength of a social reformer in the nineteen twenties. On the other hand, unlike Frank Knox and H. Styles Bridges, Bass never turned his back on the maturing progressive ideology of the twentieth century, and displayed unique talents as kingmaker and strategist who, with Winant would keep progressivism homegrown and Republican in the rolling hills of the Granite State.

---

[32] Concord Daily Monitor, September 26, 1924; Manchester Union, October 18, 1924.
[33] Concord Daily Monitor, November 15, 1924; New Hampshire Register State Year Book and Legislative Manual, No. 144 (Portland, Maine, Fred L. Tower Companies, 1941), p. 85.
[34] Manchester Union, November 17, 1924.

CHAPTER VII

"AN OVERINDULGENCE TO HUMANITY"

A Governor of New Hampshire is somewhat unique on the American political scene, for he is constantly confronted with five other "Chief Executives" in the Governor's, or Executive, Council — another barrier to autocracy written into the original Constitution.[1] Elected biennially, the Council convened periodically at the behest of the Governor, both having a veto on the other in nomination and appointment of state officials.[2] Although the Chief Executive technically initiated nominations, meetings with Councillors generally degenerated into bargaining sessions.[3] The average voter, meanwhile, rarely knew aspirants for the Council because of their immense districts, a situation which had earlier facilitated domination by the railroad. After Bass's governorship, extreme conservatives usually gained election to that body. Compounding the problem for Winant, therefore, was not only a divisive split among the legislators of his party, but an intensely reactionary group with which he must share executive responsibilities.

Within days after his election, Winant conferred with departmental heads of the Brown administration, convened a conference on State finances and studied reports of administrative agencies and commissions. What the Governor-elect learned was disturbing, if not disheartening. As a result of intense competition from the West, there had been extensive reversion of farm and pasture area to timberland, far inferior to the original forests. Over one-sixth of the State's total acreage was badly in need of forestry treatment. To facilitate the movement toward agricultural cooperative organizations, which meant

[1]   Massachusetts and Maine also have Governor's Councils.
[2]   New Hampshire Constitution, Part III, Articles 46 and 47; Ernest E. Morrill, "The Functions and Efficiency of an Executive Council in an American Commonwealth", unpublished master's thesis written for Dartmouth College, 1912.
[3]   Interview with Dr. James J. Powers, July 28, 1953. Powers was the lone Democrat on the Council in 1931-32; Executive Council Records, January 27, February 3 and 28, March 12, April 7, July 10, August 24 and September 29, 1925. Located in Drawer 8, Winant Coll. Also, Bass to Arthur E. Moreau, November 6, 1925.

greater economic production and distribution of farm crops, a standard cooperative marketing law was badly needed, in addition to expansion of agricultural Extension Work by the State College.[4]

Struggling to establish itself as a university, the State College at Durham was in dire need of an assured annual income with which it could develop long-range plans for curricular expansion, building construction and hiring of faculty. To meet the annual demand for trained teachers in the elementary and secondary schools, there was urgent necessity for expansion of the State's Normal Schools. The Highway Department was likewise confronted with a lack of funds with which to continue its road building program, or to develop a modern state map to replace the one originally compiled in 1816. Finally, complicating transportation and freight problems was the recent appeal of the Boston and Maine Railroad to the Interstate Commerce Commission to abandon approximately one-third of its trackage.[5]

As the Governor-elect developed the legislative program for his inaugural address, Robert Bass and Styles Bridges caucused to gain leadership control of both Houses. When the Legislature convened during the first week of January, 1925, a progressive, George A. Wood, won the contest for House Speaker, despite opposition from Frank Knox and the state manufacturer's association, while a similar outcome was achieved in the Senate when Charles W. Tobey was elected its president. This did not mean progressive control of both branches. Bass and Bridges had done an excellent canvassing job for two popular, respected lawmakers who, on non-economic issues, could garner majority support. When faced with regulatory, social welfare legislation involving laboring women and children, Republican and Democratic representatives from rural areas would coalesce in opposition.[6]

[4] Public Service Commission to JGW, December 1, 1924; W. R. Brown to JGW, December 15, 1924; F. E. Everett to JGW, December 20, 1924; G. M. Putnam to JGW, January 3, 1925.
[5] Public Service Commission to JGW, December 1, 1924; H. N. Spaulding to JGW, December 4, 1924; F. E. Everett to JGW, December 20, 1924; Ralph Hetzel to JGW, January 30, 1925.
[6] C. W. Tobey to Bridges, September 8, 1924; Tobey to Bass, November 11, December 6 and 10, 1924; Bass to Tobey, November 18, 1924; Bass to E. W. Snow, December 5, 1924; Bass to J. P. Richardson, November 18, 1924; S. M. Wheeler to Bridges, December 12, 1924; Bridges to Wheeler, December 22, 1924; Bridges to W. J. Randolph, December 23, 1924; Bass to F. T. Wadleigh, December 27, 1924.

The day was bright and balmy as Winant prepared to take the oath of office as the sixtieth constitutional Governor of the State. The public gallery overlooking the semi-circular sweep of benches was already packed, for a coat-laden crowd of Republican insurgents had gathered to share in the glory of their victory. A mass of lawmakers had similarly crammed the House floor, filling most every available seat and barely providing space for the twenty-four Senators who sauntered in from their adjoining chamber. Promptly at noon on January 8, 1925, the loud, steady raps of Senate President Tobey's gavel brought quiet as the retiring Governor and his restraining colleagues — the Executive Council — escorted Winant to the rostrum. For over a century, New Hampshire Governors had been sworn into office under the dome of the old State House, modeled in outline and proportioned from the celebrated cupola of the Hôtel des Invalides in Paris. While taking the oath of office, Winant's normally soft voice sounded unusually deep. Reading his inaugural address with barely a trace of self-consciousness, he impressed lawmakers and the public with his broad sweep of knowledge and understanding for the key problems confronting the state.[7]

Following the tradition of his predecessors, Winant's message stressed fiscal conditions. Without a surplus in the treasury and a critical imbalance of over $800,000 (the result of taxes illegally collected), the Legislature would have to find new sources of funds. Confronted with the threat of the Boston and Maine Railroad to cut off over one-third of existing trackage, he requested immediate authority to employ special counsel to appear before the I.C.C. in defense of those citizens who would be profoundly affected.

Disturbed, along with Governor Alfred E. Smith of New York, by an uninterrupted increase in the number of overlapping and conflicting administrative agencies, Winant urged creation of a joint legislative committee to study and suggest coordination and consolidation to facilitate a modernized form of government. Appalled by the haphazard and irresponsible manner in which State funds were generally appropriated and maintained by various State agencies, he recommended legislation providing for periodic auditing of department accounts, an inventory of all State-owned physical property and a budget system which would place increased fiscal responsibility and initiative upon the Governor.

[7] *Concord Daily Monitor,* January 8, 1925; S. S. Drury to Mrs. Frederick Winant, January 7 [*sic*], 1925; also, R. W. Drury to author, November 28, 1959.

Anxious to facilitate the growth and improve the academic standing of the State College, he advocated adoption of a tax measure which would insure automatic, annual appropriations for a developing institution of higher learning. Never losing sight of the inequities inflicted upon laboring men and women in the Granite State, he reiterated his campaign pledge for a 48-hour-work week law for women and children, in addition to ratification of the Federal Child Labor Amendment. After proposing a long overdue topographical survey of the State, he urged an increase in the gasoline tax toll to assure further construction of farm-to-market roads.[8]

Easily the State's most indefatigable Chief Executive of the twentieth century, Winant drove himself mercilessly from the day he entered the State House. He made himself available to everyone who came to his office, disrupting his official schedule and private life by this overindulgence to "humanity". An endless array of legislators, administrative officials and private citizens, with all sorts of complaints and suggestions, trooped across the Council Room on the upper floor and through two huge sliding doors which led to his unpretentious cubicle. One large desk and some chairs comfortably filled the small chamber, while glass-enclosed mahogany closets lined the sides of the private door which opened to the main corridor. While restlessly pacing the carpeted floor, the Governor could look out through the single high window to the Gothic-structured Post Office nearby.

Winant had little sense of timing for eating, sleeping or family responsibilities, rarely stopping for a hot metal or a leisurely break during long, exhausting work days. He became totally immersed in administrative decisions and, at times, with the personal problems of troubled visitors. He often left a darkened State House late at night and arrived home in time to encounter guests leaving through the front portico of his rambling, white house. Exhilarated by increasing responsibilities, the Governor frequently overlooked commitments to his wife to host a houseful of dinner guests. This grueling schedule likewise kept him away much of the time from his young children, even though he regretted missing a full family life.[9]

[8]   *Ibid.*, Paula Eldot, "Alfred E. Smith, Reforming Governor", unpublished doctoral dissertation for Yale University, 1961, chaps. II, III, pp. 429-33.
[9]   *Ibid.*; interviews with Mary Healy Harley, June 13, 1951; with Mrs. Constance R. Winant, May 19, 1959; and with Dr. James W. Jameson, July 23,

Returning home after a long day at the State House, Winant usually wandered into his favorite room, the immense book-lined library which he had added to the western wing of the structure purchased in 1922. It included shelves of first editions of Lincoln lore, Ruskin and Dickens, in addition to tooled Moroccan leather sets of well-known works in science, philosophy and literature. Just as when he was at St. Paul's, new books constantly arrived, overflowing onto large and small tables. Winant would frequently sit up much of the night reading Ruskin, or conversing with Robert Bass or lawyer-friend John McLane about intra-party developments, world affairs, the unique personality of Calvin Coolidge or oil investments in Texas. Well along into the early morning, an exhausted, drooping visitor would finally take leave of a vibrant, talkative host.[10] Burning this tremendous store of energy would eventually take its toll. With too few relaxing avocations, he seldom shared the joys and change of pace of sports, camping or other outdoor activities. On the hottest days he would decline invitations for a dip in a lake, claiming pressing business. Few had any conception of the consuming hours he devoted to official tasks.

Winant differed in political approach and strategy from Bass and Franklin D. Roosevelt. Where the latter two consulted frequently with close advisers, Winant generally kept legislative and political decisions to himself, until the very last moment. Loathe to convene liberal caucuses on his own initiative, especially in the absence of Bass, he worked through a limited number of individuals. In the process, he developed his strength in personal rather than team loyalty, and over the years could not escape being portrayed, at times, as an autocrat.[11]

To achieve a significantly constructive program in the face of the conservative bent of much of the General Court, the Governor had to approach the 400-odd lawmakers as one would a local town meeting — tactfully educate them through informal group gatherings, make personal appearances before the legislature, and consult fre-

1953. Dr. Jameson was the Winant family doctor while Mrs. Harley was one of Winant's secretaries during the 1930's. Rivington Russell Winant, the youngest of the three children, would be born on October 25, 1925.
[10] Interview with William J. Ford, December 9, 1959; Rev. John I. Daniel to author, March 6, 1962; Charles C. Davie to author, August 8, 1963.
[11] Interviews with Robert P. Bass, November 28, 1950 and June 14, 1951; with John R. McLane, December 5, 1950 and June 13, 1951; and with Robert Jackson, January 27, 1961.

quently with floor spokesmen. The executive was obliged to grasp the initiative from the moment the Legislature convened, for he would not always find Republican or Democratic discipline effective among the many individualistic lawmakers.[12]

Acclimating himself to his new post during the first few weeks of the legislative session, Winant's type of leadership managed to lose that initiative. Ambitious, yet misjudging the role of a strong executive, he awaited positive reaction to his inaugural proposals without seeking to organize or coordinate the efforts of progressive lawmakers. As a result, he wasted the groundswell of support which had voted him into office, and enabled conservative Republicans to fill the ensuing vacuum. They taught him a lesson he would not soon forget.

Hoping to forestall future progressive challenges in primary elections, Old Guard Republican leaders and Frank Knox's *Manchester Union* actively sought repeal of the direct primary law, which Bass had pushed through in 1909. In addition, Knox and his fellow conservatives organized to insure legislative rejection of the 48-hour-work week proposal and of the Federal Child Labor Amendment. In the absence of Bass from the State, now caring for an ill wife, H. Styles Bridges finally got through to Winant the dangers implicit in his policy of weak executive leadership, especially in the face of the conservative cabal in the Legislature. Finally convinced, the Governor convened a caucaus of liberal lawmakers which managed, at the last moment, to blunt the primary repeal campaign in the Lower House.[13]

Shunting aside the cynical game of power politics played by standpat G.O.P. leaders, who repudiated their own party platform, a bloc of progressives in both parties sustained defeat in the struggle for the 48-hour work law. Only Massachusetts, among the New England States, approved a 48-hour work measure. The proposed Child Labor Amendment suffered a disastrous setback in both Houses.[14] Only with proposals which avoided the conflict between

---

[12] Interviews with John R. McLane, December 5, 1950 and June 13, 1951; with Robert P. Bass, November 28, 1950 and June 14, 1951; and with Earl S. Hewitt, August 12, 1952. Hewitt had been Deputy Secretary of State under Governor Winant.

[13] Bass's telegram to Bridges, February 5, 1925; Bridges to Bass, February 6, 1925; Bridges' telegram to Bass, February 7, 1925; *Manchester Union*, February 10, 1925.

[14] *Concord Daily Monitor and Manchester Union*, February 26, March 18 and 19, 1925; JGW to John J. Coyne, March 3, 1925.

social progressivism and standpatism did Winant attain a series of victories.[15] More construction and improvement of highways and farm-to-market roads were approved than in any previous session, in addition to the most advanced cooperative marketing law in the Northeast, a reorganized Banking Commission to protect savings accounts, accurate accounting practices and records of state-owned property and resources, and purchase of that famed crag in the White Mountains called the Old Man of the Mountains. Lawmakers placed the University of New Hampshire on a firm, financial basis with which to meet the needs of the state's youth and secure it recognition as an institution of higher learning.[16]

After the Legislature gave the Governor funds with which to hire expert lawyers to oppose the Boston and Maine Railroad, legal counsel was successful in convincing the Interstate Commerce Commission to permit abandonment of only one-fifth of the original request. New Hampshire property owners were saved many millions of dollars in business and land valuation.[17]

Early in March 1925, the progressive Executive shocked many political observers when he nominated his liberal Democratic predecessor, Fred Brown, to the Public Service Commission. In some circles the move was interpreted as an indication by Brown that he would desist from entering the Senatorial race the following year against incumbent George H. Moses. This would leave the way clear for Bass or Winant to oppose the Senior Senator in the Republican primary and, if victorious, have fairly clear sailing at the November elections. Of equal significance was Brown's nomination as a warning to utility spokesmen. Winant was determined to strengthen the independence of the P.S.C. as a regulatory body, mindful of the fact that in too many states across the country, private utilities had come to dominate legislative as well as regulatory branches of government. The Governor, who could hate with vehemence, was vitriolic in his denunciation of private utilities, because of their intimate association

[15] Bridges to Bass, March 28, April 2 and 15, 1925.
[16] Laws of New Hampshire, Chapters 21, 22, 33, 47, 48, 58, 75, 110, 111, 126, 142, 143, 185, 198 and 260, 1925; Prof. James A. Tufts to JGW, May 6, 1925; Donald C. Babcock (ed.), History of the University of New Hampshire (Rochester, N.H., The Record Press, 1941), pp. 270-73. Also, interview with Ernest M. Hopkins, July 6, 1953.
[17] Laws of New Hampshire, Chapters 11 and 234, 1925; Concord Daily Monitor, January 14, 1925.

with conservative G.O.P. leaders and their general exploitation of consumers.[18]

Winant's bouts with conservatives within his own party, however, usually reached a pinnacle of frustration when he dealt with the Executive Council. Assembling at the Governor's call around a massive mahogany table in a long, high-ceilinged room, Councilors found themselves surrounded by oil portraits of State leaders dating back to Joseph Dudley who, in 1686, was the fifth President-Governor of the Province of New Hampshire. Usually composed of four standpat Republicans and a lone member of the opposition elected by Democratic voters in industrial Manchester, this extremely conservative body was constantly in conflict with the Chief Executive. Hailing from widespread, rural-oriented communities which ranged in population from a comparative handful to a few thousand, the four stalwart G.O.P. spokesmen were worlds apart from their progressive Governor. Typical was their response to Winant's nomination of Fred Brown to the Public Service Commission. Would a group sharing executive powers seriously question the designation of a former Chief Executive to a State regulatory commission? And yet it was only after intense, persistent endeavors by Winant, following a series of rejecting votes, that two G.O.P. Councilors reluctantly allied themselves with their lone Democratic colleague to approve the nomination. The Executive Council majority had originally responded to the tremendous pressure exerted by private utilities and Republican business-minded spokesmen who feared an independent regulatory Commission.[19]

Two administrations later, another equally conservative Council would release its venom against insurgent Republicans by rejecting Governor Tobey's nomination of Winant to the P.S.C., the first time in over a century that a former Governor was denied a State office by the Council.[20]

Summing up their respective appraisals of Winant's legislative and administrative record, the liberal *Concord Daily Monitor* hailed the Governor's accomplishments as significant and "farsighted", while

[18]   *Concord Daily Monitor,* March 12, 1925; interviews with Arthur J. Altmeyer, April 15, 1952, and with James M. Langley, August 11, 1952.
[19]   Executive Council Records, January 27, February 3 and 28, March 12, April 7, July 10, August 24 and September 29, 1925, located in Drawer 8, uncatalogued, Winant Coll. Bass to Arthur E. Moreau, November 6, 1925, the lone Democratic member of the Executive Council. Also, interviews with Albert S. Baker, July 25, 1953, and with Dr. James J. Powers, July 28, 1953.
[20]   Tobey to Bass, February 19, 1930; interview with Dr. Powers, July 28, 1953.

Knox's *Union* maintained that, on the whole, "negative action . . . outweighed positive action . . .".[21]

Traditionally, the Governor's work had been minimal after the departure of the Legislature, enabling him to devote considerable time to private business and family. Robert Bass, however, had broken with this tradition, and Winant finally entombed it. As Mrs. Winant put it:

Gilbert seems to be busy all the time. I thought perhaps life would not be so complicated after legislature closed, but it seems to me he has more things to do than ever. Thursday we are going to Princeton for commencement and he expects to get a degree down there. Then we dash up to Boston on Wednesday, Bunker Hill Day, then back here for a few minutes and up to Dartmouth for another commencement, and so it goes.

My children are perfectly fine and getting awfully big and awfully fresh. I do not know what I shall do to discipline them. . . .[22]

From the moment of his election in November 1924, an ambitious Winant looked longingly beyond the confines of the State House in Concord to the Senate Chamber in Washington. He conveniently ignored the consensus reached at secret planning meetings of Republican progressives in 1923, to have Bass run for the Senate three years hence against incumbent Moses. Instead, by refusing, for almost a year, to publicly endorse Bass for the senatorial nomination, the Governor placed deliberate roadblocks in the paths of many supporters, strained friendships to the breaking point, and inadvertently insured a progressive rout in the 1926 elections.[23] In an endeavor to break the resultant impasse between Bass and Winant, the two met in the latter's library in February 1925. Unless they settled the dispute immediately, the progressive struggle would be futile. The forthcoming contest would be far different from the last campaign, when many members of the G.O.P. refused to support Frank Knox because of slights he had inflicted as a Bull Mooser or as an aggressive editor. The entire machine would now unite behind Moses and his well-known gubernatorial candidate, philanthropist Huntley Spaulding.

[21] *Concord Daily Monitor*, April 30, 1925; *Manchester Union*, May 1 and 2, 1925.
[22] Constance R. Winant to Mrs. Morse, June 5, 1925. Acting upon Dr. Drury's suggestion, the President and Board of Trustees at Princeton awarded Winant an honorary Master of Arts degree.
[23] The bulk of this information was secured from an undated six-page memorandum by Bass and found in his "W" folder for 1925. Substantiating information was secured from interviews with Bass and McLane.

Bass counseled Winant to announce immediately his candidacy for re-election in 1926 and to seek the Senate seat in 1930.[24]

Impelled to respect the caucus agreement to run Bass in the 1926 Senatorial race, and accord due recognition to his immense personal contribution to the 1924 victory, Winant nevertheless wanted very much to enter the race himself. In addition, the Governor felt that his astute friend momentarily had blinded himself to political reality for Old Guard chieftains, spearheaded by Moses, sought revenge, especially for Knox's defeat in 1924. Winant maintained that Bass could not possibly overcome Moses' personal machine and the charge of traitor, which would be hurled at him because of his Bull Moose involvement twelve years earlier, and viewed himself the more available candidate for the Senate seat. When Bass left the mansion late that evening, he remained without a firm commitment.[25]

Not until nine months had passed could mutual friends convince Winant to run for re-election and permit Bass to enter the Senate race. By that time the organization candidate for Governor had secured endorsement from many key citizens who might earlier have supported the incumbent. Moses, meanwhile, had scoured the State revitalizing his machine. Nothing Bass or the Governor could do, thereafter, would change the outcome of the primary contest. Tradition, also, remained a potent foe of political holdovers in New Hampshire, for although these two progressives had sparked the spirit for social change, the more widespread feeling continued to be one of satisfaction with the half-century custom of one-term governors.[26]

While debate raged in Washington over American membership in the World Court, Winant and Bass spearheaded the New Hampshire drive for President Coolidge's proposal to affiliate. Endorsing United States membership in the Court, the Governor insisted that the nation could not afford to deny itself firsthand knowledge of European affairs. He lamented the national tendency toward isolation, contending that American apathy in the face of European developments had been responsible for America's unpreparedness for World War I.

[24] *Boston Herald,* January 11, 1925; Bass's recollection of this meeting is found in a four-page typewritten memorandum, apparently dictated the day following. "A Conversation with John Winant, February 16, 1925". Found in special folder "1925", extracted by Bass for the author shortly before the former's death in 1960. Also, Bridges to Bass, April 28, 1925.
[25] *Ibid.*
[26] Interviews with John R. McLane, June 13, 1951 and July 6-7, 1960; Bridges to Bass, April 28 and May 4, 1925; Bass to JGW, July 6, 1925; Bass to Robert E. Faulkner, November 16, 1925.

In the nation's capital, Moses would have nothing of the plan, insisting that affiliation with that judicial body would be the first step toward alliance with the League of Nations.[27]

George H. Moses in the preceding two years had become the "grandest publicity agent the State ever had." When Henry Cabot Lodge died, the day after Coolidge's election in 1924, the western bloc foresaw a swift decline of New England in legislative matters. However, when Congress reorganized in March 1925, the Upper House selected New Hampshire's Senior Senator its president pro tempore.[28]

Despite his vigorous campaigning and indictment of Moses as a leading spokesman of reaction and as the recipient of large campaign contributions from national industrial corporations, Bass suffered a tragic defeat on primary day by more than a two to one vote. Winant helped insure his own downfall by spending most of his time at the State House, hoping to convey to voters his devotion to executive responsibilties. Long before Primary Day, Mrs. Winant expected defeat. Accompanying her husband during his infrequent barnstorming, she noted, in contrast to the exhilarating campaign two years earlier, smaller turnouts at progressive rallies, but more extensive canvassing and better organized newspaper and placard coverage by the Moses forces.[29] Despite his defeat by over 5,000 votes, Winant felt vindicated. Not only did he increase his primary vote but he ran far ahead of Bass. Conservatives, however, mistakenly hailed the collapse of the progressive element.[30]

Although Republicans went on to win handsomely in New Hampshire, capturing the governorship and the Senate seat with comfortable pluralities, the G.O.P. majority in the national House of Representatives declined and the Senate divided almost equally between the two parties. The Norris-Borah group, which Moses detested, now held the balance of power in the Upper House.

A small, local newspaper, published close by the Maine border, justifiably contended in its year-end summation, that Governor-elect

[27] *Concord Daily Monitor*, November 12, 1925 and January 16, 1926; Bass to Robert E. Faulkner, November 16, 1925.
[28] *Concord Monitor*, August 20, 1920; *Manchester Union*, March 6, 1925.
[29] Bridges to Bass, March 15 and 18, 1926; Albert S. Baker to Bass, July 3, 1926; *Manchester Union*, July 30, September 7 and 13, 1926; *Concord Daily Monitor*, September 8, 1926; interview with Mrs. Constance R. Winant, May 19, 1959.
[30] *Manchester Union*, September 8 and 10, 1926. Moses ... 37,482, Bass ... 17,612; Spaulding ... 30,694, Winant ... 25,498.

Spaulding would find the affairs of state "in a healthful condition" and would be "relieved of much of the reorganization that a new governor sometimes finds necessary".[31] Within weeks after conservative Republicans took over the State House in January 1927, the New Hampshire Senate, urged on by Knox and Moses, voted to repeal the direct primary. Confident concerning a similar outcome in the Lower House, standpat leaders were shocked when a dedicated core of progressive Republicans, belatedly catalyzed into action by Winant and Bridges, joined with Democrats to defeat the move. Frank Knox now finally shelved his aspiration for the governorship as word went out that he would not be a candidate in the 1928 primary. For some years thereafter, the G.O.P. Old Guard remained on the defensive, the momentum and initiative for the governorship in the hands of progressives. Knox accepted an offer from the Hearst press which took him to Boston, and eventually to Chicago. Some fifteen years later, both Knox and Winant would work together at key appointive positions for a national Democratic administration.[32]

Having been instrumental in turning the tide for New Hampshire progressivism, Winant departed for Texas with his wife, where he spent the spring of 1927 with his wartime comrade, Arthur Coyle, trying to stimulate unproductive oil investments. For months thereafter, New Hampshire heard little from Winant. Most citizens were interested in the burgeoning stock market and a prosperity which seemed to encompass the nation. Unfortunately, little attention was paid to faltering industries, festering slums, and decreased wages in textile factories.[33]

After a series of meetings involving Winant and other G.O.P. progressives through the winter of 1927-28, it was agreed not to enter a whole slate in the election of delegates to the National Republican Convention. Only Winant and another progressive filed as delegates-at-large, favorable to Herbert Hoover.[34] There seemed to be no clear-

[31]   *Carroll County Democrat*, December 31, 1926.
[32]   Bridges to Bass, January 6 and 15, February 2, March 16, 18 and 24, 1927; Tobey to Bass, January 3 and March 23, 1927; *New York Times*, December 18, 1926; *Concord Daily Monitor*, February 23, 1927; *Manchester Union*, March 17, 1927. During much of the period between 1927 and 1930, Bass was in Arizona or South Carolina because of his wife's illness.
[33]   U.S. Department of Labor, Women's Bureau, *Eleventh Annual Report of the Director of the Women's Bureau* (Washington, U.S. Government Printing Office, 1929), p. 2.
[34]   Tobey to Bass, December 29, 1927; Bridges to Bass, February 13, 16 and March 1, 1928.

cut issue to enthuse or divide voters, and certainly not the interest which characterized the fight four years before over a pledged delegation to Coolidge, when Moses had been decisively defeated. And yet Granite State citizens flocked to the polls in record numbers in mid-March to vote in the first presidential primary of 1928. Of fourteen G.O.P. candidates running for seven delegate-at-large posts, Governor Spaulding led the slate with the Senior Senator barely behind him. Without the organizational machinery which Moses had set in motion months earlier, Winant came in a strong third. This added up to a solidly pledged delegation for Herbert Hoover. When Democratic voters gave Alfred E. Smith a clean sweep in their primary, New Hampshire had set the stage for the conventions and the election.[35]

Three months later, the former Governor accompanied the state delegation to a dull Republican Convention at Kansas City which nominated Herbert Hoover on the first ballot. Democratic delegates converged on Houston, Texas, in late June to go through the formality of nominating Governor Alfred E. Smith of New York.

Immediately after a convincing victory by New Hampshire progressives behind Charles W. Tobey in the 1928 G.O.P. gubernatorial primary, Winant returned from another stay in Texas to help stimulate the presidential campaign. As State Chairman of the Hoover Campaign Fund, he raised a considerable sum, including his own contribution of $5,000.[36] No wonder many continued to view him an extremely wealthy individual.

Prosperity, prohibition, and prejudice insured Al Smith's defeat, particularly in rural Protestant areas. While Herbert Hoover swept the Granite State, along with other G.O.P. candidates, many Republicans overlooked the significant vote accorded Smith in urban centers throughout New England and the Middle Atlantic states.[37]

With the presidential election behind him, Winant and his wife departed for Texas to spend another winter in search of a lucrative oil well. He required a huge income — to provide his wife with her

[35] Bridges to Bass, March 7 and 18, 1928; *Manchester Union*, March 14 and 20, 1928.
[36] *Manchester Union*, September 14, 1928; *Concord Daily Monitor*, August 15, 1928; *The New York Times*, January 3, 1929. JGW to George Moses, n.d. other than 1928. Located in George H. Moses Archives at New Hampshire Historical Society in Concord, N.H. An extremely limited collection of Moses' letters is to be found here, having been censored by his family.
[37] *New Hampshire Register State Year Book and Legislative Manual*, No. 144 (Portland, Maine, Fred L. Tower Companies, 1941), p. 85.

accustomed way of life, to defray the costly expenses of a burgeoning family, and to afford him the leisurely pursuit of politics.

Shortly after World War I, Arthur Coyle had purposefully secured his discharge from the Air Service in Texas. Fascinated with the potentialities of the infant oil industry, he spent the next few years working around drilling rigs in the Southwest. By the spring of 1921, impressed by favorable land structure in some 37 acres near Mexia, in eastern Texas, he wired his wartime comrade, Winant, urging him to purchase the promising lease and to provide funds with which to drill a well. Convinced by another friend's findings, Winant invested the bulk of his modest funds, enabling Coyle to proceed with the digging, laying of pipelines and storage preparations. By October, the latter brought in one of the larger oil strikes of the year. Shortly thereafter, Coyle sold the property to a leading oil company for a net return of some three quarters of a million dollars.[38]

Oilmen had to assume risks to become tycoons, and Winant had the drive and the determination necessary for the development of Texas oil fields. He lacked, however, the large bloc of uninterrupted time and peace of mind with which to make speedy decisions concerning investments. On one occasion, for example, when Coyle's study of other fields in East Texas convinced him of their potentialities and, requiring $50,000 with which to buy up these leaseholdings, he took the next train north. Arriving in Concord after several days' travel, he hurried to Governor Winant's office in the State House where he found some thirty people waiting to see the Chief Executive. Ushered into the small office through the private door, he sat listening to his restless, pacing friend discourse on the challenging problems confronting the state. Eventually realizing his friend's total absorption with official responsibilities, and without explaining the motive for his presence in Concord, Coyle excused himself and took the next available train back to Texas. Had Winant been more receptive to a discussion of issues external to New Hampshire, he might have earned greater wealth, for those who purchased that East Texas property became millionaires.[39]

The Coyle-Concord Oil Company, which Winant and six friends eventually created, began with a capitalization of $100,000. With the

[38] Interviews with John R. McLane, December 5, 1950 and July 6-7, 1960; with Arthur J. Coyle, March 13 and 19, 1952; and with Dudley Orr, July 23, 1953. Orr's father received a $40,000 return on a $4,000 investment. McLane was the attorney for this investing group.
[39] Interviews with Arthur J. Coyle, March 13 and 19, 1952.

passing years, however, they took money out of the venture but rarely put any back in. From 1924 on, a series of typical oil field misfortunes plagued the company.

Winant's income from the oil company totalled some $25,000 in 1924, but virtually nothing thereafter. Confronted with expenditures for his homes, business office, staff and insurance, which one month exceeded $30,000, and with a diminishing income from other investments, he fell back upon his capital.[40] Thus, immediately after the 1928 elections, Winant and his wife journeyed to Texas for an extended stay in search of another oil strike.

Independently wealthy, Mrs. Winant usually expended a considerable amount of time and money each year traveling abroad, shopping from their Park Avenue apartment in New York, or staying at her family's estate in Princeton, New Jersey. Her unhappiness with isolated, wintry New Hampshire remained evident, years later, when she rebelled against having walls adorned with paintings of snowy, rural scenes. Described by some as having better business acumen than her husband, Mrs. Winant might have done extremely well with Texas oil investments had she devoted herself to such ventures. Her husband, however, would never permit it.[41]

During the winter of 1928, Winant criss-crossed Texas with Arthur Coyle, assembling blocks of leases on some 25,000 acres of potential oil sites. As their car bounced along unpaved, dusty roads under a broiling Texas sun, meeting more cattle than humans and few towns, Winant sometimes unburdened himself to his wartime comrade. He spoke of a burning ambition to aid working men and women, and to prove to his parents and wealthier friends that he too could be a financial success. Once liberated from financial worries, he would again devote himself to the political scene.[42] The former Governor did not enjoy his journeys through the Lone Star State, but he gained some pleasure from the pursuit of leaseholdings and the game of chance involved in oil investment. One winter, however, remained insufficient; Winant would have to be available for immediate de-

---

[40] *Ibid.*; the itemized expenditures for March 1929, totaling $30,562.44, were found in "Nelson, Stewart" folder, Drawer 6, Winant Coll.

[41] Interviews with Constance R. Winant, May 19, 1959, and with others who prefer to remain anonymous.

[42] Constance R. Winant to Jeanette L. Winant, November 20, 1928; interviews with John R. McLane, December 5, 1950 and July 6-7, 1960, and with Arthur J. Coyle, March 13 and 19, 1952.

cisions. He could not divide his endeavors, at this stage of oil development, between active politics and business.[43]

Unable to secure another oil strike to replenish his capital, which had diminished over the years because of liberal contributions to schools, churches and civic organizations, Winant's financial situation became increasingly tenuous. As early as 1926, he requested a friend in California to return the $25,000 he had invested in the latter's fruit ranch, since he had "been hard pressed of late...".[44] By early 1929, he could no longer contribute to the Princeton Alumni Fund for undergraduate scholarships, explaining that he hoped to make a little money so that he might again "take up some sort of humanitarian work, and what little capital I own I need in my business".[45]

With the passing years, an unrealistic Winant neglected to face up to the need for increased protection of his dwindling capital. Committed to sustaining a way of life for himself and his family which strained his remaining resources, and overflowing with love for his less fortunate fellow man, his private philanthropy continued unabated. At least one unemployed friend received $50 weekly, and Winant continued to send the children of three impoverished acquaintances their college tuition and living expenses.[46] After the Great Depression fell upon New Hampshire, Concord police had a standing order to house penniless transients in jail overnight, feed them in the morning, and send the bills to Winant. He also fell into the habit of rolling up money and placing it in different pockets, the larger currency in the small upper pants slit. Upon meeting the poor and unemployed, while walking the streets of Concord, he would draw out one of these packets and transfer it in the process of shaking hands. It was not unusual for the Chief Executive to reach the railroad station empty handed and borrow money with which to purchase a ticket to Boston or New York.[47]

The rare business venture which succeeded for Winant after 1921 was his partnership in the *Concord Daily Monitor*. Initially investing $40,000 in the purchase of the newspaper in March 1923, he sold his

[43] *Ibid.*
[44] JGW to Phil Smith, November 24, 1926; Phil Smith to JGW, December 3, 1926. Letters in author's possession. Records of his extensive contributions are found in Drawer 3 of the Winant Collection at Hyde Park.
[45] JGW to Phil Drinker, March 15, 1929.
[46] Stewart Nelson to JGW, March 16 and 27, 1929. Nelson was Winant's private executive secretary. Interview with John R. McLane, July 6-7, 1960.
[47] Interviews with James J. Powers, July 28, 1953, and with John Pearson, August 13, 1952.

share for $90,000 six years later. Otherwise, he suffered a series of setbacks with the Colburn Construction Company, an endeavor to develop a road building concern in New Hampshire; with inexperienced young graduates of the University of New Hampshire who set up a dairy farming enterprise outside of Concord; with the Stevens-Winant Lumber Company; and with a wood flour venture.[48]

Turning to the stock market on the eve of the crash in 1929, the former Governor ignored the advice of his experienced brother, Frederick, and sank the bulk of his remaining capital into financial cesspools. Eternally vigilant with every cent of public funds which went across his desk, he proved reckless with his own money. What capital he had not lost with the stock market crash in October 1929 disappeared by 1935. He remained bankrupt for the rest of his life, under unyielding pressure to borrow heavily from one friend to pay another.[49]

Dedicated to the careers of Abe Lincoln and Theodore Roosevelt, Winant was repelled by the thought of devoting the bulk of his time and energies to the business world, in an endeavor to revive his income. Determined to emulate his heroes in serving the public, and in search of that Christian Socialist society for which John Ruskin had agitated and given his life, an ambitious Winant knew he must reenter the political scene in New Hampshire. He felt he had grown with his defeat in 1926, when he again demonstrated his vote-getting ability in the face of a one-term tradition. Unfortunately, as politics beckoned him anew, he would find it increasingly difficult to sustain the life of a patrician, for the pressures and frustrations arising from increased financial indebtedness would plague him in his latter years as he assumed important roles at home and abroad.

[48] Interviews with James M. Langley, April 11, 1952, and with John R. McLane, December 5, 1950 and July 6-7, 1960; and voluminous financial records located in Drawers 1-3 and 14, Winant Coll.
[49] JGW to George H. Moses, February 3, 1930; JGW to H. C. Shepherd, October 3, 1930; J. B. Teulon to JGW, November 29, 1935, in author's possession; interviews with John R. McLane, July 6-7, 1960; and with Frederick Winant, Jr., December 8, 1959. Teulon was Winant's financial secretary.

CHAPTER VIII

THE NEW DEAL IN NEW HAMPSHIRE

After his short-lived attempt at being a businessman, Winant determined to regain political office. New Hampshire and the nation, however, would soon be confronted with the most serious domestic crisis since the Civil War. The stock market collapse in 1929 not only demonstrated the vulnerability of an unsound economy but insured havoc and ruin. During the first months of the Great Depression, New Hampshire citizens seemed to have reason to be thankful for the State's economic structure. Its greatest industries, shoes and textiles, dealt in the manufacture of staple goods men were expected to need in good or bad times. As a result, the immediate emergency was not as intensive as it developed elsewhere in the nation. By the time the 1930 gubernatorial campaign reached its climax, however, the Depression had also engulfed the Granite State for every fifth factory worker was jobless, and there was an appreciable drop in wages.[1]

Throughout 1930, interest in New Hampshire increasingly centered upon decreasing industrial production, mushrooming unemployment, and rotting farm crops. Within weeks after the gubernatorial contest, twenty major textile plants would close their doors, insuring a twenty-five percent decline in the number of workers employed and the amount of wages paid in that industry.[2] For the first time since they hurled Democrats from the White House in 1921, Republicans generally found themselves on the defensive. Public complaints became bitter, invectives harsher, and voters turned Democratic.

While private charitable agencies would soon be exhausting their resources, tight-fisted New Hampshire county, city and town governments were forced to increase their expenditures for impoverished

[1] *Concord Daily Monitor,* December 1, 1931; *New Hampshire First Biennial Report of the State Planning and Development Commission* (Concord, New Hampshire State Planning and Development Commission, 1937), p. 36.
[2] *New Hampshire First Biennial Report of the State Planning and Development Commission* (Concord, New Hampshire State Planning and Development Commission, 1937), p. 39.

residents in 1930 by some 37 percent over the last prosperous year. By the following year, expenditures for the poor by governmental agencies would swell by 110 percent of the 1928 figures. Homeless unemployed could now be seen tramping the highways and byways of the State in search of jobs, or setting up "Hoovervilles" of shacks where permitted. The situation would deteriorate long before it would improve. The Great Depression would seriously hamper G.O.P. candidates whose President in Washington had been unable to preserve "Republican Prosperity".[3]

Seeking to retain the initiative gained by the gubernatorial victory of Charles W. Tobey in November 1928, progressive Republicans planned ahead for the 1930 contest. At a series of secret conclaves, inspired by Bass, insurgent delegates from all parts of the State divided in their choice between Tobey and Winant. A repetition of the disastrous 1926 primary was averted when Tobey reluctantly withdrew from consideration because of a throat condition, enabling the caucus to throw its endorsement to Winant. In February 1930, the former Governor formally entered the race against Arthur P. Morrill, the announced conservative G.O.P. candidate from Concord. In contrast to the 1924 campaign, however, Winant entered his third try for the governorship as one of the best known political figures of New Hampshire.[4]

On the campaign trail, Winant emphasized his commitment to the expansion of educational facilities, forestry conservation, workmen's compensation, cooperative farm marketing, the regulation of bank accounts, independent regulatory agencies, and the 48-hour-work law for women and children. Despite Prohibition's increasing unpopularity, he continued to support this early progressive experiment. Less concerned with a man's right to satisfy his thirst than in his obligation to provide food, clothing and shelter for his dependents, he deemed it inconceivable that the common sense of America "in a period of serious depression would want to divert the earnings of people from the ordinary channels of trade into the liquor traffic". Within two years, however, he would ally himself with Franklin D.

[3] Report of the New Hampshire Unemployment Relief Committee, Final Report, Submitted June 30, 1931 to Governor John G. Winant by Horton L. Chandler, Executive Secretary, unnumbered pages.
[4] Bridges to Bass, February 20, March 7, December 9, 19 and 24, 1929; Tobey to Bass, January 3, 1930; Bridges to Bass, January 3, 18 and 23, 1930; *Concord Daily Monitor*, February 5, 1930.

Roosevelt on this issue. In the interim, he remained "personally and politically dry".[5]

In contrast to the 1924 race, when progressive forces were able to expend considerable sums for publicity to overcome the hostile news columns of the *Manchester Union,* insurgents now found themselves severely hamstrung. Legislation, inspired by Knox and the Spaulding administration, had placed an $8,000 limitation on primary campaign expenditures. A single mailing alone, with an enclosed brochure, approached $6,000. The result was an intensified personal campaign by Winant against two primary candidates, although only conservative Morrill was a formidable contender having the backing of Senator Moses and the *Manchester Union.* The standpat nominee was also a well-known state leader, having been Speaker of the House, President of the Senate, member of the Executive Council and delegate to the 1930 constitutional convention.[6]

Three days before the primaries, Winant forces executed a coup when they inserted a full-page advertisement in the *Manchester Union* over the names of 2,300 Republican voters of Concord. Constituting over a third of the registered G.O.P. voters in the capital city, they hailed the progressive aspirant as "the best suited gubernatorial candidate".[7]

Despite an off year contest, G.O.P. voters streamed to the primary polls just short of record-breaking numbers. The progressive nominee managed to overcome the opposing machine to defeat the standpat candidate by just under 3,000 votes out of some 60,000 cast for the three candidates. If not for the amazing 3,100-vote plurality accorded Winant in his home city of Concord, he might have been in serious trouble for the rural areas gave him a mere 585 advantage. As it was, he turned out to be a minority victor for the combined vote of the two opposition candidates surpassed his by more than 5,000. The race could not have been much closer.[8] However, typifying the reaction of many who would cross party lines, a registered Democrat in Dover advised Winant that "there are a few of us down here who couldn't vote for you yesterday but we can in November". Another

---

[5] JGW to Rev. Ernest L. Converse, July 31, 1930; Winant's address dated April 23, 1930.
[6] Laws of New Hampshire, Chapter 34, 1927; JGW to Campaign representatives, July 8, 1930; *Manchester Union,* September 2 and 6, 1930.
[7] *Manchester Union,* September 6, 1930.
[8] *Manchester Union, Concord Daily Monitor,* September 10, 1930. John G. Winant 27,236, Arthur P. Morrill 24,278, Hugh K. Moore 7,824.

voter in West Epping sent congratulations from an "old Democrat. I can vote for a good Republican with a clear conscience." [9] A Florida newspaper concluded that this primary had probably brought sleepless nights to Senator Moses, who "must now gaze bleakly into the future two years hence when he will be called upon to defend his seat at Washington against this millionaire [sic] executive who has overcome New Hampshire tradition opposing two terms for a Governor". [10]

During the following weeks, Winant ranged the state as he sought to counter a Democratic tide. The theme of his campaign was that the G.O.P. would have to offer new and serious alternatives; he insisted that:

There is want in the land today and men who know the dignity of labor are idle. When we turn into the new year and sweep of winter winds and hunger and cold crowd in upon many a home, let those of us who plan to take on the duties of office and administer public funds see to it that the stigma of the pauper is never laid upon the consciousness of the willing worker, who asks help for wife and child because the wheels of industry have ceased to turn and there is no work abroad. We must plan to meet these great cycles of depression and manfully provide against them so that the poverty may be no part of modern civilization. That is the great task that confronts the American people today. [11]

And yet, while opposing measures which would levy unjust tax burdens upon citizens and insisting that the G.O.P. would have to offer new and serious programs, he continued to laud President Hoover's meaningless generalizations that any retreat from the American philosophy of constantly improving standards of living became a "retreat into perpetual unemployment and the acceptance of a cesspool of poverty for some large part of our people". [12]

In the face of a sweeping national revulsion against the G.O.P., a weak, divided Democracy in the Granite State by a narrow margin nominated an ancient war horse — elderly, bumbling Albert W. Noone. The latter found it difficult to counter the youthful, vigorous appeal of Winant's personal progressivism, political independence and popular attraction. As a result, the Republican candidate cut into

[9]   Owen Coogan to JGW; and Edwin S. Folsom to JGW, September 10, 1930.
[10] *Miami Herald,* September 18, 1930.
[11] Winant's address to Republican State Convention, September 24, 1930. Winant Coll.
[12] *Manchester Union, Concord Daily Monitor,* various issues between September 26 and November 4, 1930.

Democratic strongholds, led his party ticket, topped his 1924 plurality, and won by over 21,000 votes. New Hampshire's Republican incumbent Congressmen were reelected with him, but with greatly reduced margins.[13]

Elsewhere in the nation, voters illustrated their developing resentment against "Republican" depression. They returned the House of Representatives to Democratic control, 219 to 214. With 48 G.O.P. members, 47 Democrats and one Farmer-Laborite, the Upper House was now dominated by a coalition of Democrats and midwestern progressive Republicans. The Democrats also elected seventeen governors but the G.O.P. only twelve. The Empire State, which had barely given Franklin D. Roosevelt a plurality of 25,000 in 1928, increased it to a record-breaking 725,000 in 1930. The stage was set for the Democratic sweep two years hence. Could progressive Winant halt it again in New Hampshire?

Winant expressed a naive optimism and shortsighted view of the depression when he insisted, early in 1931, that "We are a small state, but we intend to take care of our own." Like Hoover, he recoiled against madework relief projects as an expensive method of expending relief money.[14] As the depression worsened, however, he would become more imaginative and more experimental than his Republican president. Underlining the critical nature of the times in order to stimulate legislative support for his programs, Winant still found the Senate the chief stumbling block. Increasing numbers of Democrats, however, allied with liberal Republicans to push through many of Winant's proposals, while the Executive Council swung behind the Governor as two liberal Republicans sided with the lone Democrat.[15] During one weekly radio broadcast, which illustrated his support of Hoover's "progressivism", Winant insisted that:

To do less for the unemployed than to prevent freezing and starvation is impossible in a civilized community. The hope of rectifying this condition is in maintaining a wage scale which permits a living wage . . . . The time has come . . . when particular industries must so organize their business as to eliminate the exploitation of labor as a competitive weapon. The shoe industry and particularly the textile industry can afford to make this

[13] *Concord Daily Monitor*, November 5, 1930.
[14] *Message of His Excellency John G. Winant . . . the Legislature, January 8, 1931* (Concord, Evans Printing Co., n.d.), pp. 3, 4-8, 9-12, 16.
[15] *Manchester Union*, January 8 and 9, 1931; interview with Henry P. Seidemann, April 14, 1952, a member of the Brookings Institution who undertook a number of state surveys for Governor Winant; interview with James J. Powers, July 28, 1953.

progressive move with credit to themselves and tremendous gain in human relations as affecting industry in general.[16]

The result of Winant's radio talks, personal appearances throughout the state, improved collaboration with a progressive legislative caucus, support by Democratic solons, and impact of the Depression, was the enactment of some regulatory and social welfare legislation: emergency appropriations for relief of dependent mothers and children; increased state aid to cities and towns for highway construction and maintenance; added safeguards and increased regulation of banking institutions; penalties for violation of "blue sky laws" relating to the sale of stocks and bonds; permission to towns for joint appropriation of funds for support of a community physician or for the construction and maintenance of hospitals; and a more enlightened method of employment for inmates at the State Prison.[17]

After making appointments to the Public Service Commission which insured its control by consumer-minded members,[18] the Legislature fulfilled his request to create the office of Comptroller and provide for an Executive Budget, enabling succeeding Executives to exert much greater control and coordination over state budgeting and appropriations.[19] He failed, however, to secure enactment of a 48-hour work bill, an improved workmen's compensation act, a personal and corporate income tax, a statewide teachers' retirement system, or old age pension legislation.[20]

With over twenty percent of the state's 195,000 workers unemployed by December 1930, the Governor placed unrelenting pressure on his Highway and Forestry Departments, and on city and town officials to utilize the jobless in every way possible.[21] As the situation deteriorated throughout 1931, Winant began to shift his support from

[16] *Concord Daily Monitor,* March 23, 1932.
[17] Laws of New Hampshire, Chapters 1, 7, 8, 11, 90, 96, 145 and 156, 1931. For a comparison with the accomplishments of the 1931 legislative session in New York, which show striking similarities, see Bernard Bellush, *Franklin D. Roosevelt as Governor of New York* (New York, Columbia University Press, 1955), pp. 141-43, 178-84, 201, *passim.* Also, interview with Henry P. Seidemann, April 14, 1952.
[18] Message from the Governor to the State Senate, March 31, 1931; Laws of New Hampshire, Chapter 127, 1931; Bridges to Bass, April 3, 1931.
[19] Foster, Willis and Co. to JGW, May 26, 1930; Laws of New Hampshire, Chapter 171, 1931.
[20] *Concord Daily Monitor,* May 7 and 8, 1931; *Manchester Union,* May 9, 1931.
[21] Report of the New Hampshire Unemployment Relief Committee, Final Report, submitted June 30, 1931 to Governor John G. Winant by Horton L. Chandler, Executive Secretary, unnumbered pages.

Hoover's policies; he sponsored a made work road program which employed 3,000 men.[22]

Without income from his collapsing investments, Winant found it difficult to meet his own living expenses. He readily disposed of a yacht he had barely used, but refused to go along with his wife's suggestion to reduce the staff in their Concord home. He would not add to the list of unemployed by discharging either of the nurses who had cared for their three children, the shy British maid, Orol Mears, who had joined them the year before, their cook, butler, chauffeur, financial secretary or those who cared for the grounds and his wife's dog kennels.[23]

By the end of 1931, New Hampshire was harvesting its share of the plague with over one-third of the workers jobless. Expenditures for the poor hurtled upwards, for only one-half of those unemployed could care for themselves for the remainder of the winter. In northerly Berlin, weekly payrolls fell from $235,000 to $50,000. In one community, where nine factories normally employed over 1,000 workers, only 118 remained on full-time payrolls and 200 part-time. Toward the end of the winter, with freezing cold and snow still blanketing the North Country, Chairman James Langley of the Governor's Committee on Unemployment conceded for the first time that malnutrition was a reality in many Granite State homes.[24]

With every third worker in the state unemployed, Winant moved sharply in the direction of experimental responses to the Great Depression.[25] Early that year, movie-goers throughout the country saw Winant in newsreels in which he explained a "New Hampshire Plan". Concluding that the economic crisis could no longer be attacked by individual state action, he proposed a nation-wide flexible work week of four days for each employee, the surplus man hours to be divided among additional workers without increasing operating expenses.

---

[22]   J. M. Langley to JGW, September 10, 1931. The 1931 Legislature had rejected Winant's recommendation for creation of a permanent fact-finding committee on unemployment statistics. Also, JGW to Selectmen, October 10, 1931; *Concord Daily Monitor,* October 20 and 21, 1931; "Unemployment-general" folder, Drawer 38, Winant Coll.

[23]   Interviews with Orol Mears, July 24 to 31, 1952.

[24]   James Langley to R. P. Bass, December 14, 1931; *Concord Daily Monitor,* December 1, 1931 and March 18, 1932.

[25]   JGW to Gifford Pinchot, November 1931, undated otherwise; Grace Abbott, "Children and the Depression: A National Study and A Warning", *The New York Times,* December 18, 1932; Langley to R. P. Bass, December 14, 1931; *Concord Daily Monitor,* December 1, 1931.

Despite meetings with President Hoover and spokesmen for business and labor, the plan made little headway.[26] Winant's subsequent recommendation of interstate adoption of uniform laws and regulations for the ailing textile industry was another step away from the Hoover Administration, as was his endorsement of the Garner-Wagner relief bill before Congress in July 1932. This proposal sought direct aid to individuals and a vast expansion of public works. Winant advised the President that unemployment and hunger continued unimpeded, that a third of the state's industrial population was without work, another third employed only part time, and the total payroll cut in two. "We are deeply interested in Federal action. Our relief load has increased month by month. . . ." The Governor maintained that one of the most effective means of assistance in the immediate crisis was the Garner-Wagner bill, which would enable him to adopt constructive planning to cope with the emergency situation. The time had come, he felt, for Washington to step actively into the breach for even New Hampshire would soon find it difficult to cope with increasing unemployment and hunger.[27]

The President, however, still insisted that relief was a local problem and that the Federal government could best serve the people by working through the cities and states. As Mr. Hoover put it in his reply to Winant, "If I can only strip the relief bill of its demagoguery and get it on the right track, you will find everything in it that you need and in much better form than even you suggest."[28]

When the President could not exorcise the "demagoguery" in the proposed bill, he vetoed it, calling it "impractical, dangerous," and "damaging to our whole conception of governmental relations." Congress then meekly followed his advice and passed a new relief bill which authorized the Reconstruction Finance Corporation to loan $300,000,000 to states whose resources were exhausted and an additional large sum to states and municipalities for self-liquidating public works.[29]

In September, when Winant finally appealed to Washington for funds with which to assist the needy and distressed, the Reconstruc-

[26] *New York Herald Tribune,* October 2, 1932; *Manchester Union,* August 4, 1932; JGW to William Green, June 20, 1932; Walter Lippmann to JGW, July 12, 1932; Robert J. Watt to JGW, July 18, 1932; JGW to Henry I. Harriman, July 19, 1932; JGW to Lawrence J. Richey, July 26, 1932.
[27] JGW to Herbert Hoover, July 6, 1932.
[28] Herbert Hoover to JGW, July 8, 1932.
[29] *The New York Times,* July 17, 1932.

tion Finance Corporation granted him over $600,000.[30] With the nation's economy on the verge of collapse, Winant like Governor Roosevelt of New York felt that wage cuts must be eliminated "as a weapon in competitive industry", and that reserves for unemployment insurance be set up "on the same basis as reserves for amortization of bonds and depreciation of machinery".[31]

The political pot boiled over as the ebbing economy altered the voting habits of New Hampshire citizens. In the 1932 primaries, Granite State voters would select delegates to the national conventions, candidates for Governor, the Legislature, Congress, and the Senate seat held by George H. Moses. Never was the time more propitious for a clearcut struggle between Winant's welfare state philosophy and Moses' social Darwinism. As far as the Senior Senator was concerned, recovery could be achieved only by following the hallowed methods of curtailing expenses, balancing the budget, and patiently waiting for increased business confidence.[32]

In contrast to 1926, Winant would have no difficulty securing progressive endorsement in the senatorial race. And he would be in a much stronger position to retire the standpat spokesman from politics. However, to avert a repetition of the 1926 fiasco, progressives would have to make their primary selections early. The Governor, however, procrastinated anew. Was he suddenly fearful of suffering defeat, or did he believe that the governorship might be a more efficient vehicle to the White House? As the weeks dragged into months, without a decision by Winant, progressives became more frustrated in the absence of leadership from the State House.

Only after Bass and John McLane personally urged the Governor to convene a caucus did Winant agree to a meeting in July 1931. But with Winant unable to clarify the picture as to his choice of office, the gathering was a dismal failure. Bass was obliged to return to his ill wife in Arizona, unhappy at having failed to resolve an admittedly difficult situation. Was 1926 to be repeated? [33]

When the Republican Representative from New Hampshire's First Congressional District suddenly died in October 1931, Winant again defaulted leadership in the face of a special election. Since the out-

[30] *Concord Daily Monitor*, August 17 and October 28, 1932; JGW to R.F.C., September 15, 1932.
[31] JGW to L. Conklin, September 3, 1932. See Bellush, *Roosevelt as Governor*, Chapters VI and VIII.
[32] Merrill A. Symonds, *George Higgins Moses of New Hampshire*, p. 301.
[33] Tobey to Bass, January 11, 1932.

come of this contest would have nationwide as well as local significance, the Governor should have immediately convened a caucus to
agree upon a progressive candidate. Instead, he ignored urgings from
Bass in distant Arizona and hesitated until it was too late. The three
Republicans who did announce their candidacies were all conservatives. As one insurgent leader implied, the Governor refused to convene a progressive caucus for fear that Charles W. Tobey would be
nominated, and "You ... realize that the Governor will not favor
Tobey's runnning for any office".[34]

In contrast to Bass and Tobey, the Governor refused to work closely
with others in the formulation of major policy decisions. Ambitious
for high political office, he may have feared the possibility of popular
Tobey competing with him for progressive leadership in the state. In
the absence of caucus meetings, the Governor remained the unchal-
lenged spokesman of insurgents.

Back in the First Congressional District, a conservative G.O.P.
candidate was overwhelmed in the special election by a 3,000-vote
Democratic plurality. In 1930, the Republican victor had captured
the district with a 9,000 margin. The handwriting was on the wall.[35]

Three days later, Winant jolted fellow progressives when he filed
joint papers for delegate-at-large to the Republican National Convention for Huntley Spaulding, George H. Moses and himself. The
rest of an uncontested slate was to be completed within days. This
was an astounding setback for progressives, and a breach of faith on
the part of the Governor. He had not consulted with Bass, Tobey,
Bridges or other progressive spokesmen prior to this bombshell,
although he had conferred with Moses, of all people.[36]

The ensuing uproar was tremendous, especially after Winant sought
to rationalize his action by contending that he had hoped to avoid
a strength-sapping struggle in the primary and thus save the state
for Hoover. Besides, if there was to be a fusion slate, didn't the senior
Senator merit a place on the delegation? From the high vantage
point of the State House, the Chief Executive had begun to reason
in ways strange and foreign to fellow progressives.[37]

Winant was quickly made aware of the bitterness and frustration

[34]   Bass to JGW, October 24, 1931; Bass to Bridges, October 24, 1931; Bridges
to Bass, October 31 and November 5, 1931.
[35]   *Manchester Union,* January 6, 1932.
[36]   *Concord Daily Monitor,* January 8, 1932; Tobey to Bass, January 11, 1932;
Bridges to Bass, February 11, 1932.
[37]   Tobey to Bass, March 23, 1932.

raging among friends and progressive colleagues, who felt he had gone too far and played into the hands of the conservative opposition. Only four years earlier they had fought the machine slate and elected Winant. Now, the Governor had thrown the reactionary leader a lifeline. Unless they opposed Moses all along the line, they would be in a weakened position to fight him in the senatorial campaign. In a time of national crisis which demanded enlightened leadership and ideology, Winant had strengthened the hands of reactionary spokes-men.

Disturbed by this festering anger among progressive colleagues, Winant invited Charles Tobey to his house for the first time in four-teen months. Despite lengthy endeavors at explanation and clarifica-tion, the Governor failed to regain his idealistic lustre. Furthermore, when he refused to commit himself on the senatorial race, he further neutralized his adherents who yearned for Moses' scalp. It became apparent to Tobey that the Governor would not challenge Moses in the primary. This was a sad day for insurgent Republicans in the Granite State who felt betrayed by the man they had fought for, and struggled with, these many years. As Tobey was about to leave the Winant household, the Governor suddenly blurted out: "Charles, I have been lonesome. I haven't talked with anyone in confidence as I have tonight." The surprised visitor could only remind Winant that it was his own fault. His friends had always been eager and available to speak with him.[38]

Public interest in New Hampshire's presidential primaries, the first in the nation, centered on the Democratic fight between Alfred E. Smith and Franklin D. Roosevelt. The results exceeded the New York Governor's expectations for, despite a heavy snowstorm in the northern part of the state, he decisively defeated the Happy Warrior. With no contest among Republican delegates to the national conven-tion, fewer than 23,000 G.O.P. voters bothered to give Winant a scant 600 lead over Moses.[39]

The platform adopted at a subdued national Republican conven-tion in mid-June gave Winant and western progressives little com-fort. Only on prohibition did the actors awake from their lethargy to reject efforts to endorse outright repeal of the Eighteenth Amend-ment. Eulogizing the President's leadership and praising his admin-

[38]   *Ibid.*
[39]   *Manchester Union,* March 18, 1932; Frank Freidel, *Franklin D. Roosevelt: The Triumph* (Boston, Little, Brown and Co., 1956), pp. 280-81.

istrative measures, the delegates blamed Europe for the depression and renominated Hoover on the first ballot.[40] Winant did not ally himself, at this time, with those "sons of the wild jackass" who bolted the G.O.P. Instead, he returned home to assure doubting voters that Granite State would cast its vote for Hoover "because it believes in him, and in the principles for which he stands".[41]

Victory-minded Democrats nominated Franklin D. Roosevelt on their fourth ballot, along with a platform which should have been attractive to Winant. For the general public, it offered repeal of prohibition, a balanced budget, reciprocal tariff agreements, an expanded public works program, and unemployment and old-age insurance. To farmers it promised aid on mortgages, cooperatives, crop surpluses and prices. It also pledged to enforce anti-trust laws, support conservation and water power for the public interest, the regulation of public utilities, holding companies and trading in securities and commodities. Roosevelt accepted the nomination at the convention with a promise to develop a "new deal".[42]

In late July, Winant finally announced his decision to run again for the Republican gubernatorial nomination. Sensitive to liberal criticism of his recent behavior, he rationalized his position, insisting that to leave an office of public trust in time of trouble either for promotion or retirement did not satisfy his feelings of obligation to those who had supported him.[43] During the days which followed Winant's pronouncement, a number of candidates announced their intentions to run for office; among them was former Governor Fred Brown who was up for the Democratic Senatorial nomination. The Democratic leader, apparently out of consideration for his appointment to the Public Service Commission by Winant, had confided to a Republican friend that he would not announce for the Senate seat if the Governor opposed Moses in the Republican primary.[44]

Winant did not bother to campaign against an unknown, wringing wet opponent, except for a radio address on the eve of the primary. The next day, 55,000 Republicans gave their Chief Executive a record breaking majority of 36,000 votes. Moses, unopposed, received 5,000

[40] *The New York Times*, June 15-17, 1932.
[41] JGW to Clara A. Heath, August 8, 1932.
[42] *The New York Times*, June 28-July 3, 1932.
[43] *Concord Daily Monitor*, July 21, 1932.
[44] Tobey to Bass, March 23, 1932.

fewer votes than Winant, while Fred Brown swept the Democratic contest for the Senate seat.[45]

During the weeks before the general election, Moses fought for his political life, but without any support from Winant. When a friend wrote the Governor, "I do wish someone would put a muzzle on Moses", the Chief Executive replied, "I am with you on the 'muzzle' business." [46] Fred Brown, meanwhile, persistently denounced Hoover's standpatism and Moses' cynical conservatism. Taking up the progressive cudgels which Winant had defaulted in the primaries, the Democratic candidate denounced Moses as "the tool of the corporations" and "the errand boy of the power trust". He delighted in reading off the out-of-state business contributors to the Moses campaign fund.[47]

Grateful for his original appointment to the Public Service Commission and in tune with the welfare state objectives of the Governor, Fred Brown refrained from campaigning for his own gubernatorial candidate, Henri T. Ledoux. In return, Winant never once spoke in support of Moses nor criticized Brown. Denied by Winant the opportunity to fight the caustic standpatter in the G.O.P. senatorial primaries, progressive Republicans were obliged to knife the cynical conservative in November.

On election day Roosevelt swept the nation as Democrats captured more than 70 percent of the House of Representatives and a twenty-two vote majority in the Senate. The landslide was so crushing in New York that Democrats captured the State Senate for the first time in decades. In New Hampshire, voters hesitantly awarded the state to Hoover by less than 3,000 and then turned around to hurl George H. Moses into oblivion with a scant 2,000 majority for Fred Brown. Four years before, Hoover had captured the state by 35,000, while Moses had won his last contest by 31,000. While the Democrat was reelected in the First Congressional District, Tobey won the other seat with a comfortable plurality.[48] Running far ahead of the G.O.P. ticket and winning by a 17,000-vote plurality, Winant had

[45] *Concord Daily Monitor,* September 14 and 15, 1932.
[46] *Ibid.,* September 27, 1932; George T. Hughes to JGW, September 3, 1932; JGW to Hughes, September 6, 1932.
[47] Bridges to Bass, November 9, 1932; *Concord Daily Monitor,* various issues between September 15 and November 8, 1932.
[48] Bridges to Bass, November 9, 1932; *The New York Times,* November 9, 1932; *Concord Daily Monitor,* November 9, 1932.

probably stopped the Democratic tidal wave from engulfing his presidential candidate and one of two Congressmen.[49]

The morning following election, Winant wired Hoover at Palo Alto, "New Hampshire is a small state but there are those who love it. We have four electoral votes. We cast them for you and with them goes our affectionate regard." [50]

During the interregnum in Washington, gloom and despair pervaded the atmosphere as millions verged on losing self-respect and faith in their nation. Despite efforts by Winant to tap every available source, revenues slumped so sharply during the last six months of 1932 that he was forced to appeal again to the R.F.C. for financial assistance.[51] As he hopefully awaited the changing of the guard in the nation's capital, the Governor urged New Hampshire's lawmakers to enact much-needed legislation. Emulating worried colleagues in Congress, who anxiously sought leadership from any source, many overcame their conservative inhibitions to support a number of Winant's progressive proposals, such as an emergency credit act which enabled the state to guarantee the notes of distressed political subdivisions seeking loans for governmental functions and a vastly expanded public works program. Passage of a bold reorganization of human relief to eliminate waste and inefficiency took somewhat longer.[52] This item of Winant's major emergency relief program was an outgrowth of a full-scale investigation of New Hampshire's county system by the Brookings Institution of Washington, a study undertaken at the Governor's behest. To eliminate the expensive duplication and other shortcomings pointed out in the Brookings Report, and to insure uniform direction by trained social workers, which was unattainable under local administration, Winant secured his major victory of the season with legislative endorsement of supervision of poor relief ad-

[49] Symonds, *George H. Moses of New Hampshire*, p. 316; JGW to H. Hoover, November 9, 1932; H. Hoover to JGW, November 12, 1932; Bass to Bridges, November 12, 1932. Also, *The New York Times*, November 10, 1932; *Manchester Union*, November 11, 1932; *Concord Daily Monitor*, November 15, 1932.
[50] JGW to H. Hoover, November 9, 1932.
[51] *Concord Daily Monitor*, December 15 and 20, 1932, January 5 and 16, 1933; *Manchester Union*, January 6, 1933.
[52] *Concord Daily Monitor*, March 28, 31 and April 4, 1933; Laws of New Hampshire, Chapters 63 and 150, 1933; interview with Stephen B. Story, July 23, 1953.

ministration by an administrator appointed by the Chief Executive.[53]

Despite overwhelming House approval of the 48-hour-work week measure, and personal pleas by Winant, the Senate continued to be the final stumbling block.[54] Determined that the government take a hand in the elimination of sweatshops and the exploitation of labor, he managed to sway sufficient votes to insure enactment of a minimum wage act for women and minors.[55] From the broken threads of the Great Depression, he began weaving a new pattern of labor laws designed to protect the state's industries against cutthroat competition. Some employers were affronted by the strict administering of the new minimum wage law; one of their lobbyists frankly remarked, "We didn't mind having labor legislation enacted, but we do mind having them enforced." [56] When Senator Hugo L. Black of Alabama introduced a bill to prohibit the interstate shipment of goods produced by labor working more than thirty hours a week, Winant wired his support insisting that only nationwide legislation of this kind could eliminate cutthroat competition, raise purchasing power of the workers and provide a market for the goods produced.[57]

Winant had demonstrated that state governments could assume responsibility and initiative in the face of the Great Depression. Even the carping *Manchester Union* commended Winant, albeit reluctantly, for adopting relief measures and for acting promptly in the face of the national banking emergency.[58] But the task was too great for governors alone. After Roosevelt's inaugural on March 4, 1933, with the nation deep in the valley of despair, the President and Congress became the fulcrum of the nation's political and economic structure. Henceforth, state governments would be overshadowed by the New

[53] Bridges to Bass, January 26, 1933; *Concord Daily Monitor,* June 2, 1933; interview with Edgar P. Hunter, July 1953. Hunter was one of the lawmakers involved. Also, Laws of New Hampshire, Chapter 160, 1933.
[54] *Manchester Union,* February 27 and May 15, 1933; *Concord Daily Monitor,* February 28, March 23 and May 17, 1933; JGW to Philip Heald, March 18, 1933; JGW to Mrs. Lucius Thayer, May 13, 1933; JGW to Rena Trask, May 18, 1933; Grace Abbott to JGW, May 16, 1933.
[55] Laws of New Hampshire, Chapter 87, 1933; *Concord Daily Monitor,* June 13, 1933; *Christian Science Monitor,* June 30, 1933; the state's new wage law called for the formation of wage boards for individual industries, the personnel of which was to be selected by a state administrator with the approval of the Governor and his Council. Representatives were to be equally apportioned among industry, labor and the public.
[56] Interviews with Ethel M. Johnson, May 17, 1951 and December 7, 1959. Miss Johnson was the administrator of the new law.
[57] *Concord Daily Monitor,* April 28, 1933.
[58] *Manchester Union,* June 19, 1933.

Deal in Washington, which would supply the funds, the program, and the leadership with which to revive the gasping economy.

Direction and energy, which had been lacking under Hoover, became evident immediately after March 4, 1933.[59] Throughout the first two critical years of the New Deal, New Hampshire cooperated with blossoming alphabetical agencies in the nation's capital, being the first to fill its enrollment quota in the Civilian Conservation Corps, and the first to cooperate with the National Planning Board.[60] Before autumn, 1933, Washington funds enabled Winant to launch twelve major work projects and distribute hundreds of thousands of pounds of pork, beef, butter, eggs and other staples among New Hampshire's needy.[61] Unfortunately, the summer boom, which had temporarily insured a drop in unemployment to seven percent, came to an end and Washington authorities again faced the need to recharge the economy. In October 1933, the Granite State's relief administration cared for some 40,000 men, women and children, the highest total since the advent of the depression. When the Public Works Administration failed to function quickly, Roosevelt directed Harry Hopkins to launch a vast work relief program under the Civil Works Administration and within thirty days, the CWA channeled funds to millions throughout the nation.[62] As Hopkins made clear to Winant, "We are doing a rush job ... ". By mid-January 16,000 men and women were

---

[59] H. L. Hopkins to JGW, May 23, 1933; H. A. Wallace to JGW, April 25, May 5 and June 5, 1933; JGW to H. A. Wallace, May 1, 1933; Frances Perkins to JGW, June 8, 1933; JGW to F. Perkins, June 12, 1933; *Concord Daily Monitor,* June 14, 24 and 27, 1933; Laws of New Hampshire, Chapter 162, 1933.

[60] *Concord Daily Monitor,* May 18 and 29, 1933; JGW to Charles W. Eliot, November 29, December 7 and 14, 1933; Eliot to JGW, December 9, 1933; Wesley C. Mitchell to JGW, April 5, 1934.

[61] *Concord Daily Monitor,* September 25, 1933; Harold J. Lockwood to JGW, December 1, 1933. By the end of the year the status of New Hampshire PWA projects was as follows:

	Federal	Total Cost
(1) Approved by Washington	1,183,604	2,394,136
(2) Pending in Washington	1,169,788	1,169,788
(3) Pending in Concord Office	259,806	460,415
(4) Potential in field	2,524,000	2,524,000
	5,136,198	6,548,339

At this moment Vermont had no state projects on file or approved; Massachusetts had 58 approved projects totaling $22,000,000; and Connecticut had highway projects approved totaling $6,500,000. Nothing as yet was approved for Rhode Island or Maine. Lockwood to JGW, December 1, 1933.

[62] Harold L. Ickes to JGW, June 24, 1933; *Concord Daily Monitor,* April 29, August 25, November 27 and December 2, 1933.

on the state's CWA payroll, reviving faith in themselves and their government during the debilitating winter months.[63]

By the time the CWA wound up its activities in April 1934, New Deal funds and leadership had begun to do more for the human and natural resources of New Hampshire than any previous administration since the American Revolution. New municipal parks, playgrounds, recreational buildings, outdoor swimming pools, bathing beaches, tennis courts, ski jumps and golf courses dotted the State, along with reduced highway curves, widened roads, ditches and improved drainage, forest trails, foot bridges, and cleared land. The removal of over thirteen million moth webs from apple and shade trees, and of 41,000 insect-ridden apple trees was of inestimable aid to farmers. Local projects included sewer and water development, painting and improving public buildings, town planning and airports.[64]

New Hampshire's extensive park system, a boon to contemporary tourist trade, blossomed during this period through projects begun with CWA and State emergency funds, and with the cooperation of the CCC. When CWA funds expired, the Public Works Administration helped complete or expand earlier projects. Urged on by the offer of monetary assistance from the Emergency Conservation Work program and by the impetus of the CWA, Winant directed the development of 90 state forests and reservations totaling 35,000 acres.[65] The benefits accruing North Country folk were incalculable, though immediately apparent as the CWA employment insured increased retail store receipts after November 1933, a period when industrial and commercial payrolls normally showed a decline. But the good done could not be reckoned in money alone.[66]

When 90 of the nation's business leaders recommended that the burden of relief be returned to state governments and local communities, except in cases of absolute necessity, Winant reaffirmed

---

[63] H. L. Hopkins to JGW, November 8, 10 and December 20, 1933; JGW to Hopkins, November 9, 11, 1933 and February 12, 1934; *Concord Daily Monitor*, November 9, 24, December 2, 6, 13 and 20, 1933, and April 24, 1934. Also, interview with Edgar Hunter, July 1953.

[64] W. C. O'Kane to JGW, April 14, 1934; *Concord Daily Monitor*, April 24, 1934; *Boston Globe*, July 14, 1934.

[65] JGW to Robert Fechner, December 27, 1933 and October 15, 1934; JGW to H. L. Hopkins, February 12, 1934; J. H. Foster to Ruth W. Higgins, August 31, 1934.

[66] JGW to H. L. Hopkins, February 12, 1934; H. L. Hopkins to E. Patch, February 25 and March 7, 1934; *Concord Daily Monitor*, April 24, 1934.

his support of the New Deal program. He insisted that only through the cooperation of Washington authorities had New Hampshire successfully preserved the credit of numerous local governments which otherwise would have been unable to fulfill normal commitments. Furthermore, this cooperative method of cost sharing had facilitated a reduction in the average local tax rate for the second and third times in forty years, despite large reductions in assessment of property value. The Granite State Executive reminded these businessmen that only because of the help given by federal and state governments were local units able to provide the necessary funds to feed, clothe and shelter those who, through no fault of their own, were reduced to penury.[67]

In response to bitter conservative criticism of waste, and the advice of standpatters within his own party, Roosevelt decreed the end of the CWA early in 1934. The burden of relief for the balance of the year fell upon Harry Hopkins' Federal Emergency Relief Administration which contributed over $3,000,000 to New Hampshire's general relief program.[68]

During his third term as governor Winant became increasingly involved in activities of a national scope. With the initiative for major programs increasingly assumed by Washington authorities, some governors worried about doing an effective job on their own level and about states' rights. To facilitate the development of long-range plans, programs and research for the states, the Interstate Reference Bureau and the American Legislators Association organized a more inclusive Council of State Governments in 1934. Elected as its first president, Winant set the tone for what later became the research and operating agency for the Governors' Conference and for other associations of state administrative officials. That same year, he joined the Board of Trustees of Brookings Institution, the famed research organization in Washington.[69]

Winant spearheaded the drive which resulted in the adoption of an Interstate Compact on minimum wages by the six New England States, Pennsylvania and New York. When the United States Supreme

[67] JGW to Louis J. Alber, December 20, 1933; *Concord Daily Monitor,* December 20, 1934.
[68] H. L. Hopkins to JGW, January 24, 30, February 14, April 18, May 5, June 21, October 3, 18, November 7, 27, December 16, 29, and 31, 1934; R. J. Lindquist to JGW, April 18, 1934.
[69] Henry W. Toll to JGW, December 16, 1933, August 1 and December 9, 1934; JGW to H. G. Moulton, June 18, 1934; interview with Frank Bane, December 8, 1959.

Court subsequently validated the Fair Labor Standards Act, it was no longer necessary to pursue these regional agreements which Governors Roosevelt and Winant had sponsored, anticipating the development of federal action. Furthermore, since these regional planning committees were tripartite commissions, containing representatives of labor, industry and government, the Granite State Governor unknowingly readied himself for his later work with the International Labor Organization in Geneva.[70]

In 1934, President Roosevelt appointed Winant as one of twenty-three lay members of an Advisory Council to the Committee on Economic Security. This group assisted Frances Perkins in devising the social security legislation introduced at the 1935 session of Congress. Though Winant made little contribution to this group because of excessive absences, Frances Perkins insisted that his appointment to it illustrated recognition of his progressive leadership and his role as "an outstanding liberal".[71]

In May 1933, Winant had an opportunity to display his ability as a labor-management conciliator. A strike of 8,000 textile workers in Manchester suddenly erupted into violence in the face of police provocations. The Governor rushed to the scene and, within days, through personal intervention calmed the contending forces and insured an amicable settlement in which Amoskeag management provided an immediate fifteen percent increase in salaries and pledged no discrimination against strike leaders. How different this solution from that following the tragic strike at Amoskeag in 1922.[72]

Thus, when the United Textile Workers struck the nation's textile factories on August 31, 1934, President Roosevelt made an astute decision in appointing Republican Winant to head a Special Board of Inquiry into the strike. Speedy settlement of this dispute was of vital concern to a still faltering economy. At issue was not merely interpretation of the Textile Code of the National Recovery Administration but the right of labor to organize. In the face of the President's uncertainty concerning his labor policy in 1934, and an awakening labor movement flexing its muscles against recalcitrant, backward-

---

[70] *Concord Daily Monitor,* January 3 and May 29, 1934; interview with Robert P. Bingham, July 28, 1953; interview with Ethel M. Johnson, December 7, 1959.
[71] For information about Winant's role in the Committee on Economic Security and events leading to enactment of the Social Security Act of 1935 see Edwin E. Witte, *The Development of the Social Security Act* (Madison, University of Wisconsin, 1962), pp. 3-7, 51 and *passim.*
[72] *Concord Daily Monitor,* April 28, May 18, 22, 25 and 27, 1933.

looking employers and outdated craft union leadership, a strong corps of industrial spokesmen decided the time had come to smash the drive for union recognition. In the process, labor would suffer a series of defeats across the country and pressure would increase upon the President for a new national labor policy.

Spokesmen for cotton textile manufacturers contended that labor had struck against the NRA code, that the union did not represent their employees. Furthermore, management contended, since adoption of the Textile Code child labor had been eliminated, hours of labor reduced from 52 to 40, and wage rates raised from $8 or $10 to a minimum of $12. On the other hand, union spokesmen insisted that weekly earnings per capita had declined, that there had been an increased work load resulting from a "stretch-out" system, and that the grievance machinery established in the Textile Code had collapsed in the face of employer intransigence. Senator Robert F. Wagner of New York recognized the need for replacing the NRA grievance structure with a permanent law providing for collective bargaining through unions selected by workers themselves.[73]

By the time Marion Smith of Atlanta and Raymond V. Ingersoll of Brooklyn had been added to Winant's committee, peace officers had killed ten strikers and wounded scores more in the South. In Georgia, National Guardsmen rounded up 116 men and women pickets from various mills and placed them in a "concentration camp". In the face of strikers and National Guard troops clashing in the streets of Rhode Island, that state's Democratic Governor, Theodore F. Green, advised an extraordinary session of his Legislature that they faced not merely a labor-management dispute but a "Communist uprising".[74] In New Hampshire, striking textile workers peacefully picketed their closed mills.[75]

The three members of the Board of Inquiry hurried to Washington where they worked around the clock conferring with spokesmen from labor, industry and government. Grateful for five hours sleep nightly for the next eleven days, Winant finally sped to Hyde Park to submit the Committee's report to the President. In the large, comfortable library of the family mansion, Roosevelt immediately approved the proposed compromise. Accepted with alacrity by a weak-

[73] *The New York Times*, August 27, 30, 31, September 4 and 6, 1934; *Report of the Board of Inquiry for the Cotton Textile Industry to the President* (Washington, Government Printing Office, 1935), pp. 2-5.
[74] *The New York Times*, September 12, 13 and 18, 1934.
[75] *Ibid.*, September 18, 1934.

ened union now on the defensive, textile management reluctantly gave way.[76] The report, a successful face-saving, temporary strike settlement, revived a key industry in a national economic crisis. Within days, a half million workers streamed back to factories as praise for Winant swept the country.[77] During the months which followed, however, many employers flouted and even ridiculed this effort by government to arbitrate the strike, engaging in a bitter drive to wipe out unionism in the South and deliberately victimize thousands of workers who had displayed a flicker of leadership.[78]

With the conclusion of the strike a number of Republicans began to boom Winant for the 1936 G.O.P. presidential nomination. They hailed him as the "favorite son of a rural state"; a "New England aristocrat" with "leftist ideas of the Roosevelt brand"; "a poor speaker" without a "commanding appearance" yet having "extraordinary abilities as a vote getter." [79] These presidential references stimulated Winant's interest in the White House, but he saw at the nation's helm the Champion Campaigner of them all. He could not possibly oppose Roosevelt at the polls, for he found little to criticize, let alone condemn, in the New Deal. Indeed, remaining on the scene as an available candidate could prove extremely embarrassing to a Republican who had constantly applauded the Roosevelt Administration. In an effort to remove himself from political consideration, Winant announced that he would reject a fourth term as Governor, hoping that other liberals would carry on his work in the Executive office, and instead devote himself to personal affairs.[80]

[76]   *Report of the Board ... to the President,* pp. 5-16; *The New York Times,* September 21, 22 and 23, 1934. The employees would return to their jobs while special studies were instituted by the Bureau of Labor Statistics on the hour and wage issue and by a subcommittee of the proposed Textile Labor Relations Board into the stretch-out problem. The Textile Board would be given full jurisdiction over the administration and enforcement of section 7a and over all other labor provisions of the NRA Textile Code.

[77]   *The New York Times,* September 21, 22 and 23, 1934; Emil Rieve to Alvin Knepper, in Knepper, "John Gilbert Winant and International Social Justice", pp. 83-84, unpublished doctoral dissertation for New York University, 1954. Also, interview with Frances Perkins, December 19, 1959.

[78]   Emil Rieve to Alvin Knepper, in Knepper, "John Gilbert Winant ...", pp. 83-84.

[79]   *Concord Daily Monitor,* October 6, 1933; *Worcester Telegram* and *Philadelphia Inquirer,* December 15, 1933; *Newsweek,* January 6, 1934; *Today* and *Liberty,* November 10, 1934.

[80]   Bridges to Bass, February 24, 1933; *Concord Daily Monitor,* September 12, 1933; interview with James M. Langley, August 11, 1952; interview with Robert P. Bingham, July 28, 1953. By the time the liberal Republican caucus selected

Despite this publicly stated preference for private life, Winant could never have endured an apolitical existence. Psychologically unsuited for a business career, he had, furthermore, lost virtually all his capital through poor business investments. In addition, he had little of a personal life; he had never learned to give enough of himself to his family. His wife had remained uninterested in politics and was frequently away in New York or abroad; with young Constance and John, Jr., away at private schools, and eight-year-old Rivington under the care of a governess, there was often little family to return to at the end of a long day at the State House, no respite from the intensity with which Winant thrust himself into the demanding tasks of the governorship.

Constantly requiring stimulating and demanding challenges to consume his restless energies, he remained in fact committed to serving in a public capacity. After four exhausting years laboring to preserve the spirit and self-respect of the people of his State and to conserve and utilize its human and natural resources, Winant had evolved into a national figure. With a horizon encompassing more than the hills of New Hampshire, he prepared to bid farewell to the state which had afforded him an exciting apprenticeship.

H. Styles Bridges as its nominee to succeed Winant as Governor, the latter no longer viewed Bridges as a progressive nor one to be trusted.

CHAPTER IX

"PASS ON THE TORCH"

Frightened by the Bolshevik Revolution and general unrest sweeping Europe, a handful of delegates to the Versailles Conference in 1919 sought to counter the radicalism of Marxist movements, and yet acknowledge the contributions of laboring men and women during World War I, by pushing through Part XIII of the Treaty of Versailles which created the International Labor Organization. The ILO constitution established a unique tripartite system of representation which provided for annual conferences with national delegations representing employers, labor and the government. The founders predicated tripartism on two assumptions: first, that labor and management interests remained independent of each other and of government; and second, that governments, which had the ultimate responsibility for enforcing labor legislation, should not be outnumbered by non-governmental groups. The Conference was to be composed of four member delegations from each state: two for the government; one each for employers and workers. In the Governing Body of the ILO, which met periodically between general Conferences, the same proportions obtained: twelve government delegates; six employer and six worker delegates.[1]

Equally unique was the new approach to international convention-making. To make the ILO more than a drafting committee and yet not conflict with the sovereignty of member states, the fundamental charter required that member States lay before their national parliament, for consideration, any decision agreed to at Conferences by at least a two-thirds majority.

---

[1] World Peace Foundation, *League of Nations* (Boston, World Peace Foundation, 1919), Vol. 2, No. 5, pp. 280-342; James T. Shotwell (ed.), *The Origins of the International Labor Organization* (New York, Columbia University Press, 1934), Vol. I, pp. 83-282, 424-50. For a study of the documents relating to the drafting of the constitution of the ILO and its incorporation into the Treaties of Peace, consult Volume II of Shotwell's work. Also, Bernard Beguin, "ILO and the Tripartite System", *International Conciliation*, May 1959, No. 523, pp. 411-14.

The violent opposition in the United States Senate to anything connected with the League of Nations had made American cooperation with the ILO impossible for many years. But other countries went forward with the annual IL Conferences, while its Geneva office poured out a flood of publications and labor treaties originated in the ILO which were ratified by increasing numbers of nations.[2]

Within a few months after the United States finally affiliated with the ILO in June 1934, its Director, Harold Butler, left Geneva headquarters to seek out an American as Assistant Director. Faced with the rising threats of Nazi Germany and Fascist Italy, which pointed to the imminent renewal of armed conflict, and appreciative of the industrial might of the United States, Butler sought to orient the ILO toward the Western Hemisphere.[3] Ever since he succeeded the French socialist, Albert Thomas, former British civil servant Butler devoted considerable efforts to bringing the United States into the ILO and giving that nation major responsibility.[4] He knew that he would someday return to England and sought a talented American to succeed him, convinced that Washington's commitment, America's standards of living and President Roosevelt's endeavors to achieve a better social order would enrich and broaden the effectiveness of the Geneva Organization.[5]

Arriving in the United States in late October 1934, Butler immediately met with State and Labor Department spokesmen to discuss membership on the Governing Body, financial responsibilities, and potential contributions by Americans.[6] As a result of Germany's

---

[2] Harold Butler, "American Membership in the ILO", *The American Labor Legislation Review*, December 1934, pp. 177-79.
[3] Frances Perkins to Charles E. Wyzanski, November 22, 1933; Department of State, Treaty Division, February 15, 1934, "The United States and the International Labor Organization"; F. Perkins to Sam D. McReynolds, June 9, 1934; C. E. Wyzanski to George H. Tinkham, June 18, 1934; Harold Butler to F. Perkins, June 18, 1934; Public Resolution No. 43 — 73d Congress, Approved June 19, 1934; All from the National Archives, Record Group Number 257.
[4] For a study of Thomas as ILO Director read E. J. Phelan, *Yes and Albert Thomas* (London, The Cresset Press, 1949).
[5] Butler, "American Membership in the ILO", pp. 177-179.
[6] C. E. Wyzanski to F. Perkins, September 10, 1934; F. Perkins to William Phillips, October 24, 1934; "Confidential Memorandum of Conclusions Relating to Participation of the United States in the ILO Reached at Conference held in the Office of the Secretary of Labor, Tuesday Afternoon, October 23, 1934, at 5:00 P.M."; "Confidential Memorandum of subjects relating to the participation of the United States in the ILO discussed at conference held in the Office of the Secretary of Labor ..., October 26, 1934, ..."; similar memorandum for October 29, 1934. National Archives, Record Group Number 257.

withdrawal from the ILO, he sought an American for a vacant Assistant Directorship, "well qualified to see theoretical considerations
against a background of administrative experience such as is furnished by a public office." [7] When President Roosevelt informed
Frances Perkins that he had suggested Winant as a possibility, she
asked if he desired to remove the New Hampshire Governor from
the political picture for 1936. Looking down at his desk, the President
quickly replied: "No, no. That is not my intent. Winant is a good man
for the post." [8]

On the day of his departure for Europe, Butler finally met Winant
in New York, but for only two hours. By the time he rushed off to a
Hudson River pier to board his ship, though, the ILO Director knew
that he had finally found the man to whom he could eventually
transfer the reins of leadership. As the ship slid into midstream,
Butler dashed off three quick notes. To the Secretary of Labor he
wrote that Winant was "a splendid man and the perfect one for the
job.... Please do all you can to persuade". He directed Professor
James T. Shotwell to send a copy of his book on the ILO to the New
Hampshire Governor, while to the latter he expressed the hope that
their first meeting would "lead to our being associated in the future." [9]
While Labor Department officials spent ensuing months preparing
for active participation in Geneva, the New Hampshire Governor
avoided a direct commitment to Butler and Frances Perkins.[10]

About to retire as Governor in January 1935, Winant spent considerable time weighing the implications of the ILO offer. He could
concentrate on reviving his oil ventures, but that prospect had never
challenged him sufficiently to merit his undivided attention. Would
he be satisfied to bide his time until the next Senatorial election, two
years hence? [11] Shortly after Butler offered Winant the ILO post, the
President indicated that he could have an appointment to the National

---

[7] "Confidential Memorandum of subjects relating to the participation of the
United States in the ILO discussed at a conference held in the office of the
Secretary of Labor ..., October 26, 1934, ..." National Archives, Record Group
Number 257.
[8] Interview with Frances Perkins, December 15, 1959.
[9] H. Butler to F. Perkins, November 16, 1934, National Archives, Record Group
Number 257; Butler to JGW, November 16, 1934, Winant Coll.; interview with
Carol Riegelman [Lubin], May 7, 1951 and December 12, 1959.
[10] F. Perkins to Henry A. Wallace, November 21, 1934, National Archives,
Record Group Number 257; F. Perkins to JGW, December 6, 1934; interview
with Carol Riegelman [Lubin], May 7, 1951 and December 12, 1959.
[11] *The New York Times*, March 24, 1935.

Labor Relations Board or the proposed Social Security Board. But as a leading Republican, the New Hampshire Governor hesitated to associate himself too closely with a Democratic administration, even though he was a New Dealer at heart who would never oppose Roosevelt.[12]

Equally important, however, remained Winant's devotion to social justice and world peace. As an officer of the American Association for Labor Legislation, he appreciated the real gains made by the ILO in raising standards of living throughout the world. This post in Geneva appealed to him as a strategic alternative and an ideological outlet, for it would enable him both to escape the 1936 campaign and to continue in public service. After this broadening experience, he could return to the States by 1940 as a most available candidate: progressive legislator, liberal State Executive and international public servant. After a furious exchange of cables, Butler finally advised the April 1935 meeting of the Governing Body that Winant had agreed to become the junior of three Assistant Directors at the Geneva office.[13] His appointment evoked a favorable impression throughout the United States for it indicated the high importance Roosevelt attached to the work of the ILO, especially when contrasted with American indifference to the World Court, the League of Nations and the World Bank.[14]

The day Winant sailed for Geneva with his wife, Father Coughlin addressed 23,000 cheering listeners in New York's Madison Square Garden who intermittently booed President Roosevelt, Senator Robert F. Wagner and J. P. Morgan. The nationally known clergyman insisted that capitalism would have to be voted out of existence if a decent relief pay scale was not established. The previous month 60,000 college students, symbolizing a national wave of pacifism, left their classes in a "strike for peace".[15] In the face of the isolationist temper of Americans, Winant's departure for Geneva signalled an endeavor

[12] F. Perkins to William G. Rice, April 4, 1935; C. E. Wyzanski to W. G. Rice, April 4, 1935, National Archives, Record Group Number 257; *The New York Times*, April 13, 1935; interview with F. Perkins, December 15, 1959. Rice was assigned to Geneva to head the U.S. Mission to the ILO.
[13] *Ibid.*; Wyzanski to Rice, March 7, 16 and 28, 1935, National Archives, Record Group Number 257; *The Times* (London, England), April 13, 1935; *Monthly Summary of the ILO*, April 1935, No. 4, p. 19; interview with Henri Reymond, May 16, 1962. Reymond has been a longtime member of the ILO staff, and head of the ILO Mission to the United Nations.
[14] *The New York Times*, April 13, 1935.
[15] *Ibid.*

by the President to initiate a policy of cautious international involvement. The Great Depression was not confined to the United States, and sick American industries would be vitally assisted if ILO conventions elevated conditions of labor and pay scales throughout the world. With the Soviet Union and the United States new members of the ILO, the center of gravity of the Geneva Organization began to pass from the older countries of Western Europe. The economic policies of the ILO would increasingly reflect the growing industrial might of these two nations.

During his trip across the Atlantic to take up his new post, Winant had to borrow preliminary material sent the American delegation, for the IL Office had neglected to forward him an agenda or policy papers. On the boat-train from Le Havre to Paris, he first became aware of the oath he must take before the Governing Body which would commit him to support not only the Organization but the League of Nations. Recalling the anti-League attitude of G.O.P. leaders, he feared being read out of the party. From the Carnegie Endowment Center in Paris, he wired Harold Butler that he could not take the oath and would rather return to the States and forfeit the post. After numerous exchanges, Butler agreed not to force the issue, suggesting that Winant remain in Paris until the Governing Body had concluded its session and then come on to Geneva for the IL Conference. The American would then become an Assistant Director without the oath. In the meantime, he revisited museums and art galleries he had frequented during the first World War.[16]

The 1935 IL Conference proved to be the largest and most representative in the history of the Organization. Despite its unfamiliarity with Conference procedure, the U.S. Delegation, speaking from first hand experience, played a decisive role in the adoption of the 40-hour-work week proposal. In contrast to delegations from other democratic nations which split into government, industry and worker caucuses, the United States delegation met as a unit to decide its stand on major issues. This situation resulted primarily from the advent of the New Deal, from appointments to the Labor Department of Frances Perkins and Isador Lubin, middle-class spokesmen

---

[16] Interview with Carol Riegelman [Lubin], December 12, 1959 and May 16, 1962. Not until the Governing Body accepted the resignation of Harold Butler on May 31, 1938, did Winant finally take the declaration of loyalty prescribed by staff regulations for high officials of the Office. *Monthly Summary of the ILO,* 1938, No. 5, May, p. 23.

for the more lofty ideals of labor, and from the selection of enlightened business and labor spokesmen.[17]

A contrast was the British delegation which, according to a leading English newspaper, had only an estimable civil servant, instructed to boast about the perfection of labor conditions in his country and, "while pretending to be anxious to see the raising of international standards, to try to prevent any positive action which involves responsibilities".[18]

As the 1935 Conference drew to a close, the new Assistant Director cabled Roosevelt and Perkins that they had every reason to feel "very proud" of their delegation.[19] *The Times* of London hailed the Conference as "notable", highlighted by the general draft convention of the 40-hour week, which insured it a place equal to that held by the 1919 session in Washington when the 8-hour day and 48-hour week were adopted. Its application, however, depended upon the adoption of conventions for individual industries.[20]

Winant's stay in Geneva proved brief, due to Roosevelt's insistence that he become chairman of the newly created Social Security Board.[21] During this four-month association, however, he became so concerned with the American image of the ILO that he sought to alter the rigidly formal, diplomatic language used by the staff in letters, which seemed alien to American correspondents. Furthermore, he impressed upon fellow executives the need to strengthen relations with member states in the Western Hemisphere. All this Harold Butler had hoped for when he originally urged Winant to join the Organization.[22]

In August 1935, President Roosevelt signed the "supreme achievement" of the New Deal, the Social Security Act. "If the Senate and House of Representatives in their long and arduous session had done nothing more than pass this bill", he informed a happy assemblage

[17] Grace Abbott, "The United States at the 19th International Labor Conference", *The American Labor Legislation Review,* September 1935, p. 109.
[18] *Manchester Guardian,* June 15, 1935.
[19] JGW to F. Perkins, June 17, 1935; JGW to FDR, undated cablegram; members of the American delegation included Grace Abbott, Walton Hamilton, Sam Lewisohn, Daniel Tracy, Marion Hedges and C. E. Wyzanski. See "Action Taken by the Nineteenth IL Conference", *The American Labor Legislation Review,* September 1935, p. 132.
[20] *The Times,* June 27, 1935.
[21] See fn. 71 of previous chapter.
[22] Interview with Carter Goodrich, December 18, 1959. Goodrich was U.S. Labor Commissioner in Geneva in 1937, later Chairman of the ILO Governing Body.

of Congressional supporters and Cabinet members in the White House, "the session would be regarded as historic for all time".[23]

The launching of this new system, and its subsequent strengthening, insured a lasting revolution in the United States as Roosevelt laid the foundation for a welfare state. Within two years, all states provided a schedule of unemployment insurance benefits which would afford some protection for 28,000,000 workers. In addition to a nationwide system of old-age insurance, federal aid to the states on a matching basis insured assistance to the crippled, the blind, dependent mothers and children, public health services, and to those over 65 who would have no opportunity to participate in the new old-age insurance program. The Act also established a non-partisan Social Security Board of three to initiate and administer the system.[24]

Shortly after Winant arrived in Geneva, Switzerland as the new Assistant Director of the ILO, and before the Social Security bill cleared Congress, he received a cable from Roosevelt again suggesting his appointment to the proposed Social Security Board.[25] During the days which followed, a stream of telegrams from Frances Perkins urged acceptance of the Chairmanship of the new Board.[26] He was an excellent choice because the politically aware Chief Executive wanted the Social Security Board headed by a prominent liberal Republican during its formative years. In sympathy with the Roosevelt administration, he had also demonstrated skillfulness in reconciling differing points of view.[27]

While reluctant to leave Geneva within two months after joining the ILO, or return to the domestic scene he had forsaken in order to escape political embarrassment, Winant could never ignore an op-

---

[23] *The New York Times,* April 13 and August 15, 1935.

[24] For the evolution of the Social Security Act and Winant's involvement, see: Edwin E. Witte, *The Development of the Social Security Act* (Madison, University of Wisconsin Press, 1962), pp. xiii, 3-7, 51, 56-63, 88-106, 119. Also, Joseph C. Dougherty, Jr., "The Genesis of the Social Security Act of 1935", unpublished doctoral dissertation, Georgetown University, 1955, pp. 95-224; Arthur J. Altmeyer, *The Formative Years of Social Security* (Madison, University of Wisconsin Press, 1966), pp. 3-73.

[25] Cordell Hull to American Consul, Geneva, "Message for Winant from President Roosevelt", July 2, 1935. In author's possession.

[26] Frances Perkins to JGW, July 31, August 6, 12, 13, 14 and 22, 1935; JGW to F. Perkins, August 5 and 13, 1935; JGW to C. Wyzanski, August 10, 1935. All in author's possession.

[27] F. Perkins to JGW, August 12, 1935; F. Perkins to Alvin Knepper, August 28, 1952; interview with Frances Perkins, December 15, 1959.

portunity to make a significant contribution to social justice.[28] In his last major address before leaving for Geneva, he maintained that the mere enactment of labor legislation meant little unless enforced intelligently. A statute which conferred on workers certain rights, and guaranteed them protection, remained only a scrap of paper unless conscientiously administered. The country, he insisted, needed "competent officials to administer and enforce the laws — men and women with trained intelligence, with broad sympathy and understanding, with vision and courage — executives who are experts in their fields." [29]

With such clear determination on his part, Winant could not ignore Frances Perkins' contentions that he not only understood the Social Security Act, and "cared" for its objectives, but could give the program the inspired philosophical leadership it so desperately needed at its birth. On the day the President approved the Social Security Act, Winant cabled his acceptance of the Board chairmanship.[30]

The President had strengthened the Social Security Board, but at the same time weakened Butler's organization in the eyes of those who hoped for increased American participation. Geneva associates interpreted this decision as a decline of interest by Washington and proof that Winant did not think the job worthwhile.[31] Butler, extremely disappointed, had never found anyone with whom he could work with the same feeling of confidence and harmony of aim and outlook. He felt that the two of them could do a tremendous job in Geneva and, with the passing years, possibly attain the presidency for Winant and the prime ministership for himself. "It is a secret dream of mine", wrote the Englishman, "that we might someday have the opportunity of working together in order to strengthen the sympathy and understanding between our two countries — but that is a Utopian fantasy, which the conditions of actual life are unlikely

---

[28] W. G. Rice to C. Wyzanski, August 8, 1935, National Archives, Record Group No. 257; interviews with Carol Riegelman [Lubin], May 7, 1951 and December 12, 1959. Miss Riegelman was a close associate of Winant and an American member of the ILO staff in Geneva.
[29] From the original draft of Winant's address to the National Consumers League, January 15, 1935. In author's possession.
[30] F. Perkins to JGW, August 6, 1935; JGW to F. Perkins, August 14, 1935, in author's possession; F. Perkins to JGW, August 22, 1935; *The New York Times*, August 24, 1935.
[31] H. Butler to JGW, August 27, 1935; William G. Rice to C. Wyzanski, August 30, 1935. National Archives, Record Group No. 257.

to render possible." [32] The Director advised Winant that the IL Office would do everything possible to insure the success of social security in America and that when he had "built the machine we want you back here — badly. You would perhaps be surprised to know how many people of how many nationalities have spoken to me with keen regret at your departure and how rejoiced they were at the prospect of it being only for a time." [33]

Winant's appointment insured the new Social Security Board immense prestige and good will, moving one conservative Republican to comment, "This is one of the few times where I must agree that the President made a fine selection." [34] Some friends, however, visualized the assignment as a Machiavellian move by Roosevelt to isolate Winant from the G.O.P. presidential nomination. [35]

Felix Frankfurter, the perceptive independent in American politics, correctly interpreted the significance of this designation when he wrote:

Even if you had not returned to guide one of the great civilizing agencies in the history of the United States I should have felt happier about the country now that you are with us again. The Lord knows I do not minimize the importance of the Geneva efforts and still less the influence that you were radiating there. But the Lord also knows how desperately we need you here. Your very rare (I shall not offend your modesty by saying unique) combination of character and capacity are deeply needed at home. "We live by symbols", said Mr. Justice Holmes and we greatly need you. The country does, as symbol and as promoter of wise statesmanship. [36]

The other key member of the three-man Board, serious, intellectual Arthur J. Altmeyer, had established an impressive record in Wisconsin as an associate of the La Follettes and proponent of the State's unemployment insurance system. As Second Assistant Secretary of Labor in Washington, he had played a major role in the formulation of the Social Security Act and proved himself the most knowledgeable of Board members. A technician by nature, ordinarily calm and even tempered, Altmeyer remained close to his field and seldom figured in news dispatches.

As the third member, the President named lawyer Vincent Miles,

[32] H. Butler to JGW, August 29, 1935.
[33] *Ibid.*
[34] C. W. Korell to JGW, August 28, 1935. In author's possession.
[35] Interviews with Robert P. Bingham, July 28, 1953; and with Frances Perkins, December 15, 1959.
[36] Felix Frankfurter to JGW, September 17, 1935. In author's possession.

from Little Rock, Arkansas, a concession to Senate majority leader Joseph T. Robinson. While generally well motivated, this former National Democratic Committee member lacked important qualifica-tions for the job and did not grasp public policy on welfare issues. He knew most party leaders in Washington and sought every oppor-tunity to provide loyal Democrats with positions, but usually found himself outvoted by Winant and Altmeyer who refused to permit the Washington and regional offices to become a grab bag for De-mocratic patronage. This policy quickly roused the ire of party chieftains across the country. Senate majority leader Robinson, for example, sent a confidential letter to the President complaining that Democrats did not receive "fair attention" in the appointment of the Social Security staff. California's Senator William Gibbs McAdoo also protested to the White House that appointments by the Board in his State were made without consulting him or other party leaders.[37] Yet, the success of Winant and Altmeyer, in particular, in developing what came to be recognized as an extremely efficient organization was due largely to their insistence that the initial ap-pointees be nonpolitical, dedicated and of high qualification.

This nucleus of an executive staff was given free rein "to select equally dedicated and qualified staff members" all the way down the line. Even with these criteria, the Social Security Board did not always choose wisely and well. When its members realized that one of their key Directors suffered from insufficient large-scale administrative experience, the Board was forced to call upon the Postmaster General to assume the initial responsibility of distributing applications for social security numbers through the 45,000 post offices, beginning in mid-November 1936. An impressive proportion of the initial distribu-tion of application forms was returned within three weeks, and by June 30, 1937, when the Social Security Board was competent to assume the task, 30,296,471 applications had been processed.[38]

[37] *The New York Times*, August 24, 1935; Running Record of Board Meetings, July 30 and December 26, 1936; Joseph T. Robinson to Franklin D. Roosevelt, October 1, 1936, PPF 473, F. D. Roosevelt Library; W. G. McAdoo to McIntyre, November 16, 1936, 300 Calif., M, F. D. Roosevelt Library. By the end of 1936, there were 4,189 individuals working for the Board in 12 Regional and 108 Field Offices. Interviews with Jack Tate, April 12, 1952; with John Corson, April 14, 1952; with John Pearson, August 13, 1952; and with Frances Perkins, December 15, 1959. Tate was Assistant General Counsel and Corson Assistant Executive Director of the SSB. Pearson was Regional Director of the Boston Office from 1936 to 1940.
[38] Altmeyer, *The Formative Years of Social Security*, pp. 67-70.

It was fortunate that Roosevelt and Perkins had balanced "Utopian John", as the President once described him, with Altmeyer. One without the other would have lacked either the practical or the spiritual leadership necessary at the start of this organization. But for the cold, practical, technical plodding nature of Altmeyer, the Chairman might have made a mess of the Board during its organizational period. While Altmeyer loved figures, tables and charts, they repelled Winant because they lacked the human quality. Where the former proved careful, meticulous, and well organized, the latter carried around memoranda and letters in bulging pockets. Where Winant combined the intellectual with the emotional, his practical associate remained coldly intellectual. Although a suspicious and cautious man, Winant came to trust his Wisconsin colleague implicitly and often embarrassed him with the responsibility for decision making. A devoted nucleus in the Washington and regional offices eased the challenging burdens suddenly thrust upon the Board. Frank Bane, a soft spoken southerner who served as Executive Director during the crucial three years of its birth was particularly effective. With extensive knowledge gleaned from many years of work in the welfare field, Bane exerted a singularly constructive influence upon Board member Miles and kept the organization headed in the right direction.

Despite the absence of appropriate funds with which to operate during the first four months of its existence — the result of a filibuster by Senator Huey Long during the last hours of the legislative session — and the barest skeleton of a staff, Board members would be responsible for creating, within one year, a national organization where none had existed before — 12 Regional offices and 108 field offices — and would supervise or direct the hiring of over 4,000 civil service employees. They would act upon requests of Governors, welfare agencies, and legislative groups for advice in the framing of enabling legislation, and then review and generally approve, state laws dealing with unemployment compensation, old-age assistance plans and aid to the blind and to dependent children. Board members would be responsible for disbursing, within the first year, over $41,000,000 to 36 states to help finance old-age benefit programs, and $1,500,000 to states to aid in the administration of unemployment insurance acts.[39]

[39]   *The New York Times*, August 27, 1935.

By the end of August 1935, the three-man Social Security Board met daily in the Department of Labor Building in borrowed offices with a borrowed staff from the liquidating National Industrial Recovery Administration. "Research funds" to develop ways and means of putting the Social Security Act into operation were supplied by the Federal Emergency Relief Administration.[40] The members set to work at such a pace that within days, FERA Administrator Harry L. Hopkins humorously advised the new Chairman that "just because I am going away is no reason why you should try to take all our money. Take it easy".[41]

There was nothing outwardly efficient in Winant's labors. He usually went at things in a "roundabout way", often causing Altmeyer to lament his colleague's indecisiveness. Though conceding his foresight in social thinking, many a public administrator felt that the Board Chairman did not carry it over to administrative techniques.[42] A visitor to his large office would usually observe huge piles of letters on his desk awaiting his signature. Although two assistants formulated replies to a tremendous quantity of inquiries, Winant impractically adhered to Justice Brandeis' earlier advice to read and sign all letters emanating from his office. On one occasion, when reading a message drafted by one of his assistants who had inserted Christmas greetings from both Mr. and Mrs. Winant, the Board Chairman immediately advised his subordinate that this would not do. No one could speak for Mrs. Winant, who was out of town at that moment! This expenditure of extremely valuable time and energy, and his refusal to delegate much work, exasperated co-workers, while endearing him to thousands of citizens who read his small, scrawling signature.[43]

While he may have expended unnecessary energy on detail, Winant's talents tended toward other directions. Board meetings, for example, illustrated his awareness of individual problems and feeling for human needs. With attendance varying from ten to thirty, he involved everyone in the ensuing discussion. Participants left these

[40]   Ibid., September 22, 1935; Official Board Minutes of the Social Security Board, October 16, 1935; Altmeyer, The Formative Years of Social Security, pp. 44-45.
[41]   Harry L. Hopkins to JGW, September 26, 1935, Papers of Harry L. Hopkins, Correspondence, 1933-40, F. D. Roosevelt Library.
[42]   Interviews with Arthur J. Altmeyer, April 15, 1952; and with Frances Perkins, December 15, 1959.
[43]   Interviews with Maurine Mulliner, May 16, 1951; with John Corson and Henry P. Seidemann, April 14, 1952.

meetings feeling they had had a say in the determination of policy, even if the Board rejected their recommendations.[44]

During his visits to Capitol Hill, the Board Chairman demonstrated his political astuteness, experiencing a minimum of difficulty with Congressmen from either party. While explaining budgetary requests and clarifying the work and objectives of the Board in his characteristically soft, harmonizing manner, committee members eventually found themselves conversing in hushed tones. An absolute spendthrift with time, he often kept Congressmen waiting in the outer office, while he spoke at length with private citizens. Clothing, also, remained an unimportant factor in his life, for he frequently wore darned trousers and frayed shirts. One would never know that his unpressed suits came from Brooks Brothers in New York, or that he had a considerable number of belts at home the day he walked into the office with a necktie holding up his trousers.[45]

As Felix Frankfurter had suggested, Winant came to symbolize social security to the nation. While politicians and New Deal spokesmen avoided the imposing task of educating the public, the former Governor stumped the country speaking to interested groups in support of the Act. "Security", he maintained, "must always be relative". Old age insurance and unemployment compensation represented an honest effort to give greater security to the wage earner in industry. The Act, however, could not be viewed as a panacea for the economic ills of the nation which had made depressions possible. It sought to remove the fear of poverty during unemployment, and destitution in old age which for generations had constantly hung over the heads of millions of wage earners. He urged greater realism in attitudes toward unemployment, insisting that the idea that private indolence had been preying on public generosity had finally been shown to be a pretense.[46]

The psychological block which had hampered earlier speaking

[44]   Interviews with Maurine Mulliner, May 16, 1951; with Jack Tate, April 12, 1952; with John Corson, April 14, 1952; with A. J. Altmeyer, April 15, 1952; with Frank Bane, December 8, 1959; and with Frances Perkins, December 15, 1959. With the exception of Madame Perkins, all were key members of the Washington staff and participants at Board meetings.

[45]   Interviews with Arthur J. Altmeyer, April 15, 1952; with Frank Bane, December 8, 1959; with Maurine Mulliner, December 7, 1959 and June 12, 1960; and with Elizabeth Green, December 9, 1959. Mrs. Green was one of the Board secretaries.

[46]   *New York Herald Tribune,* October 16, 1935; interview with Elizabeth Green, December 9, 1959.

endeavors continued to plague Winant in his new role as spokesman for social security. As he confided to his eldest son, who had just entered St. Paul's School, "I am spending my time locked up in an office or on airplanes or on trains. I like working better than I do talking and I have a good deal of talking to do." [47]

During these trying months, Winant's family life was depressing. Seldom would he leave the office before evening; he spent Saturday and Sunday in the empty and silent Labor Department Building. He returned for late dinners to a cold, quiet and imposing house which he had rented in Georgetown. Mrs. Winant, meanwhile, continued to be busy with her social life and displayed little interest in the work of her husband. The three children were away at private schools. The sadness which young Gil had felt in his childhood enveloped him anew in this Georgetown mansion. When a St. Paul's schoolmaster queried John, Jr. as to being homesick, the youth replied that he had been away from home too much for that sort of thing. "Sis" was at an exclusive girl's school, while "Riv", the youngest, was at St. Bernards.[48]

Winant's increasing financial indebtedness aggravated the situation, forcing him at one stage to borrow the savings of his British maid in order to pay the house rent. He had already taken loans of thousands on extensive life insurance, only to forfeit the policies when he could no longer meet the premiums.[49] Years later, while walking through the Georgetown area, Winant suddenly found himself in front of this large dwelling on Thirty-Fourth Street. Halting for a moment, he looked up at the building and sadly commented to a friend, "I was more miserable in that house than ever in my life. That was a nightmare." [50]

Although he became 47 in February 1936, he continued to convey a surprisingly youthful impression. His hair and eyebrows remained thick and dark, his grayish eyes thoughtful. He smiled easily, "like a human being rather than a politician". He maneuvered around his

[47] JGW to JGW, Jr., October 22, 1936.
[48] JGW to JGW, Jr., December 6, 1935 and October 22, 1936; Archer Harman to JGW, October 21, 1936. In author's possession.
[49] J. B. Teulon to JGW, January 30, 1936; JGW to Thomas H. Barber, June 30, 1937; Life Insurance for the Winants, December 20, 1934, Drawer 7, Uncatalogued Folder, Winant Coll. Also, interview with Orol Mears, July 24-30, 1952.
[50] Interview with Maurine Mulliner, June 12, 1960.

office quickly with a slight stoop and a gait that falsely suggested a youth spent on a farm.[51]

Despite the fact that Wisconsin passed an unemployment compensation act before 1935 and six states enacted laws while Congress considered the Social Security Act, in the remaining states the machinery and procedures to collect contributions, keep records, and pay benefits, had to be built from the ground up. By February 1936, with the first Federal grants, 38 State plans had been approved. State laws dealing with unemployment compensation started slowly, with only 15 of the 48 adopting enabling laws through much of 1936. Late that year, twenty States called special legislative sessions and speedily adopted unemployment compensation acts in order to allow their employers to take credit against the Federal payroll tax before January 1, 1937. Largely as a result of the position of the Board that Federal funds be made available as soon as a State met the requirements of the Act, the initial phase — rapid legislative development throughout the States — passed its peak within a comparatively short period. By the middle of 1937, every State had enacted unemployment compensation laws and all had been approved by the Board. By the fall of 1938 all the States had approved old-age assistance plans and most were taking part in both aid to the blind and dependent children.[52]

Despite his return to Washington and his deep involvement with the emerging social security program, Winant maintained close liaison with ILO developments. During his brief sojourn in Geneva, he had quickly grasped the role the ILO could play in the inevitable struggle between the democracies and the Rome-Berlin Axis. Geneva documents streamed across his desk, as well as lengthy letters from Carol

---

[51] *The New York Times,* January 5, 1936.
[52] "A Summary of Accomplishments in the First Year of the Administration of the Social Security Act", Official File 1710, Social Security Board, Correspondence 1935-37, F. D. Roosevelt Library; *The New York Times,* August 9, 1936. Also, V. O. Key, Jr., "State Administration of the Social Security Act", *Annals of the American Academy of Political and Social Science,* March 1939, pp. 153-54; Frank Bane, "The Social Security Board and State Organizations", *Annals of the American Academy of Political and Social Science,* March 1939, pp. 137-44. Also, for a detailed study of the administrative accomplishments and organizational structure of the Social Security Board see Sayid Zafar Hasan, "Policy Formulation and Development in Public Assistance, A Study of the Role of the Federal Government in the First Five Years of the Social Security Act, 1935-1940", doctoral dissertation, New York School of Social Work, Columbia University, 1958; Altmeyer, *The Formative Years of Social Security,* pp. 43-73.

Riegelman, his former assistant, and copies of communications to and from the U.S. Labor Commissioner in Geneva. As he journeyed across the nation meeting Governors, State labor commissioners and the public, he spread news of the ILO.[53] When Butler arrived in the United States for a brief stay in February 1936, he was "astonished" by Winant's knowledge of the Organization's activities, and, therefore, felt free to request the Social Security head to keep a keen eye upon the ILO's Washington office.[54]

Winant remained officially involved with the ILO when Roosevelt appointed him Chairman of the American delegation to the 1936 Conference in Geneva.[55] Throughout this meeting the former Governor happily enunciated governmental policies in accord with his social welfare philosophy. Since the previous Conference had adopted a general 40-hour-work week convention, the 1936 gathering sought to extend the reform to four specific industries. With United States delegates taking the lead, the draft convention on public works secured the necessary two-thirds vote, though the other three lost by extremely close margins.[56]

Departing delegations left Geneva with a picture of a thriving Organization, while in the decaying League of Nations, the major powers exhibited cowardice in the face of despotism, refugees from Nazi Germany, and approaching worldwide upheaval. When the Emperor of Ethiopia pleaded with a cowed Assembly of the League of Nations for aid to help throw back invading Italian troops, he rose from the very seat which Winant, as Vice Chairman of the IL Conference had occupied the previous week.

As Italy and Germany pressed on with their interventions in Africa and Spain, and Europe became an armed camp, Americans remained generally preoccupied with domestic issues: the lingering depression,

---

[53] Interviews with Carol Riegelman [Lubin], December 12, 1959 and May 16, 1962; with Frances Perkins, December 15, 1959. Also, C. Wyzanski to W. G. Rice, September 14, 1935; Rice to Wyzanski, October 21 and 29, 1935, National Archives, Record Group No. 257; Isador Lubin to JGW, November 19, 1935; C. Riegelman to JGW, May 11, 1937.

[54] JGW to H. Butler, November 5, 1935; Butler to JGW, November 15, 1935; H. Butler to JGW, February 11, 1936.

[55] *The New York Times,* May 15 and 21, 1936. Representing the Government on the delegation were Miss Frieda Miller, for the employers Marion Folsom, and for labor Emil Rieve.

[56] U.S. Bureau of Labor Statistics, *Monthly Labor Review,* XLIII (April 1936), 953; ILO, *Verbatim Record,* 20th Conference, Annex, pp. 742-44, 746; *The New York Times,* June 25, 1936.

the quadrennial race for the presidency and a national debate over
the president's proposal to reform the Supreme Court.

With the familiar trappings of an old-fashioned national party
convention, the undergraduate body of Oberlin College gathered
under a gigantic canvas tent in May 1936, for their Nineteenth Mock
Republican Convention. Shortly before it convened, the *Oberlin
Review* advised Winant that he would be one of the nominees. Favorable "delegates" learned from the Board Chairman that he preferred
"not to be a nominee. Trying very hard to keep entirely out of partisan
politics as it has no place in social security. Appreciate the compli-
ment. Hope you have lots of fun." [57] After leading on the first two
ballots, Winant fell behind Senator Arthur Vandenberg and others
for several counts, only to break through on the seventh ballot and
sweep the nomination.[58] A Cleveland newspaper concluded that while
these mock conventions had frequently picked winners, the aim of
most participants had usually been to name those who should be
president, not those who necessarily would be. Oberlin students expressed the feeling of a vast number of young voters of the 1930's
that irrespective of party labels, the man chosen to the highest office
should be an outstanding aggressive liberal.[59]

Winant never actively sought the presidential nomination, though
he hoped the call would come some day. Ever since the decisive
Republican defeat in 1932, increasing numbers of liberal G.O.P. voters
had turned to him to head the ticket.[60] For some time, journalist
William Allen White lauded the former New Hampshire Governor
as the leading Republican on the horizon, but lamented his lack of
showmanship. In 1935, the Kansas newsman had turned the presidential spotlight on Winant at meetings in the midwest and in New
York, but to no avail. Everybody loved him, White insisted, "but he
was just impossible", for he didn't have his speech written when he
got out West, and instead of passing out advance copies, he buried
himself in his hotel room to write it, and then had to read it. "He
just never got himself across. It was the same in New York. I had
the people at a luncheon that a politician needs to meet. But he had

57 JGW to Allen M. Bailey, May 7, 1936.
58 *The New York Times,* May 10, 1936.
59 *Cleveland Plain Dealer,* May 11, 1936.
60 H. C. Holland to JGW, May 4, 1935; A. Robertson to JGW, November 25,
1935; G. W. Hanley to JGW, June 2, 1936, were typical of letters urging Winant
to seek the Republican presidential nomination.

to hurry away to work on his speech, and it wasn't worth the trouble." Unable to build a bonfire under Winant, White turned elsewhere.[61] The call would never come again.

William Allen White then threw his support to Governor Alfred M. Landon of Kansas. Colonel Frank Knox, publisher of the *Chicago Daily News*, whose attempt to start a political career in New Hampshire had been blunted by young Winant in 1924, vigorously pursued the presidential nomination but aroused little popular support. Landon captured the candidacy even before the Republicans met in Cleveland in June 1936, while Knox's preconvention campaigning won him the vice presidential nomination when Senator Vandenberg refused to be considered for the post.[62]

The G.O.P. platform sought to satisfy all elements in the party. After indicting the New Deal administration for misdeeds and usurpations of state prerogatives, it invited all citizens to join in the defense of American institutions — unemployment should be solved by private business and the removal of hampering governmental regulation; relief returned to local control with Federal grants-in-aid; more adequate old-age pensions offered in place of the Social Security Act; and New Deal financing condemned and a balanced budget promised. The agricultural section basically accepted the administration farm program, while promising collective bargaining in labor disputes along with state laws and interstate compacts to protect women and children in industry. Extreme isolation characterized the foreign policy planks.[63]

The Democratic convention in Philadelphia abrogated the century-old two-thirds rule, renominating Roosevelt and Garner after a marathon of seconding speeches. Roosevelt's denunciation of "economic royalists" in his acceptance address set the tone for the Democratic campaign. The party platform declared unemployment to be a national problem and promised a continuation of work relief where needed, and a balanced budget at the earliest possible moment as relief requirements declined and national income increased. It pledged to continue the "Good Neighbor" policy, take the profits out of war and guard against involvement in hostilities. The election issue would

---

[61] *Boston Globe,* October 29, 1935; John Pearson to JGW, June 27, 1935; Harlan C. Pearson to JGW, June 20, 1935.
[62] *The New York Times,* June 7-12, 1936.
[63] *Ibid.,* June 12, 1936.

be the G.O.P., which would regiment the people in the service of privileged groups, and an administration which believed in equal opportunity for all.[64]

Former Bull Mooser Landon proved colorless as a candidate and uninspiring as a speaker. Despite support from "Jeffersonian Democrats" John W. Davis and Alfred E. Smith, and from the overwhelming bulk of the nation's newspapers, the pronounced conservatism of the G.O.P. cost Republicans far more votes through defections among their liberals than they gained from recruiting on the right. They also lost Winant in the process.

While not a harsh word had been uttered against the Winant-led Board, there had been increasing Republican sniping at provisions of the Social Security Act. Disturbed by the refusal of G.O.P. convention delegates to ratify Congressional approval of the Act, the Board Chairman had hoped that Landon would endorse it during the campaign.

In the White House, meanwhile, Mrs. Eleanor Roosevelt astutely advised her husband that the provisions and objectives of social security could be better known to the general public and suggested that "Governor Winant . . . should let go to non-partisan meetings all the people he possibly can, in order that they may explain the Social Security Act. This is not campaigning." [65] Shortly thereafter, the President informed the Board Chairman that "opponents of social legislation (who incidentally, are also, of course, opponents of the administration) are spreading abroad much deliberate misinformation about the Social Security Act." While conceding that the Board should abstain from politics he, nevertheless, felt it neither fair nor right to sit back and let these attacks go unanswered. The Chief Executive expressed the hope that Winant would encourage his personnel "to go to non-partisan meetings as much as possible — not to party rallies but gatherings of all kinds of organizations willing to hear the truth about the act and the progress we are making".[66]

Correctly interpreting overwhelming public support for social security, the President would be satisfied with speeches throughout the country by staff members of the SSB explaining the workings of

---

[64] *Ibid.*, June 25-28, 1936.
[65] Memorandum for the President from M.A.L., August 12, 1936. F. D. Roosevelt Library.
[66] F. D. Roosevelt to JGW, August 22, 1936. In author's possession.

the Act. Winant's endorsement of the New Deal would be most welcome, though hardly to be expected, for it would carry great weight
with the liberal wing of the G.O.P.

But it was Landon, not Roosevelt, who finally thrust Winant into
the political cauldron. During the last weekend in September, Landon followed up his earlier criticisms with a slashing attack on the
Social Security Act. Before 10,000 cheering Republicans in Milwaukee,
he denounced the enactment as "unjust, unworkable, stupidly drafted,
and wastefully financed". The Roosevelt method of financing old-
age pensions by a payroll tax on employers and employees, he
charged, was a "cruel hoax" on the workers, and the creation of a
"needless" reserve of $47,000,000,000 would encourage increased
Federal extravagance. To call this social security was a "fraud on
the workingman", for when the aged sought payment of their pensions they would find in the government strong box only bundles
of "I.O.U's". He advocated, as a substitute, State experimentation
with different plans.[67]

Winant, appalled by Landon's denunciations, saw his hopes for
bi-partisan support quashed. Momentarily bewildered by this new
turn of events, he sought a way out from a frustrating dilemma. In
the face of repudiation by his party leader, could he, in good conscience, continue as the lone G.O.P. member of the Board and remain
silent? Only six weeks earlier he had celebrated the first anniversary
of the legislation by informing a nationwide radio audience that "The
Social Security Act in my judgment, is the most humane document
written into law in this century." [68]

Surprising two staff members on the SSB with telephone calls, he
elicited from the more experienced the sage conclusion that resigning
from the Board in an endeavor to refute Landon would mean
repudiation of his party affiliation and political suicide. After hours
of agonizing appraisal in his Georgetown home, he telephoned Hyde
Park to alert the President to his imminent resignation. Roosevelt
immediately cautioned against a precipitate decision and urged re-
consideration. Winant, however, had made up his mind and would
have none of the reasoning of friends who pleaded with him to with-

---

[67] *The New York Times*, September 27, 1936.
[68] Address by John G. Winant, "Reviewing the First Year of Social Security
in the United States". Broadcast over a network of the National Broadcasting
Company, Thursday, August 13, 1936. In author's possession.

draw his resignation so as to preserve his political career as a presidential aspirant.[69]

Imbued with a sense of destiny and sparked by a messianic streak, the former Governor may have believed that his resignation and defense of Roosevelt would have great significance for the United States as well as the world. During his brief sojourn in Geneva, developing war clouds had convinced him of the urgent need for determined leadership in the White House. In the Far East, the Japanese had penetrated China. In Europe, Hitler rearmed Germany and inaugurated conscription, while Mussolini rejected mediation by the League of Nations and overwhelmed Ethiopia by May 1936. After the Rome-Berlin Axis began its rape of democratic Spain, the Germans and Japanese joined forces in an Anti-Comintern Pact. While great numbers of Americans sought to hide behind a curtain of isolation, Winant foresaw another World War. Faced with this threat, the International Labor Organization, and other democratic forces throughout the world, would need a warm, understanding friend in Washington. With Roosevelt defeated, there would be little hope for a reasonable world after the projected conflagration.

Within moments after telegraphing Winant's letter of resignation to Hyde Park, an aide advised Roosevelt that the document offered him an excellent opportunity to make a statement on Social Security in the nature of a reply or acceptance of the Governor's resignation. But he suggested that this be timed as a follow-up story and not written for immediate release. "The Winant story is big enough to stand alone tonight." [70]

Accusing the G.O.P. candidate of rejecting the Act for a "dole with a means test", the resigning Board Chairman defended it as a nonpartisan, humanitarian measure. Landon's address had not been a plea for improvement of the Act but a demand that it be scrapped. Since the Kansas Governor had made social security a major issue in the campaign, Winant could not support him and, therefore, felt

---

[69] Interview with Mary Healy Harley, June 13, 1951; M. H. Harley to author, January 26, 1960. Mrs. Harley had been a secretary for Winant in Concord, Geneva and Washington, and was with him when he decided to resign from the Board. Interview with Ethel M. Johnson, December 7, 1959.

[70] Steve [Early?] to F. D. Roosevelt, September 28, 1936. F. D. Roosevelt Library. Two days later, the President issued a press release assailing the foes of the Social Security Act, contending they were resorting to "partisan hostility". At the same time he hailed the contributions of Board Chairman Winant, while lamenting his decision to resign. *The New York Times*, October 1, 1936.

it incumbent to resign as the minority member of the Board so as to be free to defend it alongside Roosevelt.

Having seen the tragedy of war, I have been consistently interested in the ways of peace. Having seen some of the cruelties of the depression, I have wanted to help with others in lessening the hardships, the suffering and the humiliations forced upon American citizens because of our previous failure as a nation to provide effective social machinery for meeting the problems of dependency and unemployment. The Social Security Act is America's answer to this great human need.[71]

In a nationwide radio address the following evening, Winant insisted that "either the nominee has not read the Social Security Act or his advisers have misled him as to its essential provisions". The Act remained a first, not a last, step in protecting the people against the major hazards of an industrial society. It made a promising beginning in the protection of maternity and childhood, in guarding against the grosser hazards of unemployment, and in making a minimum provision for old age. The call to retreat, he insisted, was written large in the whole tissue of the Republican position.[72]

In response to Landon's desire to use the States as laboratories, the former Board Chairman illustrated the flexibility and opportunity for experimentation provided by the Act when he demonstrated that of fourteen unemployment compensation laws already in effect, twelve were of the pooled fund type, one of the employer reserve type, and one combined elements of both. Under some laws, contributions were made by employers only; in other cases, by both employers and employees. Some laws contained merit rating provisions; others didn't. The waiting periods and the size of benefits varied with the desires of State Legislatures. In short, the Act facilitated the very experimental State laboratory method which the G.O.P. nominee advocated. In a final challenge to Landon and conservative G.O.P. chieftains, Winant warned that, "An advance has begun — and no man has a right to call 'halt'." [73]

His faltering campaign momentarily stranded by Winant's resignation and open attack, Landon responded by releasing a hitherto unpublished report of the Twentieth Century Fund, on which he had based his Milwaukee address. The document identified nearly two-thirds of the people of the country as being outside the old-age

[71] *The New York Times,* September 29, 1935.
[72] Address of John G. Winant on the Social Security Act, Columbia network, September 29, 1936, in author's possession.
[73] *Ibid.*

assistance section of the Act and held the proposed reserve fund unnecessary and dangerous.[74] Embarrassed officials of the Fund were obliged to advise Landon that this report was the tentative work of only one member of its research staff, that it had not been approved or rejected by the Fund's committee on old-age security, and that it had been sent to him with the stipulation that it be treated as confidential. The Kansas Governor had also overlooked a key phrase in the report which held that "in considering the inadequacies and shortcomings of the act full credit should be given to it as a real achievement and as a real foundation on which a satisfactory structure for old-age security may eventually be built".[75]

A midwestern newspaper appraised the situation correctly when it concluded that Winant's "sincerity and disinterestedness" in support of social security would not be challenged by partisans in either camp. "Yet he felt obliged to resign to qualify as its champion. We are still puzzled. Why must Winant, almost alone among high officials, resign in order to educate." [76] In New Hampshire, John McLane lamented the end of Winant's political career, especially in light of Styles Bridges' increasing conservatism and control of Granite State politics.[77]

Feeling that he had done more than his share to counter Landon's attacks on social security, especially as a Republican, Winant remained reluctant to become further involved in the campaign. The President, however, would not let him rest and dashed off a pencilled note to "Gill" [sic] urging him to reconsider his hesitancy to speak at pro-Roosevelt rallies. Where once he cautioned against resignation from the SSB, the President now pressed for increased involvement, insisting that an Ohio meeting "... must be called off if you don't go.... And next week New England! Don't hesitate to repeat and reiterate — it's the only way to get the story across".[78]

Republicans, again, facilitated Winant's renewed involvement in the campaign when the Industrial Division of the G.O.P. National Committee revived a technique which had been extremely successful

---

74   *The New York Times*, October 1, 2 and 4, 1936.
75   *Ibid.*, October 2 and 4, 1936.
76   *Ibid.*; *Des Moines Register* editorial reprinted in *The New York Times*, October 11, 1936.
77   John R. McLane to JGW, October 2, 1936.
78   Undated letter from F. D. Roosevelt to JGW, apparently sent shortly before Winant's address from Cincinnati given the last day in October 1936. In author's possession.

during the Bryan-McKinley contest in 1896. A week before the election employers were flooded with millions of pamphlets, posters, and pay envelope inserts attacking the old age insurance system, many of which were forced upon workers on payday.[79] This tactic so infuriated Winant that he went on the air to charge these employers and the Republican National Committee with "shoddy politics". Finding no recourse, with peace and social security involved, he forsook personal friendship and political attachments to denounce the printed insertions in pay envelopes. This sort of propaganda did not give a square deal to the worker, nor insure fair play, and was inconsistent with the principles of democratic government. "Any political message in a worker's pay envelope is coercion. It is a new form of the old threat to shut down the mill if the employer's candidate isn't elected. We're supposed to be beyond that in this country." The dissident Republican then asserted that he would cast his vote for Roosevelt, "one of the finest human beings" he had ever known, and "because I believe that the interests of economic security will be best forwarded by a continuation of the present administration".[80]

That same night, Alfred E. Smith bitterly denounced Roosevelt in a nationwide radio address, insisting that the President was preparing the way for Communist conquest of the nation and appealed to Democrats to vote for Landon. The "Happy Warrior" had turned his back on progress and on the great contributions he had made to the evolution of the welfare state as Governor of New York — a tragic ending for so courageous and devoted a public servant.[81]

The social security issue had set one party against the other. The Republican candidate would have the nation destroy what had generally been regarded as an essential and excellent feature of the Act, namely its contributory provision. Speaking for the President, Winant had expressed general support of the existing law, though acknow-

[79] *The New York Times,* October 27, 1936. Typical of these slips prepared by the Republican National Committee was the following:

Pay Deduction

Effective January 1937, we are compelled by a Roosevelt "New Deal" law, to make a 1% deduction from your wages and turn it over to the government. Finally this may go as high as 4%. You might get this money back in future years . . . but only if Congress decides to make the appropriation for that purpose. There is NO guarantee. Decide, before November 3 — election day, whether or not you wish to take these chances.

Photostatic copies of this and similar leaflets are in the author's possession.

[80] *The New York Times,* October 27 and November 1, 1936; JGW to James M. Langley, November 12, 1936.

[81] *Ibid.*

ledging the need for modification and revision.[82] The voters responded
with resounding affirmation of the New Deal.

Only Maine and Vermont went to Landon while some 60 percent
of the total popular vote was cast for Roosevelt. Running far ahead
of his ticket, the Champion Campaigner all but destroyed the radical
forces on the right and left.[83] Voters in Republican New Hampshire
followed the lead of their former Governor when they converted a
3,000-vote defeat for Roosevelt in 1932 to a 4,400 plurality for the
White House incumbent.[84]

Dean Christian Gauss of Princeton University expressed the feelings
of many Winant admirers, who viewed social security as the most
fundamental issue in the campaign, when he advised the former
Governor that "the most satisfying single event that happened through
it all was your own courageous and high minded stand. May I tell
you how proud I am to remember that it was taken by a Prince-
tonian. . . ." [85]

Appointed anew to the Social Security Board to break an impasse
between Altmeyer and Miles, Winant submitted his final resignation
after the start of the New Year. It was rare for him to hold onto a job
for too long a period. His restlessness could only be managed when
confronted with challenging tasks. He could not sustain constructive
interest or drive after the major crisis had been hurdled and the work
had become routine.

The President responded to Winant's second resignation with the
wish that "after what I hope will be a short period of time — I count
on your returning to national public service". Roosevelt's expectation
of appointing him head of the proposed Department of Public Welfare was soon quashed when Congress revolted against the Chief
Executive's proposed reorganization of the Federal judiciary and, in
the process, shunted aside the new cabinet department.[86]

---

[82]   In 1937, the Social Security Board initiated a study which resulted in a complete legislative overhaul of the old-age retirement program within two years.
[83]   Congressman William Lemke, a Nonpartisan League Republican from North
Dakota who ran on a "Union Party" ticket for President, and was endorsed by
Father Charles E. Coughlin and Dr. Francis E. Townsend, polled less than a
million votes. The tally for Normann Thomas was the smallest Socialist vote since
1900, while in New York the Communist Party lost its legal status when it was
unable secure the necessary 50,000 ballots.
[84]   *The New York Times*, November 5, 1936.
[85]   Christian Gauss to JGW, November 4, 1936.
[86]   F. D. Roosevelt to JGW, February 19, 1937; *The New York Times*, February
19, 1937.

As soon as Harold Butler learned of Winant's resignation from the Social Security Board, he became feverishly active in negotiating for the latter's return. With war clouds enveloping Europe, the ILO head became more convinced than ever that only through active involvement of Washington and Winant could the Organization survive. While attending an ILO World Textile Conference in the United States during the Spring of 1937, Butler hinted to Roosevelt and Frances Perkins that he planned to retire and wanted Winant to replace him.[87]

Disappointed by Congressional rejection of Roosevelt's proposed Department of Public Welfare, and no longer available for a presidential nomination or, indeed, any elective office, Winant acceded to the urgings of Butler and Miss Perkins. When the Governing Body convened in May 1937, the Director almost inaudibly remarked with restrained joy that the members would be pleased to know that Mr. Winant would be resuming his position as Assistant Director.[88]

In the Europe to which Winant returned in 1937, rearmament and the imminence of war had become accepted premises of industry and labor spokesmen. Observers did not need the sight of new barbed wire entanglements on French frontier fortifications to appreciate the significance of war preparations as a background for discussions by staff members and friends of the ILO. British labor leader Ernest Bevin observed that workers in Great Britain, delighted with having employment again after many slack years, no longer pressured for shorter hours. He offered this as one reason why the Labor Party had not made any serious protest against the Government's military program. In fact, the British labor movement completed the reversal of its pacifist position later that year when the Trade Union Congress cautiously endorsed the government's armament program.[89]

Since American affiliation, Washington spokesmen had thrown their support behind far-sighted conventions. They again illustrated this at the 1937 IL Conference when, over the opposition of the British, delegates adopted the 40-hour Textile Convention proposal as a result

[87] H. Butler to JGW, August 29, 1935 and October 5, 1936; interview with Frances Perkins, December 15, 1959; Alvin Knepper "John Gilbert Winant and International Social Justice", p. 148.
[88] Carol Riegelman [Lubin] to JGW, May 11, 1937; Carter Goodrich to Isador Lubin, May 14, 1937, National Archives, Record Group No. 257; *Monthly Summary of the ILO*, 1937, No. 5, May, p. 30.
[89] C. Goodrich to I. Lubin, February 16, 1937; W. E. Chalmers to I. Lubin, September 21, 1937, National Archives, Record Group No. 257.

of collaboration between Washington and Paris and extensive lobbying efforts by U.S. spokesmen among Latin American delegates.[90]

Shortly after his return to Geneva, Winant was followed there by his wife, attractive sixteen-year-old Constance, twelve-year-old Rivington, Dr. Drury's daughter Edith, and Mary Healy, a secretary. The Winant children attended an international school in the Swiss city, except for John, Jr., who remained in the States to complete his schooling in Arizona. Mrs. Winant frequently occupied herself with French lessons, shopping in Paris, and visiting nearby casinos. Unable to remain in one place for too long she would periodically journey to the United States. After the Harold Butlers returned to England, the Winant family moved into La Fenêtre, a large attractive house located on beautiful grounds belonging to the League of Nations. During their brief stay at La Fenêtre the Winants did considerable entertaining for delegates attending conferences or Governing Body meetings. On one occasion, when the American was pouring sherry for the wife of a delegate, the visitor remarked that the host would make an excellent butler. Winant demurred, explaining that "I don't drink enough". At Geneva, however, the former prohibitionist started tippling. On their eighteenth wedding anniversary in December 1937, Mrs. Winant was crossing the Atlantic while her husband labored in Geneva. Terribly frustrated by increasing financial indebtedness, he found it impossible to meet the bills of students he had been sustaining at the University of New Hampshire. Despite these stringencies, however, he continued to cable flowers to friends on festive occasions and to wire get-well messages to Harry Hopkins and others.[91]

Winant met daily at cabinet meetings with Butler, E. J. Phelan, Henri Reymond and André Tixier, top officials of the IL Office. He hardly spoke at these gatherings but, as Phelan recalled, he did through "his silences". His pockets remained his desk where he kept important wires and communications and quite often lost them to the dismay of fellow executives. He rarely ate at regular periods and, if not for a solicitous secretary, often forgot lunch or dinner, usually working through the evening. A rare form of relaxation in which he sometimes indulged was a long walk along the beautiful shores of

[90] C. Goodrich to I. Lubin, June 30, 1937, National Archives, Record Group No. 257.

[91] Constance Winant to JGW, December 20, 1937; Harry Hopkins to JGW, January 14, 1938. Pertinent material on his financial condition was located in Drawer 9, uncatalogued, Winant Coll.

Lac Leman with a sandwich in his pocket, often ending up in the heart of Geneva to look at charming old houses.[92]

Toward the end of 1937, Italy notified the ILO of its withdrawal. Three months later, German troops marched into Austria and proclaimed the Anschluss with no opposition from the European democracies. The event, however, which significantly altered Winant's career was Harold Butler's decision to retire to an academic life in England. Personally committed to the American as his successor, the ILO head had carefully prepared the groundwork for his resignation.[93] Determined to preserve the Organization by transferring leadership and responsibility to Washington, Butler took advantage of a controversy with the French government to advise the Governing Body, in April 1938, that he had accepted appointment as head of Nuffield College at Oxford.[94] At a closed meeting, the Director frankly lamented the diminished interest of European powers in the ILO, which he contrasted with increasing activity by the U.S. and other non-European members. Suggesting that the Organization's center of gravity had shifted during the previous five years, he felt it was time for a change.[95]

In the ensuing weeks, a strong movement developed to have the Directorship pass out of the hands of Great Britain. Of the two Assistant Directors senior to Winant, the Frenchman Tixier was not friendly with Butler and not a serious contender, while Edward Phelan, who had been with the Organization since its birth, appeared handicapped because he came from a small country, Ireland. Butler, meanwhile, had worked quietly through intermediaries like Frances Perkins, and had alerted Winant weeks before. The American had immediately wired Roosevelt, "Want very much to help you at home. Opportunity to do useful service here. Would you cable me to come

[92] Interviews with Edward J. Phelan, July 21, 1951; and with Henri Reymond and Carol Riegelman [Lubin], May 16, 1962.

[93] Interviews with C. Wilfred Jenks, July 23, 1951; with Lewis Lorwin, December 17, 1959; and with Frances Perkins, December 15, 1959. Jenks was an advisor on international law to the ILO; Lorwin was a key ILO employee on economics.

[94] Cable from Howard Bucknell, Jr. to Secretary of State, April 27, 1938; *The Times*, April 28, 1938; for Labor Lubin from Saunders, April 29, 1938, State Department, Historical Office Files, National Archives, Record Group No. 257; and interview with Carter Goodrich, December 18, 1959. Bucknell was the American Consul in Geneva.

[95] ILO, *Minutes*, 84th Session ... Governing Body (Private) ..., Appendix 1, pp. 21-22; *The New York Times*, April 28 and 29, 1938; *The Times*, April 29, 1938.

on to Washington for conference." Not until the ILO head submitted his resignation, however, did the President direct Winant to return to the States.[96]

Butler's plans for his successor became complicated, however, by extensive support for Phelan. A key staff member since its birth in 1919, and Assistant Director for many years, he had exhibited marked administrative skill and masterful knowledge of the Organization's internal structure. Schooled in the British Civil Service, and widely known for his adeptness at securing decisions on major policy matters at Conferences and Governing Body meetings, Phelan had helped develop the tripartite system and in contrast to Winant, loved the machinery of the Organization and the managing of it. Through the years he had assiduously cultivated the leaders of the various delegations and mastered the intricacies of internal maneuverings. What he lacked was the fire, the imagination and the foresight needed in the developing crisis. Although he had worked closely with Butler in a fruitful way, the two had never been close, personal friends.[97]

Despite his impressive background as Governor and Chairman of the Social Security Board, Winant had remained a comparative newcomer to veteran members of the Governing Body. Most of them hardly knew him, while some deemed him too transient an individual with his earlier resignation and frequent journeys between Geneva and the United States. Among factors working against him were his meagre knowledge of French, and his extreme progressivism, in the eyes of some members of the employers' group. The uncertainty of Washington's continued membership carried most weight with certain members of the Governing Body requiring, as a result, active involvement by the U.S. government to insure Winant's election.[98]

The American, however, had certain personality traits which harmonized with the type of Directorship created by its first two office-

[96] JGW to F. D. Roosevelt, April 9, 1938; M. H. McIntyre to JGW, April 29, 1938, President's Personal File 2, F. D. Roosevelt Library; Bucknell to Secretary of State, May 3, 1938, State Dept., Historical Office Files. Also interviews with C. Wilfred Jenks, July 23, 1951; with Frances Perkins, December 15, 1959.
[97] Interviews with C. Wilfred Jenks, July 23, 1951; and with Henri Reymond, May 16, 1962.
[98] Ibid.; H. Bucknell, Jr., to Secretary of State, May 5, 1938, State Department, Historical Office Files, National Archives, Record Group No. 257; undated letter from Carol Riegelman [Lubin] to Carter [Goodrich]. In all likelihood sent between Winant's sudden departure for the United States and his return to Geneva before the Governing Body meeting the end of May 1938. This letter is in the possession of Mrs. Lubin.

holders. As a result of the pioneering endeavors of Albert Thomas and Butler, the Director occupied an eminent international position, his influence on the daily life of millions of laboring men and women throughout the world being in many respects more important than that of the Secretary-General of the League of Nations. The Director determined the course of the Organization to a far greater extent than was the case with the head of the parent unit. Thomas had vested in the Directorship a power of initiative and vital participation in the shaping of policy. He devised it as a living organism, as an instrument of action, not just for collecting and sifting information, or for passively existing under the Governing Body. Less colorful but with a shrewd judgment of political forces and a keen perception of inevitable alterations in power relationships, Butler had adapted, not changed, this role.

Many members of the Governing Body recalled Winant as a tall, youthful-looking individual who seemed so shy and self-conscious that they instinctively sought to put him at ease. While he gave delegates a firm, abrupt handshake, he was not the back-slapping type of politician. He smiled readily and, as one Geneva observer put it, had an "almost mystic quality of intensity in his grayish eyes". He tended to be somewhat of a recluse, though at his conversational best with a very small group.[99] A perceptive English correspondent portrayed him as the very "antithesis of the American public man of the cinema screen". In films, governors and senators seemed to delight in reeling off long and impassioned statements to the press wherever they went, but Winant, though anxious to be of assistance to newsmen, remained "singularly unproductive of 'copy'". He was, in fact, the shyest American this correspondent had ever interviewed.[100]

Immediately following Butler's resignation, Roosevelt discussed the question of his successor with Frances Perkins and Cordell Hull at a cabinet meeting. The President not only sought to repay a political debt to Winant, but appeared anxious to strengthen his own social welfare program by worldwide improvement of labor conditions through the ILO. In addition, the election of an American might offer proof to many nations that Washington had moved away from isola-

[99] Interviews with Edward J. Phelan, July 21, 1951; with Frances Perkins, December 15, 1959; and with Henri Reymond, May 16, 1962. Also, The New York Times Magazine, June 19, 1938.
[100] Newcastle Journal, June 8, 1938; interview with Thomas C. Blaisdell, November 12, 1959. Blaisdell was an American member of the ILO staff.

tion.[101] An American correspondent correctly interpreted the significance of this strategy when she pointed out that while the world's greatest powers had lost faith in the efficacy of the League of Nations and in international cooperation, the greatest non-member finally took cautious steps to join the world of nation-states.[102]

After lengthy conferences in Washington with the President and other cabinet members, Winant finally consented to become an avowed candidate. When Roosevelt learned, however, that the latter's election was in jeopardy, due to Phelan's extensive support, he immediately cabled the heads of state of Governing Body members, including the Soviet Union, conveying his wish that Winant be selected as the new Director.[103] The Champion Campaigner of them all, Franklin D. Roosevelt, resorted to a diplomatic strategy unique in ILO annals by direct lobbying with national governmental leaders. Neither in the selection of Thomas nor Butler had any single nation member initiated such a massive diplomatic campaign.

By the time the Governing Body reconvened in June, Roosevelt's lobbying had proved too much for Phelan — all the government delegates, in addition to a scattering of worker and employer spokesmen, gave the American a majority.[104] When Winant agreed to ap-

---

[101] Memo to Mr. Welles, Undersecretary of State from PM [Pierrepont Moffat?], April 29, 1938; Sumner Welles memo for Moffat, April 30, 1938; G. S. Messersmith memo to Hull, May 5, 1938, State Dept., Historical Office Files.

[102] *The New York Times,* June 6, 1938.

[103] Memo to Mr. Welles, Undersecretary of State from PM [Pierrepont Moffat?], April 29, 1938; Cordell Hull to American Consul, Geneva, May 17, 1938; Cordell Hull to Amembassy London, Cordell Hull to Amlegation, Ottawa, Hull to Amembassy Rio de Janeiro, Hull to Amembassy Hankow, Hull to Amembassy Mexico, Hull to Amembassy Santiago, Hull to Amembassy Paris, Hull to Amembassy Moscow, Hull to Amembassy Warsaw, Hull to Amembassy Barcelona, Hull to Amlegation Oslo, Hull to Amlegation Belgrade, all dated May 18, 1938. Also, interviews with Frances Perkins, December 15, 1959; and with Carter Goodrich, December 18, 1959. The cables dispatched by Hull are found in State Dept., Historical Office Files, National Archives, Record Group No. 257.

[104] Armour to Secretary of State, from Chile, May 19, 1938; Caffery to Secretary of State, from Brazil, May 19, 1938; Boal to Secretary of State, from Mexico, May 19, 1938; Johnson to Secretary of State, from China, May 20, 1938; Bullitt to Secretary of State, from Paris, May 20, 1938; Kennedy to Secretary of State, from London, May 21, 1938; Lane to Secretary of State, from Yugoslavia, May 21, 1938; Bucknell to Secretary of State, from Geneva, May 23, 1938; Biddle to Secretary of State, from Warsaw, May 23, 1938; Davies to Secretary of State, from Moscow, May 26, 1938; Grew to Secretary of State, from Tokyo, May 27, 1938; Armour to Secretary of State from Santiago, May 19, 1938; Hull to American Consul, Geneva, May 31, 1938; Bucknell to Secretary of State, May 31, 1938, State Dept., Historical Office Files, National Archives, Record Group

point Phelan to the new office of Deputy Director, with an increase in salary, the latter withdrew his candidacy. Nevertheless, two of the thirty ballots cast for a new Director remained blank, and immediately after the chairman announced the election of Winant, the British workers' delegate and the Danish employers' spokesman publicly lamented the resort to "prior arrangements made through ... machinery extraneous to the Organization".[105] It was ironic that despite Winant's more pronounced pro-labor inclinations than Phelan, the former was reluctantly accepted by leaders of the workers' group. The basic explanation was the lack of familiarity with the American and their distaste for the unprecedented lobbying tactics by Washington.[106]

In his first address to the Governing Body, Winant sought to ease the tenseness of the meeting by relating an incident in the life of Calvin Coolidge. Shortly after he succeeded to the presidency of the United States, Coolidge learned from a voter in his home state that although he had great respect for the political leader as Governor of Massachusetts, he did not feel he was big enough to be President of the United States. Coolidge responded, "Well, if you feel that way, how do you think I feel?" After warmly praising his predecessors, Winant made clear his severance with the American political scene when he remarked:

No one accepted public office today ... without a realization of its responsibilities, and no one could accept this office without a knowledge that it closes many other ways of life. I had always looked forward to working in more familiar fields, perhaps closer to home, and I want you to know that I realize in taking on the obligations of this office that it is necessary to turn away from many things that I have planned to do, and to have you know that everything that is in me that is worth the having is dedicated to the service before me.

As his voice trailed off at the end, he concluded, "the world rightly

No. 257. Also, undated cable from Harriman to Hans C. Oersted, sent from mid-Atlantic as American delegation headed for Geneva meeting of Governing Body. In possession of C. Riegelman [Lubin].
[105] Bucknell and Goodrich for State and Labor, June 4, 1938; Bucknell to Secretary of State, June 9, 1938; International Labour Office, *Minutes of the Second, Fourth, Fifth and Seventh Sittings — Private — of the Eighty Fourth Session of the Governing Body.* Geneva — 31 May — 17 June 1938, pp. 4-7, 9-11; *The Times,* June 6, 1938.
[106] Paul Ramadier to JGW, undated. Located in Winant Collection folder "Congratulations on Directorship", Drawer 16.

belongs to those who really care. I shall try to do my part." [107]

Harold Butler was delighted with the knowledge that the Office would henceforth be in the hands of "the only person to whom I could pass on the torch without the gravest misgivings and with a feeling of the warmest personal satisfaction".[108] Frances Perkins, who had fulfilled a personal pledge to attend the 1938 Conference, recalled for delegates Winant's integrity, devotion to high purposes and unique contributions. "We have tried him in the fire. He has been faithful. . . ." [109]

During the next decade, Winant would find himself far from Washington and his beloved New Hampshire. Having served his apprenticeship as a social welfare-minded Governor, and as a pioneering Chairman of the Social Security Board, he looked forward with eagerness to the new challenges confronting him at Geneva. From this vantage point he could hope to exert, in the tradition of Albert Thomas and Harold Butler, profound influence in elevating the status and health of laboring men and women everywhere — if the world remained at peace.

[107]   "Speech of acceptance of Mr. Winant to the Governing Body, June 6, 1938". In author's possession.
[108]   H. Butler to JGW, June 4, 1938.
[109]   Located in Winant Collection folder, "Congratulations on Directorship".

CHAPTER X

"A WEAPON FOR EMBATTLED DEMOCRACIES"

Overshadowed by war preparations throughout Europe, domestic labor issues were viewed as of secondary concern by delegates to the annual IL Conference in June 1938. Besides endorsing Winant's plans for a second Conference of American States, little was accomplished, and little would be until the end of the inevitable war.[1]

When the Governing Body convened in London that October, the European crisis remained the overriding issue. In the face of demands by Hitler for his solution to the Sudeten problem, Prime Minister Neville Chamberlain and French Premier Edouard Daladier had agreed, at Munich in September, to dismember Czechoslovakia without the latter's presence or permission. Chamberlain's return to London with his "it is peace in our time", was hailed by the populace, parliament and the press. In London, the ILO Governing Body developed plans for the Labor Conference of American States in Cuba, for the Annual Session, and then offered a series of tributes to Harold Butler, attending his last meeting as Director.[2] A vital decision, taken at a closed meeting, prepared for the Organization's functioning in wartime.[3]

Shortly after taking the oath of office as Director in February 1939, Winant was swept into the crisis by political events. The withdrawal of Germany, Italy and Japan from the League meant a drastic reduction in budgetary appropriations. Fiscal restrictions fell hardest upon the ILO at a time when there was need for expansion of its activities into rapidly developing industrial countries.[4] Confronted with the unpalatable task of discharging one-eighth of the 400 employees —

[1] *The Times*, June 14 and 23, 1938; *Monthly Summary of the ILO*, 1938, No. 6, June, pp. 25-39.
[2] *The Times*, October 26, 27 and 28, 1938; *Monthly Summary of the ILO*, 1938, No. 10, October, pp. 45-49.
[3] International Labour Office, *Minutes of the Eighth Sitting — Private — of the 85th Session of the Governing Body*; Carter Goodrich to Cordell Hull, November 25, 1938, State Dept., Historical Office Files.
[4] *The Times*, December 14 and 31, 1938.

eventually he would be forced to reduce the staff by more than eighty per cent — Winant convened an emergency staff meeting. Conveying a warmth and egalitarianism traditionally foreign to the Geneva staff, he underscored the two contending forces competing for world loyalties. In a world in which nations spent some 13 billion dollars on armaments, and placed over 8 million men under arms, the dedicated handful of the ILO staff, devoted to peace and social justice, had to maintain standards above reproach.

In members we are less than a single regiment, trying to make the world understand that peaceful cooperation and human justice must prevail. And that means we have to put to one side many things that are second rate: we have to maintain within our own group a morale that is expected in every first-class regiment that ever moved forward on a battlefield. We cannot deal lightly with things about which we feel deeply.[5]

Immediately, thereafter, he cabled the ILO representative in the United States to discontinue all codes, to send mail only on ships of member states, to consult with designated individuals in the Labor and State Departments in Washington, and to cable him in Geneva before making any vital, external decisions.[6] From this moment on there would be the closest of working relationships between the new ILO Director in Geneva and President Roosevelt in Washington. Though pledged to conduct his Office as an impartial, international civil servant, Winant could rarely, thereafter, make major policy decisions without prior consultation with the Chief Executive of the United States.

At a closed session in March, the Governing Body appointed an Emergency Committee of eight members to assume its powers during wartime. If members could not attend, then the officers would constitute a quorum and make decisions.[7]

Within days, Winant sped to the United States to meet with Roosevelt on the European crisis and to plan for the protection of the Office. Since a hurried visit to Czechoslovakia before the Munich agreement, information from Czech contacts had convinced him that the Nazis would not only engulf Czechoslovakia but seek to conquer

[5] "Address to the Staff of the ILO, January 18, 1939", Drawer 18, Winant Coll.; Interviews with Henri Reymond and Carol Riegelman [Lubin], May 16, 1962.
[6] JGW to E. M. Johnson, January 14, 1939. W. E. Chalmers was the Labor Department contact, and Theodore Achilles in the State Department.
[7] IL Office, *Minutes of the 5th and 6th Sittings — Private — of the 86th Session of the Governing Body*, Geneva — 2-4 February 1939.

all Europe. During the 1938 Conference, Winant had spoken with Frances Perkins about the oncoming war and the possibility of transferring his staff to the United States.[8] Shortly after his arrival in Washington in March 1939, the Director made clear to Roosevelt that he must prepare the nation for the inevitable conflict and help save the ILO. Winant pinpointed such strategic defense and transportation centers as Dakar in Africa, which he felt would have major significance in the general strategy of a world conflict. By the end of this meeting, the two agreed that the Organization must plan for survival, but not attempt policy development during the months ahead.[9]

In mid-March, with Winant still in Washington, German troops suddenly crossed the Czech frontier and Hitler proclaimed the "Protectorate of Bohemia and Moravia." The following month, Italian Fascists invaded Albania and the British announced the start of compulsory military training. Within weeks, Hitler denounced the Naval Agreement with Britain and its Non-Aggression Pact with Poland, demanded the city of Danzig and a road through the Polish Corridor. Diplomats in the Soviet Union observed a changing of the guard when the comparatively western-oriented Maxim Litvinov was replaced as Foreign Commissar by hardbitten V. M. Molotov.

After returning to Geneva, Winant busied himself with meetings, preparation of the Annual Report, and continued retrenchment. Convinced of the inevitability of democracy's success in the forthcoming conflict, Winant insisted that the ILO prepare for the end of the war, when it must clarify and implement the social objectives of a lasting peace.[10] Those who read carefully the foreword to his Annual Report sensed his determination to make the ILO a vital force for democracy during the conflict. Like Albert Thomas, he spoke his mind on the great contemporary issues related to the work and mission of the Organization. Like Harold Butler, he attacked the folly and social disaster of war and arms competition. Where the Englishman had used the weapons of the intellect, the American colored his offensive with an emotional awareness of what war meant to the common man. He could not, and would not, remain above the battle sweeping across Europe.

[8] Interviews with Frances Perkins, December 15, 1959; with Carol Riegelman [Lubin] and Henri Reymond, May 16, 1962.
[9] I. Lubin to C. Goodrich, March 29, 1939; John G. Winant, *Letter From Grosvenor Square* (Boston, Houghton Mifflin Co., 1947), pp. 137-38, 249.
[10] *Report of the Director to the 25th Session of the IL Conference, June 1939,* IL Office, Geneva, 1939, pp. 5, 7-11; *The Times,* May 31, 1939.

After consulting with Roosevelt and Labor Department spokesmen in Washington, he called a halt to further progress in the ILO. He advised postponement of the proposal for reduced working hours at the 1939 Conference, for with Britain and France resorting to increased conscription and war economies, longer hours of labor would be required of their workers. Unfortunately, these were not times for economic and social reform.[11] At stake were the ILO Office and the tripartite cooperative spirit. Upon recommendation by the Emergency Committee, the Governing Body decided that the Office would remain in Geneva until operation there proved impossible. In case of invasion of Switzerland, the Director was authorized to accept a French invitation to move to Vichy.[12]

In the midst of the Annual Conference in June 1939, with more than 300 delegates and advisers milling about corridors and meeting halls, Winant singled out Chester H. Rowell, Republican leader, former Bull Moose spokesman in California, editor of the *San Francisco Chronicle*, and an Adviser to the United States Employers' delegate. Asking Rowell to his house for lunch, he proposed a fantastic plan which the newspaperman would have immediately rejected, had Winant not been its proponent. The Director was convinced that war would commence immediately after the German harvest that summer, for Nazi authorities had hurried the collection of crops, even calling upon women students in Universities to help work in the fields. The Germans, he knew, would not believe assurances from Great Britain and the United States that they could get "legitimate economic rights and needs" without resorting to armed conflict. If war was to be averted, it must be done quickly by giving the Germans this commitment through some source whose sincerity they would trust. Winant thought the ILO might be that source, but he could not initiate such a move personally since that would make it official and he had no authorization. Nor could he ask any govern-

[11] *IL Conference, 25th Session, Geneva, 1939,* IL Office, Geneva, 1939, pp. 26-44; *The Times,* June 13, 1939; *The New York Times,* June 24, 1939.
[12] ILO, *Minutes of the 1st and 2nd (Private) Sessions of the Emergency Committee,* April 18-21, 1939 and May 9 to June 5, 1939; *Minutes of the Second and Third Sittings — Private — of the 88th Session of the Governing Body,* Geneva, 6-13 June 1939; IL Office, *Official Bulletin,* 27 December 1939, Vol. XXIV, No. 4, pp. 99-101; IL Office, *A Report to the Governments, Employers and Workers of Member States of the International Labor Organization,* 1941, pp. 6-7. Also, Bucknell and Goodrich for State and Labor, April 18, 1939, State Dept., Historical Files.

ment to undertake the task. He had decided that Rowell should do it. While the newsman protested that he had no contacts with the Nazi Government and did not know where to start, he followed through on one of Winant's suggestions: to communicate with the new German Consul in San Francisco through a mutual friend. It seemed rather grotesque to Rowell to make an approach to Germany, from Switzerland, by way of San Francisco.[13]

More grotesque, however, was the fact that Winant had permitted his idealism and abhorrence of war momentarily to isolate him from reality and from history. He, above all others, knew full well that attempts to appease Hitler since 1933 had only intensified this dictator's hunger for land and conquest. Only months before, democratic Czechoslovakia had been destroyed by Neville Chamberlain's appeasement at Munich. And yet, in June 1939, this devotee of political and economic democracy was apparently willing to offer "assurances" to Hitler in hopes of warding off another world war.

In the intervening weeks between July and September, Germany rushed headlong into war and the Soviet Union hurled its own bombshell with the signing of a Soviet-German Non-Aggression Pact. Less than two weeks afterward, the German Army crashed into Poland and the Second World War officially began.

After a quick flight to Washington and then Havana, Cuba to arrange for the November Conference, Winant returned to Geneva just before the final assault on Poland by German and Russian troops. The Governing Body meeting in Oslo cancelled, the Emergency Committee took over, elected the American government delegate, Carter Goodrich, as Chairman and directed Winant to proceed with the Havana Conference.[14] To the members of the Emergency Committee the Director stressed the need for planning for postwar years. Winant promised to use the ILO to prevent a situation where laborers returning to their jobs after demobilization might find the standard of working conditions permanently lowered by the demands of wartime productivity. He quoted Albert Thomas to the effect, "If you wish for peace, cultivate justice." [15]

---

[13] C. H. Rowell to Myrtle [Rowell?], June 25, 1939, Chester H. Rowell Papers, Bancroft Library, University of California. Also, interview with Henri Reymond, May 16, 1962.
[14] F. Perkins to C. Goodrich, September 7, 1939; ILO, *Minutes of the 3rd Session of the Emergency Committee — Private —* Geneva, 20-21 September 1939.
[15] From Mr. Gambs, in the American Consulate in Geneva, to Mr. Lubin, October 17, 1939, State Dept., Historical Office Files.

At the Havana Conference, Winant, thirty staff members and delegates from sixteen nations in North and South America achieved three major objectives: first, they indicated to the world that the ILO would carry on for democracy despite the war; second, they reaffirmed the pressing need for cooperative action and social justice in a world gone mad; and third, the Director proved to doubting staff members and to others that the Havana Conference could serve as a link between America and the democratic European nations involved in the conflict.[16]

The "phony war" on the Western front, meanwhile, lulled Americans and even Britishers into believing that the Germans would go no further. On November 30, Russia invaded Finland and two weeks later was expelled by the League of Nations. As a result of the comparative quiet which hung over the battlelines, the Governing Body met in Geneva in February to plan for the 1940 Annual Conference and to expel the Soviet Union for having invaded a member ILO state.[17]

Four days after Prime Minister Chamberlain confidently advised the House of Commons that "Hitler has missed the bus", German troops swarmed over Denmark and Norway, and "Quisling" became part of the world's vocabulary. By early May, a miserably equipped Allied Force was driven out of Norway into the Atlantic. These developments found the ILO Director in Washington on the eve of a much publicized visit to South American countries. Alerted by cables from Geneva, he involved the State Department in cancelling his projected trip and facilitating his return to Europe. At LaGuardia Airport in New York, twenty expectant passengers watched their places aboard a scheduled seaplane taken by over 7,000 pounds of mail and seating space provided for the ILO Director alone.[18]

[16] H. H. Tittman to Secretary of State, October 20, 1939, State Dept., Historical Office Files. Tittman was American Consul General in Geneva; *The New York Times*, November 22 and 23, 1939. For a report of the Havana Conference read IL Office, *The ILO Month by Month*, Vol. II, Nos. 1-3, January-March 1940, pp. 9-16; Carter Goodrich, "The ILO in Wartime", *The American Labor Legislation Review*, March 1940, pp. 41-43. Interviews with Carter Goodrich, December 18, 1959; with Carol Riegelman [Lubin] and Henri Reymond, May 16, 1962.
[17] IL Office, *Minutes of the 6th Sitting — Private — of the 89th Session*, Geneva, February 5, 1940; IL Office, *Minutes of the 89th Session of the Governing Body*, Geneva, 3-5 February 1940, p. 49; *The Times*, February 6, 1940.
[18] JGW to Hull, March 27, 1940; Hull to American Embassy, Rio de Janeiro, Brazil, April 11, 1940, State Dept., Historical Office Files; Phelan to JGW, JGW to Phelan, C. Goodrich to JGW, all dated April 11, 1940; JGW to Goodrich, April 14, 1940; E. M. Johnson to JGW, April 30 and May 4, 1940.

During the night of May 9, with German troops poised to invade Holland, Belgium and Luxemburg, Winant in Geneva wired Emergency Committee members, successfully urging cancellation of the Annual Conference.

With the passing days, the safety of the Organization became increasingly precarious as German forces moved across Europe and armored divisions broke through at Sedan and threatened to destroy the entire British Expeditionary Force. Trains bound for France ground to a halt, as did buses and commercial planes. Telegraph and telephone lines running through France ceased to carry messages. Masses of letters, newspapers, periodicals and packages piled up in French post offices, some not to be delivered until a year later. Flooded with rumors, and with little reliable information available in Geneva, Winant's hopes for the ILO appeared dashed as he visualized the Organization cut off from the democratic world.

Frightened by sweeping Nazi victories, Swiss authorities placed stringent regulations upon the Office, hampering the free discussion which Winant considered essential for continued existence. The Office would have to be transferred, and the logical place was the United States.[19] Over Phelan's opposition, Winant sought approval of the Emergency Committee for transfer of the Office.[20] His problem, however, was to reach British and French members and those who might have escaped from Norway, Denmark and Belgium. Unable to rely upon letters or telegrams, the Director suddenly left his headquarters as Allied remnants began their retreat across Dunkirk's beaches.

Much as Winant was prepared to make a speedy, personal decision to transfer the Office from Geneva to America, he could not legitimately do so without majority consent of the Emergency Committee. Furthermore, he was uncertain as to the attitude of key member states like France and Great Britain as to locating the Office in the United States, and feared that without such prior approval the parent League of Nations — overwhelmed in isolated Geneva — and disgruntled member states, would deny him the necessary annual appropriations and membership contributions necessary to defray organizational expenses.

[19] For State and Labor from commissioner and Consulate (Geneva), May 23, 1940, State Dept., Historical Files.
[20] Interviews with Henri Reymond and Carol Riegelman [Lubin], May 16, 1962.

As a sobered Britain gathered in surviving soldiers, the Director and his chef du cabinet, T. T. Scott, managed a plane flight across the channel to London. On June 10, Winant met with Foreign Under Secretary, R. A. Butler, who informed him that Italy had just declared war on France and Great Britain. After being assured of governmental support for removal of the Office to America, Winant hurried across Whitehall to the Labour Building where he spoke with Ernest Bevin. One of Labour's most forceful and colorful spokesmen, Bevin, who had recently joined Winston Churchill's coalition cabinet as Minister of Labour and National Service, agreed that every effort should be made to transfer the ILO to the United States. If impossible, the next logical site should be Canada. The Organization, he insisted, must be preserved for important postwar responsibilities.[21]

From London, Winant flew to Paris, where he found French forces retiring across the Marne and government agencies moving to Tours. Passing shocked Parisians, the Director hurried to meetings with remaining governmental, labor and industry officials. After securing general approval of his transfer plans, and with bombs dropping in the vicinity, he commandeered a car and drove southeast to the Swiss frontier. He barely escaped the onrushing Germans who entered the French capital within twenty-four hours after his departure. Winant's slow journey to Geneva evoked deep emotional distress as he passed thousands of fleeing French refugees.[22]

Back in Geneva, he ordered staff members to have knapsacks handy with two days' provisions, travelers checks, and passports, and be ready to leave at a moment's notice to hike over the mountains toward unoccupied France to avoid the expected German invasion of Switzerland. When Winant ignored his own directives, Mrs. Carter Goodrich purchased provisions and readied a knapsack for him.[23] Fast-moving German motorcycle units frustrated these plans when they occupied French frontier posts, temporarily isolating Geneva from the democratic world. Not until the eventual withdrawal of

---

[21]   Interviews with T. T. Scott, July 13, 1951; and with C. Wilfred Jenks, July 23. 1951; Winant, *Letter From Grosvenor Square*, pp. 216-17.
[22]   *Ibid.*
[23]   Interview with Carter Goodrich, December 18, 1949. Also, interview of Herbert L. May, p. 83, in the Oral History Office Collection, Special Collections Library, Columbia University. May was a staff member of the League of Nations in 1940.

German troops from Unoccupied France, following the Armistice between Marshal Henri Pétain and the Nazis, did the Office staff have an opportunity to escape. Through these trying days, Winant displayed a profound sense of loyalty to his colleagues, particularly the Jewish members of his staff and others with international reputations who, he felt, would be cruelly mistreated if they fell into Nazi hands. Winant never ceased worrying about the people "in his outfit".[24]

On the day German troops entered a stilled Paris, Winant and Carter Goodrich had appealed to Cordell Hull and Frances Perkins for permission to transfer a nucleus of the Office to the United States, insisting that it remained the one promising chance of preserving the Organization as a functioning democratic institution. Unless a favorable decision was granted before German-Franco armistice terms were agreed upon, "it would become difficult, if not impossible, to transfer the most valued members of the staff".[25]

During the evening of June 17, Frances Perkins convinced Roosevelt to approve Winant's request. The following morning, however, upon receipt of a directive from the President granting refuge to the ILO, Assistant Secretary of State Breckinridge Long, who had fought this move from the start, appealed the decision to Cordell Hull. Long persuaded the Secretary of State that the Geneva Organization should not be invited, on the grounds that among the personnel were at least a dozen natives of Germany and other Axis-dominated states who "were objectionable to the United States and whom we would have to keep constant track of if they were admitted even as members of that committee". In addition, Long insisted that it would be bad politically, because inviting the ILO would hold out the promise of possible refuge for the political sections of the League of Nations. He advised the Secretary of State that the ILO would be confronted with a situation in the United States where it would have very little to do and would, as a result, "immediately turn to investigation of our own labor conditions and no doubt with a little more time on their hands would begin investigating matters in Latin America and stirring up trouble there just at a time when we are

[24] Interview with Carter Goodrich, December 18, 1959.
[25] For State and Labor From Commissioner and Labor (From Geneva), June 14, 1940; For State and Labor From Commissioner and Consul (Geneva), June 18, 1940, State Dept., Historical Office Files.

trying to keep our relations with those countries on very cordial terms." [26]

Cordell Hull, who had never been overly friendly toward the ILO, readily accepted Long's objections and sought to reverse Roosevelt's decision. Strengthened by an erosion of isolationist sentiments at home, the President would shortly make one of the momentous decisions of his career, to gamble on the survival of the British. And yet, faced with an appeal for refuge from Winant, he finally listened to the fearful voices of Breckinridge Long and Cordell Hull, and retracted the invitation. When Frances Perkins relayed a subsequent message from Winant contending that refusal to transfer the Office might result in liquidation of twenty-four of the best members of the staff, she was informed by Llewelyn E. Thompson that the State Department postion remained the same. In the face of a collapsing France, of an England alone fighting the battle against totalitarianism, and the United States the most powerful member of the ILO, all that Thompson could say for the State Department was that the matter had been very carefully considered and that "no exception to the visa laws and regulations could be made". Transit visas would be issued if staff members could show their intention to proceed to another country and if they satisfied the officer issuing the visa that they would in fact be admitted to the country of destination.[27]

Bitterly frustrated, Frances Perkins felt that the State Department had "let the ILO down very badly . . .". Winant then made it a matter of record that the list of personnel involved had been selected on the basis of unquestioned loyalty to democratic principles.[28] But the President at that moment was totally immersed in his determination to aid Britain, to "scrape the bottom of the barrel" and turn over to private firms for re-sale to the British all available guns and ammunition. During this exchange of cables between Geneva and the State Department, Roosevelt was also laying the groundwork for the transfer of overage destroyers to London. In the developing national debate over foreign policy, the Chief Executive did n ot

[26] Diary of Breckinridge Long, entry for June 18, 1940, Library of Congress; Memorandum by Llewelyn E. Thompson to PM [Pierrepont Moffat?], May 15, 1940, State Dept., Historical Office Files.
[27] Memorandum of Conversation. Subject: Transfer of the International Labor Office. Participants: Secretary of Labor, Mr. L. E. Thompson, Division of European Affairs, June 19, 1940. State Dept., Historical Office Files.
[28] Ibid.; For State and Labor From Commissioner and Consul (Geneva), June 20, 1940, State Dept., Historical Office Files.

want to detract in any way from the proponents of aid for Britain.[29]

Early one mid-July morning, Winant and a chauffeur drove quietly out of Geneva. Forced now to seek a haven elsewhere, he headed for Lisbon, by way of Marseilles and the Spanish border. Over the opposition of key Assistants, and in the face of increasing pressure from the German and Italian governments, he personally carried the IL Office to the new world.[30]

Shortly after reaching the Portuguese capital, a Pan American Clipper winged him to New York. Within days after his arrival in Washington, he secured permission from authorities in Ottawa to transfer the Office to Canada along with staff members and their families who would be admitted on visitors' visas issued at London or Lisbon.[31] Within 48 hours after the Canadian government had granted a refuge to the ILO, the State Department in Washington began issuing transit visas to key staff members of the Geneva Organization.[32] Shortly thereafter, Dr. Wilder Penfield of the Montreal Neurological Institute of McGill University received an unexpected telephone call from Winant, his Princeton classmate. The latter inquired if it would be possible for the ILO to use the University as a mailing address until it found a home somewhere in Canada. After speedily contacting University authorities, Penfield wired back that the IL Office could not only use McGill as a mailing address but as a home for the duration.[33]

The main contingent, some fifteen members and a dozen dependents, left Geneva by bus on August 7. At the Spanish frontier regulations required such a protracted time that they missed connections with the train for Barcelona, extending the trip to Lisbon to five tiresome days. After three weeks at the Portuguese seaport, they

[29] Tittman, Secstate Washington, No. 98, June 23, 1940, Winant Coll.; Benjamin V. Cohen to M. LeHand, June 21, 1940; Cordell Hull to JGW, June 27, 1940. "OK'd by FDR, June 28, 1940", Official files of F. D. Roosevelt 499. 1940-41. ILO Labor Conf. F. D. Roosevelt Library.

[30] Ambassador Kennedy (London) to Secretary of State, July 14, 1940, State Dept., Historical Office Files; interviews with Henri Reymond and Carol Riegelman [Lubin], May 16, 1962.

[31] The Historical Office of the Department of State could not permit specific citation of this communication dated July 26, 1940.

[32] Sumner Welles to American Consul, Geneva, July 27, 1940; Tittman (Geneva) to Secretary of State, for State and Labor, August 8, 14, 31, September 6 and October 10, 1940, State Dept., Historical Office Files.

[33] "Presentation of Tablet Commemorates Wartime Work of International Labour Organization", The Labour Gazette, Vol. L, No. 11, November 1950, p. 1883; Wilder Penfield to author, May 25, 1962.

boarded American and Greek vessels headed for New York. Carter Goodrich, Phelan and the remaining Office staff got to Lisbon as best they could in an assorted array of private cars or by chartered bus.[34] By mid-September the bulk of the small staff reached Montreal.

Finally reaching Lisbon, Phelan, however, refused to leave until he secured ratification of the proposed budget for the forthcoming year by at least a majority of the Emergency Committee. Typifying the stolid, legalistically minded civil servant, the Deputy Director correctly reasoned that without a legitimately ratified budget, the ILO would have to go begging to Member States for funds with which to maintain the Montreal office. Despite a speedy flight by Winant to Lisbon in early September to hasten Phelan's transfer, the Deputy Director and Carter Goodrich would not budge for eleven weeks until four other members of the Emergency Committee managed to reach them, including two who had escaped to Britain from the clutches of the Nazis. After securing the Committee's approval, Phelan and Goodrich finally headed for Montreal.[35]

The transfer completed and the ILO saved, research and publishing resumed. A small custodial group remained in Geneva to look after the 500-room structure and the half million books and pamphlets. The rest of the staff which had not gone on to Montreal, returned to their native countries as national correspondents or attached to branch offices. Winant, meanwhile, spent much of his time in Washington in the midst of the presidential campaign. At this critical stage in international developments, Roosevelt fought his most effective opponent, Wendell Willkie. Despite opposition from staff members who felt that their Director ought not to become actively involved, Winant insisted that the world struggle for the democratic way of life depended on Roosevelt's reelection and that he could not, therefore, remain silent.[36]

Under the auspices of an independent committee headed by Senator George W. Norris of Nebraska, Winant addressed the nation in a radio broadcast from Boston, two days before the elections. In the confines of a private studio, without a visible audience to disconcert him, the Republican New Dealer replied to third-term critics,

[34] Smith Simpson, "The ILO in Wartime", *The American Labor Legislation Review*, Vol. XXXI, No. 3, Sept. 1941, pp. 121-22; interview with Carter Goodrich, December 19, 1959.
[35] *The New York Times*, September 9, 1940; interviews with Edward J. Phelan, July 21, 1951; and with Carter Goodrich, December 19, 1959.
[36] Interview with C. Wilfred Jenks, July 23, 1951.

insisting that Roosevelt was a candidate through force of circumstances. Recalling some of the recent tragedies he had witnessed in Western Europe, he insisted that even a temporary interruption through change of government might have fateful results, not only to Great Britain but to the United States. On another occasion he had maintained that he knew of no other man who had the trust of the common people of all the democratic countries in the world. He expressed his accord with the President when the latter told the world after Munich:

There can be no peace if the reign of law is to be replaced by a recurrent sanctification of sheer force. There can be no peace if national policy adopts as a deliberate instrument the threat of war. There can be no peace if national policy adopts as a deliberate instrument the dispersion all over the world of millions of helpless and persecuted wanderers with no place to lay their heads. There can be no peace if humble men and women are not free to think their own thoughts, to express their own feelings, to worship God.[37]

Despite unending crises, Winant never lost sight of the need to widen the base of the ILO. He had converted a primarily British-French civil service agency, somewhat hostile to the United States, into an international body strengthened by the new world as well as the old; he helped insure that United States delegations would consistently play progressive roles on key issues at Conferences and Governing Body meetings. Mindful of the past, his eye remained constantly on the future. And the future of the ILO in 1940 depended primarily upon the decisions of one man — Winant. The effectiveness of the Organization would be determined by the calibre of some forty remaining staff members selected for transfer to Montreal. He could afford few mistakes.

　　Transfer to Canada resulted from a desire to preserve the Organization, as well as a deliberate design to use it as a propaganda weapon for embattled democracies and as a contact between Allied nations, the United States and neutral governments. Spokesmen for underground labor movements in occupied countries were strengthened by the knowledge that the ILO had been preserved and transferred to an unconquered democratic nation. Winant enabled the Organization to keep open its lines of communications with the free world and to insure that it would remain a force for freedom and social justice. When hostilities finally ceased, delegates to the new United

[37]　*The Nation*, October 26, 1940; *The New York Times*, November 4, 1940.

Nations Organization agreed that the one major unit of the old League to be admitted as an integral part of the new international framework would be the ILO.

With the Office safely in Montreal, the remainder of the war years could provide only housekeeping tasks for its Director. Lacking the challenge and dynamics of a highly active and demanding responsibility, Winant could not contemplate remaining in a safe Canadian city isolated from the heart of the crucial battle.

CHAPTER XI

"SEND US JOHN WINANT"

During the unending series of diplomatic setbacks and crushing military defeats sustained by the British through the autumn of 1940, the American spokesmen in London and at the ILO in Geneva represented two conflicting philosophies. Emotionally repelled by Nazism and Fascism, Winant had frequently alerted Roosevelt to the inevitability of U.S. involvement in the war and to the need for long-range military preparations. Britain's war, he felt, was America's war. At the Court of St. James's in London, Joseph P. Kennedy, a business-minded, conservative Democrat, supported Chamberlain's policy of appeasement.[1] In sharp contrast to his fellow New Englander in Geneva, Kennedy was "electric, articulate, breezy, direct, ... indiscreet".[2] He was at home with British businessmen who had sought to avoid war by refusing to aid democracy in Spain, Czechoslovakia or elsewhere.[3] He knew Conservatives well, but hardly a Laborite. Kennedy was against the war and America's involvement in it. There developed, as a result, a profound dissonance between the Ambassador and his President as to the fundamental issues at stake in the world.

In October 1940, Kennedy returned home amid rumors that he would retire because of disagreement with American foreign policy. Nevertheless, during the presidential campaign, he urged Roosevelt's reelection, in hopes of keeping the U.S. out of war. At a lengthy, informal meeting with Cordell Hull, Sumner Welles and Assistant Secretary of State Breckinridge Long, the Ambassador insisted that England was "gone." Not only had German bombs paralyzed industry

[1] *The Memoirs of Cordell Hull* (New York, The Macmillan Co., 1948), p. 763; William L. Langer and S. Everett Gleason, *The Undeclared War 1940-1941* (New York, Harper and Brothers, 1953), pp. 56, 208; Eduard Beneš, *Memoirs of Dr. Eduard Beneš* (London, George Allen and Unwin, 1954), p. 172; John Morton Blum, *From the Morgenthau Diaries* (Boston, Houghton Mifflin Co., 1959), p. 518.
[2] Taken from a broadcast by Raymond Gram Swing over the British Broadcasting Corporation, February 8, 1941. Copy in author's possession.
[3] For a study of British appeasement, see Martin Gilbert and Richard Gott, *The Appeasers* (Boston, Houghton Mifflin Co., 1963).

and communication lines, spreading a sense of defeatism throughout the nation, but Britain was bankrupt and would soon go off the gold standard, unable to meet commitments to the United States. With "the British Empire ... gone; ... the British Navy ... gone," and Hitler rampant on European soil and dominant over England, he visualized the United States excluded from markets in Europe, the Far East and South America. He thought that America should institute a realistic policy through economic collaboration with Germany and Japan.

Misinterpreting increased British governmental regulations since the outbreak of war, Kennedy concluded that England was as much a "socialistic state" under Winston Churchill as were Nazi Germany and Fascist Italy. He ignored the basic fact that the British tendency toward greater economic control by the state sprang from a philosophical conception fundamentally opposed to totalitarianism. He never fully appreciated the independence of British political parties, the dynamics of the Parliamentary system, nor the effectiveness of a critical press and the country's trade union movement.

Kennedy believed that the British could not hold out unless America took over the airplane production and furnished them with "thousands and thousands and thousands of planes." Though Allied combat aircraft and pilots had proved superior to the Germans, the latter came through in such great numbers and with such devastating effect that the British would soon be battered into a desire for some understanding with the Third Reich. The spirit and morale of the world, he maintained, was broken, for the people had lost faith in God. Displaying an ambivalence and confusion as to the issues involved in the struggle against Nazism, Kennedy insisted that the United States would have to assume a Fascist form of government to survive in a world of concentrated and centralized power.[4]

In the United States, the population experienced one of the most heated debates since the Civil War; to what extent should the nation cooperate with Great Britain in her lone stand against the European dictators? The House Foreign Affairs Committee would soon conduct hearings on the Administration-sponsored Lend-Lease bill which would facilitate the distribution of arms and material to a financially

[4] Detailed information concerning this conference in the State Department is to be found in the Breckinridge Long diary, entries for November 6 and 7, 1940, pp. 196-99 in the 1940 volume. Also, *The New York Times*, November 12, 22, 23 and December 2, 1940.

hard-pressed Britain.[5] Spearheading national support for this proposal would be the "Committee to Defend America by Aiding the Allies", led by Kansan William Allen White. Channeling most of the opposition to this legislation, and to further involvement in the European conflict, would be the America First Committee with Senator Burton K. Wheeler and Charles A. Lindbergh as its most noted spokesmen.

On December 1, 1940 Kennedy advised the press that he had resigned as Ambassador so that he might devote his time to "the greatest cause in the world today, to help the President keep the United States out of war". Echoing the keynote sounded by Wheeler and Lindbergh, Kennedy insisted that "This is not our war. We were not consulted when it began. We had no veto power over its continuance. England's own leaders have told us why they are fighting. They are fighting for their very existence." [6]

Franklin D. Roosevelt, during the final months of Kennedy's tenure, had developed his own contacts with Prime Minister Winston Churchill and with other vital sources in London, enabling him not only to circumvent his defeatist Envoy but to foresee the possibility of a "new order" evolving in England by the end of the conflict. The Country Gentleman type, the landed and industrial aristocracy which had ruled Britain and the Empire for many years through the Tory Conservative party, was being crowded out of its traditional position by an economic and social revolution engendered by the war. If Churchill fell, any new government would be composed of more popular interests and led by men whom Kennedy, Cordell Hull and Breckinridge Long deemed "radical". This would mean a government out of sympathy with the "present and past influences in controlling groups". Viewing this as a distinct possibility, Roosevelt knew he must choose a new envoy whose background, interests and human sympathies would enable him to establish contact not only with the Prime Minister but with those Laborites who might lead the British government in the future.[7]

[5] In effect, this bill wiped out the restrictions of the existent Neutrality Act for it granted to the President the power to "sell, transfer, lease, lend or otherwise dispose of" munitions and defense articles to any power whose defense was "deemed vital to the defense of the United States". The bill became law on March 11, 1941.

[6] The New York Times, November 12, 22, 23, December 2, 1940 and January 14, 1941.

[7] Breckinridge Long diary. Entry for February 15, 1941, pp. 23-24 of 1941 volume. Library of Congress; New York Herald Tribune, February 6, 1941; The

The President wanted an understanding emissary who could re-organize the work in the London Embassy so that the United States would benefit from British war experiences. Such a spokesman would have to be sympathetic while urging patience during Washington's preparations for greater commitment. Expanded military training had begun under the Selective Service Act; American industry was being keyed to war production; Lend-Lease was pending before Congress, and fifty overage destroyers had been transferred to Great Britain.[8]

In the nation's capital, three names were mentioned as possible successors to Kennedy — William C. Bullitt, who had resigned as Ambassador to France; J. Anthony Drexel Biddle, Ambassador to the Polish Government-in-Exile located in London; and Winant.[9] In England, a leading Socialist intellectual voiced the sentiments of many Britishers when he urged friends in the United States to "send us John Winant as Ambassador; and . . . even more . . . secure the permanent end of Joe Kennedy's political career". While Harold Laski felt that things, on the whole, went well, he feared that in the next three months the British would face their biggest challenge. Confident of inevitable victory, he viewed the crisis as one of material aid.[10] At home, a close friend of Mrs. Roosevelt urged Winant's selection because, she felt, a new type of Ambassador was needed with a new type of courage.[11]

Winant was an ideal choice to succeed Kennedy. The latter's defeatism and enchantment with totalitarian power would be more than counterbalanced by the former's utter devotion to the British, and by his contention that the war remained a life and death struggle for peace and "social democracy". Since the start of the conflict he had insisted that the social content of democracy had to be expanded, for London and Paris could no longer expect its laboring men and

---

New York Times, February 7, 1941; Washington Post, February 9, 1941; Washington Star, February 9, 1941.

[8] Winant, Letter from Grosvenor Square, pp. 21-22.

[9] The New York Times, December 2, 1940.

[10] Harold J. Laski to Freda Kirchwey, January 20, 1941. A copy was forwarded to Winant.

[11] Esther Lape to Eleanor Roosevelt, November 8, 1940. In a postscript, Miss Lape added, "My impression is that the 'suggestion' that there's a loose bridk [sic] in Gil's handling of his own or his wife's finances is a purposeful creation. I don't believe it." Attached to the above letter was a memo for the President from Mrs. Roosevelt: "I think you had better check with Henry Morgenthau on some of the things he told me if you are at all interested in this suggestion of Esther's." President's Personal File 42, Franklin D. Roosevelt Library.

women, who had suffered through "depression democracy", to give their faith and their lives for the preservation of empty promises. Badly needed, in addition, was a tightening of the lines of friendship between Britain and the United States, as well as significant expressions of faith in the ultimate outcome of the war. Winant's commitment, shyness and reserved type of leadership would insure him personal acceptance by the British.[12]

Within days after his third inaugural, when the President warned that the task of the people was to "save the nation and its institutions from disruption from without", Roosevelt ordered Winant to the White House.[13] In the waiting room of the Executive Office, he learned that the President planned to drive to Annapolis that rainy afternoon to meet Lord Halifax, the new British Ambassador. Roosevelt queried the ILO Director about Britain and social and economic conditions in Europe. He discussed London's precarious military position and the urgent need for equipment and supplies, but not a word about the Court of St. James's.[14] Winant learned of his appointment as Ambassador through the Canadian newspapers. With the exception of a rare discordant note struck by Arthur Krock, the appointment met universal approval. Krock worried lest the designation of this "dreamer on a brave new world" would promote the "socialization of industry in both nations", as advocated by Bevin and Laski in England and stimulated by the President and Supreme Court Justice Felix Frankfurter.[15]

Throughout the Allied world, however, the selection was warmly hailed. Argentina's Secretary of the Federation of Trade Unions cabled "congratulations and ... fraternal greetings of the working class and our own". A Minister in Czechoslovakia's Government-in-Exile hailed the new Envoy as a "real democrat and friend of our nation". The Polish Minister of Labor voiced the sentiments of many former colleagues at the ILO when he insisted that his years of work for social progress had made him "an eloquent symbol of the Ameri-

---

[12] "The Citizen's Responsibilities in Foreign Policy". An address by Winant before the luncheon meeting of the N.Y.C. League of Women Voters, February 8, 1941. Copy in author's possession.
[13] *The New York Times,* January 21, 1941.
[14] Winant, *Letter from Grosvenor Square,* pp. 10-14.
[15] February 7, 1941 issues of *The New York Times, Washington Post, Washington Star, New York Herald Tribune, Baltimore Sun* and *Philadelphia Inquirer.* Also, *The New York Times,* February 8, 10 and 11, 1941.

can tradition of liberty". Edward R. Murrow in London concluded, "This is indeed good news." [16]

Contrary to speculation, neither Laski nor his close friend, Felix Frankfurter, exerted influence in the selection of this new envoy whose appointment displeased Breckinridge Long and other key members of the State Department.[17] A photograph of the new Ambassador wearing high laced shoes moved one newspaper to comment, "The old line about stepping into another man's shoes doesn't go with Winant. . . . Mr. Kennedy, you can bet, hasn't worn high tops like those Winant brogans for years and years." [18]

In Britain, conservative Lord Beaverbrook, who headed the Ministry of Aircraft Production, hailed the appointment, as did Laborite Laski, while Harold Butler viewed it as a "good augury" for the future. *The Times* of London came closest to the mark when it described the new Envoy as "a man slow to reach a decision but inflexible when convinced, and today as fully awake to the tremendous moral and social issues of the conflict of which he will be a spectator as anyone alive. Britons will discover they are dealing with a man in whom confidences can be placed unhesitatingly." [19]

In response to an invitation to address a joint session of the new Hampshire Legislature, the new Envoy made a hurried trip to Concord, which also facilitated a rare family reunion at the Pleasant Street mansion. Daughter Constance had just flown home from schooling in Peru with a husband, following an elopement, while his sons hastened from Deerfield Academy to join him. Tall, handsome John Jr., now nineteen, looked and acted like his restless father, while Rivington Russell, fifteen, seemed overawed by the excitement of hovering newspapermen. Mrs. Winant appeared excited and happy in the spotlight of international importance.

After breakfast in the large, sunlit dining room, the family drove the short distance to the imposing State House, to be escorted into

[16] Jose Domenech to JGW, January 15, 1941; Allende to JGW, January 19, 1941; Stanczyk to JGW, February 9, 1941; E. R. Murrow to JGW, February 7, 1941.
[17] Interview with Felix Frankfurter, December 9, 1959; Langer and Gleason, *The Undeclared War*, p. 419 fn; Breckinridge Long diary, entry for February 15, 1941, pp. 23-24 of 1941 volume.
[18] *Washington Daily News*, February 7, 1941.
[19] Beaverbrook to JGW, February 10, 1941; H. Laski to JGW, February 7, 1941; H. Butler to JGW, February 8, 1941; *The Times*, February 7, 1941. Also, the February 7, 1941 issues of *Daily Express, Daily Telegraph, Daily Mail, Daily Herald, News Chronicle* and *Manchester Guardian*.

Representatives Hall. Bursting with an excited audience of legislators, citizens and school children, these North Country folk had come to pay homage to their renowned son. Deeply moved by the warm reception and by the rush of memories, Winant spoke slowly as he stood beneath the portrait of George Washington. In a voice which quivered with emotion, he recalled that a quarter of a century had gone by since he first served in this hall as a member of the General Court, and the memory remained real of those he had worked with in the struggle for social justice. Here he had learned, during the Great Depression, that critical problems reached beyond State lines and across national frontiers. Because he realized that security, a stabilized economy and peace remained essential to the happiness of people everywhere that, whether in Washington or Europe, "I felt that I was still working for you here at home."

At this juncture, the Ambassador extemporized on the theme closest to his heart. His eyes blazed, more deeply sunken than usual from loss of sleep, and his unkempt forelocks fell over his brow as he spoke of men and women he had known in Europe. Rapping his fist sharply on the lectern before him, he recalled friends who had been killed, imprisoned, or driven from their homes by the Nazis.

All those things men have fought for in this country, all those things this country is founded upon have been wiped out in Europe. Today the peace of the world is menaced by those who have put aside reason and orderly procedures for wanton violence and brute force.

We are today the "arsenal of democracy", the service of supply against aggressor nations.

England has asked that we give them the tools that they "might finish the job". We can stand with them as free men in the comradeship of hard work, not asking but giving, with unity of purpose in defense of liberty under law, of government answerable to the people.[20]

As the former Governor concluded his remarks with the statement that no matter where he might be in the world "this place is forever home to me", the audience rose in tumultuous acclaim.

After exchanging farewells with many friends, the new Ambassador took leave of his family and hurried to Washington for additional briefings. A few hours before boarding a plane for England, he had a sobering meeting with Harry Hopkins, who had just returned from a lengthy stay in London. The ailing confidant to the President spoke

---

[20] *Concord Daily Monitor*, February 18, 1941; *The New York Times, The Times*, February 19, 1941.

particularly of German U-boats scouring the Atlantic and sinking hundreds of thousands of vital British tonnage while Nazi troops marched steadily across the world's battlefields.[21] The Pan American Clipper hurried Winant to Lisbon, where a British plane sped him to the Bristol airport in southwestern England. Arriving earlier than expected, the pilot circled the landing field for an hour in a thunderstorm. King George's younger brother, the Duke of Kent, finally made his appearance after the passengers had debarked. Obviously embarrased, he hurried to the waiting room and greeted the new arrivals who returned obligingly to the plane to pose for pictures, as if the Duke had been waiting all the time. To inquiring reporters, the American Envoy, at first, remarked that he hadn't much to say, but after nervously shifting from one foot to the other and biting his lip, he suddenly exclaimed in a loud, clear voice: "I'm glad to be here. There's no place I'd rather be than in England." [22]

On the motor trip to the railway station, Winant observed extensive destruction of British homes and deep wounds inflicted by the German Luftwaffe, a sight he would become familiar with in London, Cardiff, Coventry and elsewhere during pilgrimages through Britain. As the special train sped across southern England, the Duke explained that the King would be waiting for them at Windsor station, to reciprocate Roosevelt's journey to Annapolis to greet Viscount Halifax. When the rolling stock finally came to a halt alongside this historic town, King George VI stood on a windswept station platform to greet the new Ambassador. The Envoy quickly reached the open door of his special car and the King, spruce in the uniform of a Field Marshal, impulsively reached out and pumped Winant's hand, saying warmly, "I am glad to welcome you here". An interesting contrast was the American's crumpled navy blue overcoat and gray suit, and a worn white shirt. After a brief visit with the King and Queen at nearby Windsor Castle, Winant returned to the waiting train which then proceeded to London.[23]

In March 1941, when Winant reached England, Londoners still

[21]   Robert E. Sherwood, *Roosevelt and Hopkins: An Intimate History* (New York, Harper and Brothers, 1948), p. 262.

[22]   *The New York Times*, February 28, March 1 and 2, 1941.

[23]   *Ibid.*, March 2, 1941; *The Observer*, March 2, 1941; *Evening Standard*, *Manchester Guardian*, March 3, 1941; JGW telegram to FDR and Cordell Hull, March 5, 1941, copy in author's possession. Unless otherwise identified, all telegrams subsequently referred to as from Winant are in the possession of the author. They are duplicates of official telegrams which the retiring Envoy brought back with him to the United States.

experienced heavy, periodic night attacks, even though the Battle of Britain had been won the previous September by radar, the superior armament of Spitfires and Hurricanes, and the daring of British, Czech and Polish airmen. In the face of disastrous air losses, German armored divisions could no longer reach the English beaches and the Luftwaffe shifted to less perilous and less effective night attacks.

During his first night in the British capital, the Ambassador blurted out to key Embassy aides, "Now that I am here, what can I do to help?" He framed his entire approach in human terms, as when he directed staff members to prepare papers on economic and social developments "in the form of shoes, in the form of clothing and pork chops for each and every individual in Britain." Those in trouble were apt to receive priority over cabinet ministers and diplomatic officials when they appealed directly to the Ambassador. He saw people at all hours in his large Embassy office overlooking Grosvenor Square, or in his private flat next door. He was accessible to the char-woman, to historian R. H. Tawney, to Harold Laski, to Anthony Eden and to the five young American volunteers who had joined the Kings Royal Rifle Corps. Some staff members, however, found him inaccessible for regular appointments, which did not help matters at the Embassy.

Because of former Ambassador Kennedy's attitude, a considerable portion of the Embassy staff had been ridden with friction and dissatisfaction. After Winant's arrival, much of this discord disappeared, partly because of his personality and his devotion to the British cause. Although he rarely remembered the names of his many staff members, he became familiar with their job assignments.

Long before America became involved in the conflict, the new Ambassador reorganized the work of the Embassy as the President had wanted and funneled an unending stream of vital news to the United States. He coordinated scientific information, insuring that all surgical advances in the treatment of wounds, burns, arctic and tropical diseases were immediately transmitted to Washington; he reported on the use of radar in air control, on the new designs of British fighting planes used in building America's own production program, and on the defects of British tank treads which Washington eliminated from its own. Hardly a phase of fighting equipment, tactic or strategy that the British developed from their war experience was not known to the United States before Japan struck at Pearl Harbor. In addition, almost every American governmental department and war bureau had representation in London, with all civilian agencies responsible to the Embassy, including those charged with carrying out policy on the economic front, Lend-Lease, shipping, coal and oil. This required Winant to do business with more than twenty-two ministries of government.

With more than a thousand employees of varied wartime missions under his supervision, the new Ambassador granted extensive responsibility and freedom of decision to immediate subordinates. While he kept himself fairly well informed on Embassy activities, he did not inject himself unduly into its day-by-day work. With independent-minded individuals this policy worked well; with others who required greater direction and guidelines, this turned out to be a major weakness of Winant's administration. Though he loved people, the shy Envoy could not move freely among large groups, even in the Embassy.

On the other hand, there is the not unusual story of the American GI from Akron, Ohio, who wanted to see the interior of the American Embassy one Sunday morning. The military policeman at the front door had turned him away and he was walking dejectedly down a nearby street. A tall man in civilian clothing hailed him, introduced himself as a fellow American, and asked him how things were going. When the GI explained about the Embassy, the stranger responded, "I know the MP at the door, maybe I can get him to let us look around. I work at the Embassy too." The GI not only got to tour the building but stayed for lunch. He was struck speechless for a few moments, however, when a passing aide hailed the host as "Mr. Ambassador".[24]

The Ambassador endeavored to organize his own brains trust but did not always use it to maximum effectiveness.[25] Abreast of economic, social and political developments in Britain, he sought to keep Washington attuned to the needs and thinking of the people as well as the government. Unfortunately, he remained handcuffed to too many administrative responsibilities by his own personality and

[24] *Chicago Daily News*, November 8, 1943.
[25] George Soloveytchik, "London Embassy", *Survey Graphic*, June 1944, pp. 277-79; interviews with P. Sargent Florence, July 1, 1951; with Virginia Crawley, July 3, 1951; with Herbert Agar, July 11, 1951; and with Wallace Carroll, June 13, 1960. Assisting the Ambassador were Winfield William Riefler of the Princeton Institute for Advanced Study; Philip D. Reed, former Board Chairman of General Electric; newsman Wallace Carroll; Pulitzer prize winner Herbert Agar; youthful Samuel Berger; and economists P. Sargent Florence and Ernest F. Penrose, among others.

by what America's Envoy to Ireland called, the lack of sufficient
"first rate men in the London Embassy".[26] Winant frequently lamented
the fact that some key staff people could not make original contributions, having been trained to do errands assigned them by Washington. When confronted with legitimate criticism of administrative
weaknesses, particularly poor communications within the Embassy,
he insisted that the State Department had not assigned him competent personnel.[27]

A forty-year veteran of the State Department, who headed the
London Branch of the Office of Strategic Services, concluded that
something in the Ambassador's makeup "created confusion in his
office". Of singular disturbance to this exacting observer was Winant's
inability to keep abreast of his schedule for visitors. He never seemed
to catch up with activity around him and found it exceedingly difficult to answer invitations from British sources. "He had the best will
in the world but to translate good intentions into actions was difficult
for him." [28] As well, Winant was a constant security worry to his
subordinates; he wandered around London with top secret papers
indiscriminately thrown into bulging pockets of crumpled suits, and
left secret telegrams in different locations.[29]

On the other hand, when United States Senator Owen Brewster
of Maine returned home from a 35,000-mile trip around the world to
study American diplomatic representation, he advised a select group
of listeners that at every post he visited, except two, United States
delegations were "inadequate". Of the two exceptions, the Embassy
in London and the Legation in Canberra, Senator Brewster felt that
only Winant maintained a completely harmonious official family in
which the representatives of the various agencies had been integrated
into an effective team.[30]

[26]   David Gray to JGW, November 24, 1942. Box f-802, 18220, State Department, Historical Office Files.
[27]   Diary of Maurine Mulliner, entries for September 19, 21 and October 31,
1945; JGW telegram "To the Undersecretary", June 20, 1944.
[28]   Interview of William Phillips in the Oral History Office Collection, Special
Collections Library, Columbia University, p. 135.
[29]   The bulk of the foregoing information on Winant's role as Ambassador was
secured from interviews with Theodore Achilles, July 6, 1951; with Fred Nor-
berry, Embassy chauffeur, July 6, 1951; with Miss Mary Dawson, Embassy char-
woman, July 6, 1951; with Mrs. P. Sargent Florence, Embassy researcher, July 1,
1951; and with Miss Ruth Russell, Embassy staff member, April 16, 1952.
[30]   H. Freeman Matthews to JGW, November 19, 1943; JGW telegram "To the
Secretary", August 4, 1943.

Ignoring the luxurious residence of American Ambassadors at 14 Princess Gate, Winant leased a comfortable third floor furnished flat at 3 Grosvenor Square, next door to the Embassy. The apartment contained three bedrooms, a large living room, dining area, kitchenette and long hall. His shy housekeeper, Orol Mears, looked after his meals and cared for visitors. Plain furniture, plenty of pacing room, and the absence of frills made this a typical man's flat. When he left the Embassy late at night, he would walk to his apartment and devote the remainder of the evening to preparing and receiving cables from Washington. Equipped with protected telephones, assigned constant messenger service with Army and Navy signals and with the Embassy code room, and always on "duty" because of the time differential in the United States, he was often awakened in the middle of the night to be handed urgent cables from Washington. Not infrequently, the code room messenger found the Ambassador reading novels in bed.

He never attended a tea party and lived exclusively on British civil rations. The only formal dinners he gave enabled General Dwight D. Eisenhower to meet the British cabinet on his arrival in London, and Mrs. Roosevelt to pay tribute to the wartime contribution of British women. At the sole formal luncheon, Winant decorated members of the British Chiefs of Staff and other high ranking British officers, at the request of President Truman.

These long, tense working hours in the Embassy, with Anthony Eden in the Foreign Office, at Chequers with the Prime Minister, and pilgrimages throughout embattled Britain, became an unending stimulant to the Ambassador who had no social life and few moments of relaxation. Perpetually working at top speed with paper flowing endlessly across his desk, kept him at a constantly high pitch, and with the passing months and years, the strings of life became increasingly taut.[31]

Most of his creative work was done in his apartment, particularly preparing speeches. As a result of his pervading fear of public addresses, he would delay preparation of talks until the last possible moment. Isolating himself for a day or two, he would often complete his remarks on the train or car headed for the meeting. He smoked

[31] Interviews with Eileen Mason, July 2, 1951; with Theodore Achilles, July 6, 1951; with Anthony Eden, July 7-8, 1951; with Grace Hogarth, July 10, 1951; and with Orol Mears, July 24 to 31, 1952. Also, Wilder Penfield to author, May 25, 1962. Miss Mason was an Embassy librarian and secretary; Achilles was a key staff member in the Embassy; and Miss Hogarth assisted Winant as a secretary during the writing of his book.

cigars endlessly, a practice he had acquired during his governorship, and Orol Mears tucked them away throughout the flat so that he could find them most anywhere. Winant, however, gave so many to vistors that his secretaries frequently had to scour the town to purchase these scarce items.

Idolizing this unusual personality, English-born Orol Mears realized that the Ambassador labored under tremendous tension. She sought to provide him rare evenings of relaxation by extending dinner invitations to American volunteers in the British army, and subsequently to GI's from the States. These young men helped the Envoy forget his official self momentarily, as he recalled days as a schoolmaster and political leader, or spoke of his hopes for a postwar world. The young visitors who made the greatest impact were five American college graduates who had joined Anthony Eden's old army unit, the 60th King's Royal Rifle Corps. These "Five Musketeers", as he called them, would journey to London together on leave and, when their money ran out, come up to his flat late at night to spend hours in discussion and debate and then fall asleep on the floor. As Winant's contact with life, "with all that youth and fineness means in the world today", they helped him keep faith with America and faith in the ultimate willingness of the American nation to sacrifice and to fight. Of these five who went on to North Africa, three survived.[32] As soon as the Envoy learned that one of his young American friends had been killed in North Africa, he labored over a letter to the father. No young man he had met during his stay in Britain had meant as much to him as Jack Brister, not only for what he was but for what he would have been in building a world of the future. Jack had gone in helping to save what "we have got, in protecting what was given to us." Benét was correct when he said: "We who are alive today did not make our free institutions. We got them from the past, and we hold them in trust for the future." Jack had joined his physician-father in paying that debt. "In all that was human he was above reproach, whether it was eating griddle cakes or making love or giving life." [33]

Mrs. Winant arrived in mid-April 1941, just before one of the heaviest Luftwaffe attacks. German bombers came over early that night and Londoners soon knew this was a major raid. Working in

---

[32]   *Ibid.*; Charles G. Bolté to JGW, June 15, 1943; JGW to Dr. F. E. Brister, July 1, 1943. Also, interview with Mrs. Herbert Agar, July 11, 1951.
[33]   JGW to Dr. F. E. Brister, July 1, 1943.

his office, the Ambassador realized the proportions of the attack when a bomb dropped across the street, shattering Embassy windows, and he hurried to his flat to urge his wife and Miss Mears to take cover in a cellar shelter. Mrs. Winant suggested, instead, that they go to the roof to see the effects of the raid. From there, all London seemed ablaze as anti-aircraft guns boomed, bombers droned overhead and high explosives and incendiary bombs burst all about them. The residential district surrounding the Embassy seemed to be receiving the brunt of the attack, with two houses on Grosvenor Square destroyed and others ablaze.

Almost overpowered by the human tragedy associated with this destruction, the Envoy put his wife and Miss Mears to bed on sofas in his office and then went out into the night with key Embassy aide Theodore Achilles. The streets were bright as day from the glare of burning structures, as enemy planes continued to fly overhead; it was an eery and frightening experience. Nevertheless, the brooding Ambassador with his soft crumpled felt hat, and his assistant in a tin helmet, walked for hours. When the Emissary inquired of harassed air raid wardens if he could be of help, the reply was an inevitable "No". His aid was not to be material — the lifting of helpless victims, the removal of burning debris — rather it would be a pervading spiritual support which would spread throughout Britain; for his very presence in the streets of burning London, or when visiting crowded shelters, conveyed profound confidence and an emotional identity with tragedy.

The two Americans paced the streets of London that memorable night until the rays of dawn appeared over a scarred and smoking city. When some Londoners, coming out of shelters, spotted the Ambassador wearily trudging back to Grosvenor Square, newspapers and the radio quickly spread the news to every corner of Britain. The story gave suffering people a feeling of intimate association with Americans, greater hope in the future, and an understanding of how deeply the new Envoy cared.[34]

By his behavior and dedication, Winant quickly undid the damage of his predecessor. As Prime Minister Clement Attlee put it, years

[34] JGW telegram "To Secstate", April 20, 1941; interviews with Theodore Achilles, July 6, 1951, and with Mrs. Herbert Agar, July 11, 1951. Mrs. Winant remained in Britain through the end of August 1941, visiting hospitals and service clubs. *The Times*, July 21, August 1, 21, 26 and 30, 1941.

later, he "brought a feeling of warmth, confidence and courage to the British people in their time of greatest need".[35] The American Envoy seldom forgot that there were real people about him, people who were not ambassadors or civil servants or statesmen, just plain people who loved and laughed and cried and died for their country.

[35] Interview with Clement R. Attlee, July 4, 1951.

CHAPTER XII

WINSTON CHURCHILL AND THE AMBASSADOR
WHO REMAINED AN AMERICAN

Hours after Winant arrived in London as the new Ambassador, staff members had alerted him to an impasse in negotiations within the Joint Base Lease Commission. The destroyer-naval base deal, during the summer of 1940, had been the first concrete endeavor by the United States to assist Britain in her hour of great peril. In return for fifty overage destroyers from Washington, the British Government had committed itself not to surrender its fleet to Germany, to transfer to the United States, as an outright gift, air and naval bases in Newfoundland and Bermuda, and finally to grant ninety-nine-year leases for additional bases in the Bahamas, Jamaica, St. Lucia, Trinidad, British Guiana and Antigua.

Although the agreement had been incorporated in an earlier exchange of letters between Secretary Cordell Hull and the British Ambassador, Lord Lothian, Colonial and Dominion representatives were now raising objections to what Washington thought necessary concessions for naval bases on these British islands near the American coast. Determined to facilitate agreements which would protect American shipping against U-boats ravaging the Atlantic coast, the new Envoy did nothing more than raise the problem of the impasse with the Prime Minister at their first dinner meeting at the "Annex" in Whitehall.[1]

The following day, when the Joint Base Lease Commission convened in conference at Downing Street with the Prime Minister, Winant, who sat by as a spectator, observed the British leader display his unique talents as an administrator and leader. Short and stocky, with a slight stoop, Winston Churchill knew the United States

[1] Henry L. Stimson and McGeorge Bundy, *On Active Service in Peace and War* (New York, Harper and Bros., 1948), pp. 83-84, 564-68.
    While regular day conferences were held at 10 Downing Street, the Prime Minister and Mrs. Churchill lived on the first floor of an administration building in Whitehall which had been reinforced with steel and concrete. In the basement was the communications and map room and the nerve center of the war control system, to which Winant was frequently invited.

almost as well as he knew his own country. Quickly grasping the rationale of the American delegation, it took him less than five minutes to sweep away three quarters of the objections raised by his negotiators, as immaterial, and then he overruled his own military and naval advisors.[2] In little more than two weeks, the Commission approved the Anglo-American Leased Bases Agreement, implementing the "destroyers for bases" deal of the previous September. The compact insured a great boon to Allied shipping off the American coast.[3]

In April 1941, Churchill and Winant were off on one of their periodic pilgrimages, this time to severely damaged cities in southwest England and Wales. After visiting bomb-shattered Swansea, they spent the night in a train on a siding near the Severn tunnel, observing a heavy air raid over Bristol. The next morning the Prime Minister, as Chancellor of Bristol University, would award Winant an honorary degree. When they finally reached this busy seaport, they found much of it destroyed or in flames with delayed-action bombs exploding at intervals. Driving through rubble-strewn streets, the Prime Minister's party observed determined women "busy cooking breakfast in half-demolished homes or over stoves in front gardens". The procession and rituals in the hall of the University proceeded as if nothing had happened, despite the fact that many an academic robe hid gum boots and civil defense uniforms soaked from a full night's work. As Churchill conferred the honorary degree, the acrid smell of burning buildings drifted through shattered windows.[4]

During this early period of his Ambassadorship, Winant spent many weekends at Chequers, the Prime Minister's official country home in the heart of Buckinghamshire — a lovely part of England, isolated from the clamor of cities and industry and a peaceful haven through the war years.[5] These weekends found the Prime Minister and the

[2] JGW telegram, "To the President and the Secretary", March 5, 1941; *The New York Times*, March 5, 1941; Winant, *Letter From Grosvenor Square*, p. 36.
[3] JGW telegram "for the President and the Secretary", March 12, 1941; *The New York Times*, March 28, 1941; *Daily Telegraph*, March 28, 1941.
[4] *The Times*, April 12 and 14, 1941; Gerald Pawle, *The War and Colonel Warden* (New York, Alfred E. Knopf, 1963), pp. 90-91.
[5] Mr. Winant's Visits to Chequers, March 15-August 23, 1941. "Chequers" folder located in light tan valise of Winant Collection at F. D. Roosevelt Library. Chequers was owned originally by Lord Lee of Fareham and when he died he left his estate to the nation. The order of succession of the house was first to the Prime Minister, second to the Chancellor of the Exchequer, and third, in memory of his American wife, to the American Ambassador.

Ambassador sparring with one another, with a distinct tactical advantage accruing the Britisher. Winant usually reached this retreat about noon on Saturday, when he would lunch with the Prime Minister and a cabinet member or some head of a governmental agency. The two Britishers would then have a "go" at the American on some crucial issue which Churchill wanted pressed in Washington. As the hour approached three, the Prime Minister would excuse himself and wander off, leaving his colleague arguing with the Envoy. After a refreshing nap, the British leader reappeared to intensify the pressure on the tired Ambassador. After a while, Winant dreaded visiting Chequers.[6]

From these meetings at Chequers and Downing Street, the Prime Minister could ascertain the extent of the Ambassador's loyalty to Washington and to Roosevelt. When subsequently contrasting Winant with Walter Hines Page, America's World War I anglophile emissary, Churchill underscored the fact that the former was first and foremost the representative of the United States. Winant, he insisted, always put Britain's role "in the best light before the American people, and yet would still do it as a patriotic American".[7]

The Ambassador managed, infrequently, to return to the States for brief breaks from his debilitating labors in London. During these short stays at home, however, he would rush around Washington stimulating increased material and moral support for the British. By the end of May 1941, for example, he had learned enough of the critical situation in Britain to desire talks at home with military and economic leaders. For weeks he had been under tremendous pressure from Churchill who felt that the one decisive counter-weight to continued British setbacks abroad "would be if the United States were immediately to range herself with us as a belligerent power".[8] Despite American neutrality, Winant felt that his nation must increase its commitment to Britain.

Greatly concerned by the serious loss of British merchant vessels by U-boat attacks and the shortage of protective ships for convoy, despite the earlier transfer of destroyers, Winant sought to secure an extension of the American patrol of the Western Atlantic in order

[6] Interviews with Winston S. Churchill, July 4, 1951; and with Jacob Beam, July 26, 1951.
[7] Interview with Winston S. Churchill, July 4, 1951. See Edward Grey, *Twenty-five Years, 1892-1916* (New York, Frederick A. Stokes, 1937), p. 110.
[8] JGW telegram "From Former Naval Person to President Roosevelt", May 3, 1941.

to relieve the pressure on the hard-pressed British navy. Concluding that reporting by cable was ineffective, he flew back to press the case in person.[9] The United States to which he returned seemed more divided than when he had left three months earlier. The America First Committee had covered the nation with leaflets and held gigantic rallies, as Lindbergh and Senator Burton K. Wheeler urged the country to shun the war and return to a policy of isolation.[10] Nonetheless, a steady shift toward aiding the British was taking place in public sentiment and this would be helpful to the Ambassador.

Directed by telephone from Hyde Park to proceed to the White House to await the President's return, Winant took the night train from New York to Washington. Instead of sleeping in a Pullman berth, he sat up in a coach car and conversed with fellow passengers about developments at home. The following morning, an unshaven Ambassador in a crumpled suit and worn shirt turned up in a friend's office in the State Department building. Before shaving, he emptied bulging pockets of scraps of paper on which he had noted some of his train conversations, one of them concerning a recent enlistee who was anxious to become a pharmacist's mate.[11]

Hurrying from one meeting to another with Hopkins, Stimson, Knox, General Marshall, and finally with the President at the White House, Winant vigorously endorsed Churchill's pleas for extended American naval activity and for American troops to replace British forces in Iceland.[12] Already alerted to imminent invasion of Russia by Germany, the Chief Executive acceded to Winant's requests, reasoning that the Nazis would be too preoccupied to retaliate effectively in the North Atlantic.[13] (When Winant had first walked into the President's office in the White House, Roosevelt took one look at him and suggested, as he would repeatedly at subsequent meetings, that as soon as the conference was over he had for the nearest barber

[9]   JGW telegrams "For the President and the Secretary Only", April 27, 1941; "To the Secretary for the President", May 20, 1941; Langer and Gleason, *Undeclared War*, p. 523.
[10]   *The New York Times*, May 24, 1941.
[11]   Interview with Theodore Achilles, July 6, 1951.
[12]   Winant, *Letter from Grosvenor Square*, pp. 194-95, 203; Stetson Conn and Byron Fairchild, *The Framework of Hemisphere Defense* (Washington, Office of the Chief of Military History, Department of the Army, 1960), p. 123.
[13]   Stimson diary, entries of June 5, 6 and 18, 1941, as noted in Conn and Fairchild, *The Framework of Hemisphere Defense*, p. 124. Also, Winant, *Letter from Grosvenor Square*, p. 204; Hull, *Memoirs*, II, 973.

shop and get himself a haircut.)[14] At a subsequent meeting with Vice President Henry Wallace and the Agriculture Secretary, the Ambassador successfully pressed for a significant increase in exports to Britain of dried milk, pork, bacon and dehydrated foods.[15]

Before returning to England, Winant hurried to Deerfield Academy in Massachusetts for a thirty-minute middle-of-the-night reunion with his two sleepy sons. After a long flight across the Atlantic, the Envoy reached Chequers forty-eight hours before the Nazi onslaught upon Russia.

Six months after the start of this Russian campaign, by which time Hitler had hoped to conquer the USSR, the Germans had taken the Crimea, but not Sevastopol, had assaulted Moscow from three sides and beleaguered Leningrad. Despite serious early losses, the Red Army improved daily and the bitter cold and heavy snows of a rigorous Russian winter came to the aid of the Soviets. The Russian Air Corps also recovered slowly from the disaster which had enveloped it during the first days of the invasion. Sensitive to Russia's need for encouragement, the American Envoy had sought to do more than extend mere personal interest to the Russian Ambassador in London, scholarly Ivan Maisky. When Harry Hopkins arrived in the British capital in July 1941, to discuss Lend-Lease with the Prime Minister, Winant urged that some generous gesture be extended to Russia to strengthen sagging morale. What did Hopkins think of the Ambassador's flying to Moscow with some concrete offer from the President, especially in light of his amicable relations with Maisky and other Soviet spokesmen previously associated with the ILO? After a moment's hesitation, the New Dealer, who cherished his close relationship with the President, replied, "What would you think of my going from here?"

Winant realized that a visit by Hopkins would have much greater significance because of his intimate association with the President, and his major role in facilitating the shipment of Lend-Lease supplies to Britain. Following speedy approval by Roosevelt, a telephone call from Winant brought Maisky hurrying to London from his country retreat where, in his own handwriting, he inscribed permission for the flight to the USSR. With this unique visa, the American

---

[14]   Interview with Theodore Achilles, July 6, 1951.
[15]   *The New York Times*, June 4-8, 1941; Winant, *Letter from Grosvenor Square*, pp. 195-99.

Ambassador rushed to the railway station in time to hand it to Hopkins through an open window as the train pulled out for an airfield in distant Scotland. Hopkins' eventful journey to Moscow helped turn the tide of war for, through Lend-Lease, the United States put much of the Russian Army on wheels and made up many of the deficiencies resulting from its frightful early losses.[16]

In July 1941, Winant again toured Wales, this time in the company of Clement R. Attlee, Labor's key spokesman in the coalition cabinet. The Welsh people, on the whole, are moved by oratory, but Gil Winant was no Aneurin Bevan. Nevertheless, his warmth, sincerity and understanding shone through to miners as he journeyed through the countryside. In one poor mining town near Neath, as some coal diggers conversed with the Ambassador, the men suddenly burst into a series of Welsh songs. Attlee never forgot this incident, which he interpreted as a universal sign of respect and a tribute to the Envoy.[17]

Back in London, however, Winant found himself frustrated by increasing numbers of independent American missions and handicapped by a lack of clarity in the directives he received from Washington. On numerous occasions he learned that representations of the State Department sent through other agencies in the British capital had not been telegraphed to him. A number of delegations, particularly W. Averell Harriman's Lend-Lease group, negotiated with the British without definite assignment to the Embassy. In the midst of Allied preparations for the assault on Europe, this proliferation of missions and agencies led to a serious decline in his ambassadorial authority.[18] But he was just one of many American envoys during the war and postwar years who suffered such a fate. Even though Roosevelt issued memoranda to the effect that "The Chief of the United States Diplomatic Mission in a foreign country is the officer of the United States in charge in that country under whose supervision are coordinated the activities there of all the official representatives of the United States", the President's appointment of special missions to London undermined this Emissary.[19]

After the arrival of Harriman, the relationship between Churchill and Winant became increasingly estranged. Whereas the Lend-Lease administrator appeared a virtual Santa Claus, eager to supply the

16   Winant, *Letter from Grosvenor Square*, pp. 206-09; Sherwood, *Roosevelt and Hopkins*, p. 318.
17   Interview with Clement R. Attlee, July 4, 1951.
18   *The New York Times*, August 5, 1963.
19   *Ibid.*

British with their greatest needs, Washington often placed the Ambassador in the position of saying "no" to many of the Prime Minister's requests. This did not make for friendly contacts between Winant and Harriman, especially after the latter became a popular weekend guest at Chequers.[20]

The diffusion of responsibility and leadership became so frustrating that by August 1941, Winant pleaded with Hull and Hopkins for clarification of his authority. The Ambassador found himself frequently at cross-purposes or in complete ignorance of key developments, for efforts to reach agreements on both sides of the water at the same time, without keeping him informed, seriously hampered the work of the Embassy. The more times he contacted British agencies, only to learn that other American delegations had solved the problem or were already in consultation, the less effective he became. He wanted friendly and orderly relations with the British so that he could insure a mutual confidence which would permit continuing trust and cooperation. But how could he under these circumstances? "Please help me", were the concluding words of a cable to Hopkins.[21]

The climax came late in 1943 when a distraught Ambassador disclosed that the business delegated to him could be done by an efficient Foreign Service officer. "I have been by-passed continuously", he lamented. "I have had no contacts with the Prime Minister except on two occasions when he invited me to meet with him so that he could bring me up to date on Anglo-American relations. Officials of the British Government have been friendly and frank with me but they are quick to appreciate when one in my position has been deprived of his authority." [22]

His changed relationship with Brendan Bracken, Churchill's Parliamentary Secretary and confidant, typified the situation. He had originally seen Bracken at least once and even three or four times a week, but during the previous six months had not seen him at all, except by chance in the street or at some function. By this time, not only had Lord Beaverbrook cabled Hopkins directly on a subject

[20] Sherwood, *Roosevelt and Hopkins*, p. 269; interviews with Anthony Eden, July 7-8, 1951; with Jacob Beam, July 26, 1951; and with Wallace Carroll, June 13, 1960.
[21] JGW telegram "To Secstate", April 4, 1941; JGW telegram "to the Secretary of State for Mr. Hopkins", August 22, 1941.
[22] JGW telegrams, "For Hopkins", October 20, 1943; "To the Undersecretary", October 26, 1943.

which Winant had labored on for weeks, but the Ambassador had even lost control over those selected in the United States to visit England.[23] Rumors had persisted for months that he would be replaced by Harriman. Now, the Envoy cabled home, London newspapers had identified Hopkins as his successor. These reports "would do no damage were it not for the fact that you and Averell have done a considerable part of the exchange of communications that normally should be done by the Ambassador. I think the President and Stettinius should know that no Ambassador can be an effective representative here in London unless he is given more information and more support than I am receiving." [24]

This persevering Envoy had been shunted aside by a set of circumstances beyond his control and which, with the passing months, sharply curtailed his ability to make any significant impact upon major policy decisions. Since Churchill viewed Lend-Lease as a "matter of wartime life or death" which involved his department as Minister of Defense, and since Harriman spoke for Hopkins, the Prime Minister all but ignored the Ambassador. There also developed an unique exchange of correspondence between Churchill and Roosevelt, completely bypassing Winant and even Foreign Secretary Eden. Whenever the Prime Minister wanted to sound out the President's view on important proposals, he would address a private cable to Hopkins, or telephone the President directly. Years later, the wartime Prime Minister conceded that he had often dealt directly with the President, insisting, however, that "this did not necessarily make things more difficult" for the American Ambassador. In fact, he contended, he always kept Winant abreast of his telephone conversations with Roosevelt, afterwards. Churchill sought to explain this unusual procedure by maintaining that his "relationship with President Roosevelt superseded both the Foreign Office of my nation and the American Embassy". He, nevertheless, concluded that Winant had "exerted great influence on the formulation of British policy for he was recognized as the American spokesman". Britain's wartime leader displayed unusual kindness to the memory of a former envoy.[25]

In the midst of these depressing developments, there evolved an

[23] JGW telegrams "For the Secretary", September 18, 1943; "To the Undersecretary", October 26, 1943; Sherwood, *Roosevelt and Hopkins*, p. 755.
[24] JGW telegrams, "For Hopkins", October 20, 1943; "To the Undersecretary", October 26, 1943; Sherwood, *Roosevelt and Hopkins*, pp. 754-55.
[25] Interview with Winston S. Churchill, July 4, 1951; Sherwood, *Roosevelt and Hopkins*, p. 269.

unprecedented collaboration between the Ambassador and Churchill's youthful Foreign Secretary, Anthony Eden. After their initial meetings in the Foreign Office, a warm friendship blossomed between the two, strengthened by the fact that both were overshadowed and bypassed by two great men. Shortly after beginning their joint endeavors, often meeting twice a day, they dispensed with the traditional exchange of written memoranda of conversations. Time remained limited and, besides, they had developed complete faith in each other. The nattily dressed Foreign Secretary became totally devoted to the American Envoy, whom he once described as caring "much for his work, little for party politics, not at all for himself". Prior to Winant, it had been normal procedure for foreign embassies to deal with British departments through the Foreign Office. When the war effort made it imperative for the American to coordinate endeavors with many of these departments, avoiding the usual frustrating delays, Eden granted him permission to deal directly with other ministers.[26] On the eve of Eden's departure for Moscow, in December 1941, to discuss war aims with Josef Stalin, the Foreign Minister spent hours with Winant disclosing British policy positions.[27] At the behest of the Britisher, the Ambassador visited the Foreign Office daily to read Eden's communications from Moscow and relay them to Roosevelt. Consequently, the President was advised of proposed Anglo-Russian agreements before they had been seen by Churchill and his cabinet.[28]

On at least a dozen weekends during the war, Eden brought Winant to his gracious Georgian country home outside Chichester, to afford the American some escape from the constant drive and debilitating pressure of his responsibilities. While a relaxed Foreign Secretary spent warm days stripped to the waist tending his beautiful rose garden, Winant absentmindedly mowed the lawn, unable to forget his work in London. He did not join his friend for a brisk set on the tennis court, as he had sometimes done with his eldest son before the war. Only during conversations in the beautiful, book-lined library which housed a rare collection of Persian literature, did

---

[26] Interview with Anthony Eden, July 7 and 8, 1951; Winant, *Letter from Grosvenor Square*, pp. 71-73, 96-97; Dennis Bardens, *Portrait of a Statesman* (New York, Philosophical Library, 1956), p. 229.

[27] JGW telegram "For the Secretary and the President", December 4, 1941.

[28] JGW telegrams "For the Secretary", December 19, 1941; "To the Secretary and the President", December 21, 1941; "To the Secretary and for the President", January 19, 1942.

the Envoy seem to unbend. Otherwise, he remained constantly "on duty".[29]

Sensitive to public opinion, the Ambassador worried about little things which might disturb amicable relations between the Allies, such as the occasion when he journeyed to Winchester to witness the commissioning of new officers of Eden's old army unit. When the band commander asked the American whether he had any objection to the playing of the traditional concluding selection, "Marching Through Georgia", the Envoy expressed no reservations and the ceremonies proceeded. Later that evening, however, as the Foreign Secretary listened to a broadcast of the formalities being beamed to the United States, he became perplexed when he did not hear the familiar march. Raising the issue with Winant the next day, he learned that the Envoy had subsequently requested its deletion, hoping to prevent the British from alienating a single Southerner who might still be fighting the Civil War.[30]

Immediately after Pearl Harbor, and before American GI's came streaming across the Atlantic, Winant worried about the reaction of his young countrymen to British customs and traditions: the absence of ice cream parlors, rationing, afternoon tea breaks, and queuing up for buses. He projected the feelings of British soldiers who would find their girls dated by better dressed, higher paid Americans, who would also drink up the beer in neighborhood pubs. Fortunately, well-paid Canadian soldiers had been in Britain since 1939 and the Ambassador profited from talks with British and Canadian military leaders. The Envoy then planned with American military spokesmen for the peaceful "invasion" of the British Isles. By the time GI's left the United States, most received indoctrination lectures and a pamphlet depicting some unfamiliar British traditions.[31] Shortly after the arrival of early contingents of United States troops, the Ambassador read in a local newspaper that a court had sentenced an American GI to a whipping for violating a civil law. Contemplating reactions at home, he immediately set to work with General Eisenhower and Eden to avert repetitions of such incidents. In a remarkably short space of time, and with amazingly little opposition — despite the fact that no similar grant had ever been made within the British Isles —

29 Interview with Anthony Eden, July 7-8, 1951.
30 *Ibid.; The Times*, November 3, 1941.
31 Interviews with Eileen Mason, July 6, 1951; with Theodore Achilles, July 6, 1951; with Anthony Eden, July 7-8, 1951; and with Dwight D. Eisenhower, August 8, 1951.

Parliament enacted Winant's proposal to turn over to the United States military, exclusive jurisdiction in respect of criminal offenses committed by members of the American forces.[32]

Noting the weakened physical state of Winant toward the end of his second year in London, America's Envoy to Ireland, David Gray, deplored Washington's neglect to provide additional "first rate men in the London Embassy" to remove part of the burden of detail from his colleague's shoulders. ". . . if you break down", he lamented, "what does any of it amount to? Your personality and sense of values is the important thing and, if necessary, you should be kept in a glass case or, better yet, spend two or three days a week in the country, walking yourself tired and doing what you should to recover from the trouble that continually pulls you down." [33]

When the well-known neuro-surgeon, Wilder Penfield, stopped off in London on his way to Russia with a medical mission, he remained baffled by the grueling schedule of his Princeton classmate. Though seriously concerned about Winant's endless and driven devotion to duty, the Canadian doctor failed on numerous occasions to convince the Ambassador to spend a weekend in the nearby countryside.[34]

Constantly propelled by this deep inner need to work day and night, the Ambassador revived himself through meetings with eminent intellectuals. From the moment of his arrival in London, his flat became a center for discussions with R. H. Tawney, Harold Laski, Sir William Beveridge, H. G. Wells and others who helped stimulate his thinking and satisfy his yearning for friendship. When alone with one of these challenging minds, his shyness disappeared, to be replaced by a relaxed and easy manner as he drew upon his deep fund of political knowledge and experience. Only subsequently did these intellectual statesmen realize that they had been conversing with a stranger as though he were an old friend.[35] One of the more challenging friendships developed with Harold Laski. Academician and Socialist theoretician, he sought to influence Winant's thinking and decisions along foreign policy lines which, at times, came into sharp conflict with President Roosevelt and Cordell Hull. All of these men,

[32] *Ibid.*, and JGW telegram "To the President", August 22, 1942.
[33] David Gray to JGW, November 24, 1942. Box F-802, 18220, State Dept., Historical Office files.
[34] Wilder Penfield to author, May 25, 1962.
[35] R. H. Tawney to author, July 10, 1951; interviews with Clement R. Attlee, July 4, 1951; and with Kingsley Martin, July 9, 1951.

however, helped stimulate the Envoy's interest in, and planning for, the welfare state of the postwar world.[36]

It was unique in the history of Britain for an Ambassador to the Court of St. James's to become a personality with a public appeal to intellectuals as well as to workingmen and women, for envoys generally remained specialists without contacts outside the diplomatic world. As one British historian put it, "His obvious sincerity was more effective than the most finished eloquence could have been. It was clear that he spoke from the heart and meant what he said." [37]

[36] JGW to Freda Kirchwey, March 17, 1941; William Beveridge to JGW, March 29, 1941; H. J. Laski to JGW, May 1, 1941; JGW to H. G. Wells, May 16, 1941; H. G. Wells to JGW, May 20, 1941; interview with Mrs. Harold J. Laski, July 10, 1951.
[37] R. H. Tawney to author, July 10, 1951; interviews with Clement R. Attlee, July 4, 1951; and with Kingsley Martin, July 9, 1951.

CHAPTER XIII

THE WAR FOR A PEOPLE'S DEMOCRACY

Early in 1942, as the Allies suffered disastrous military setbacks, Winant noted that despondency, weariness, and anxiety dominated the British spirit. While hopeful about the ultimate outcome, victory seemed so distant and the goals and purposes of the government so vague, that a disquieting doubt began to pervade Britain. There seemed to be no impelling incentive for great numbers of Britishers "to finish the job", merely to return to the old order of pre-war days.[1]

Churchill also sensed this ebb of enthusiasm in the war effort and, as a result, shuffled his cabinet in mid-February, making Laborite leader Clement Attlee the Deputy Prime Minister. But he refused to be diverted from the military objectives by pressing forward with major domestic reforms, maintaining that "... we ought to win the war first, and then in a free country the issues of socialism and free enterprise can be fought out in a constitutional manner. ... I think it would be a pity to break up the national unity in the war, and that I believe is the opinion of the mass of the people." Harold Laski, and other Laborites, however, feared that without a definitive statement of the economic and social objectives of the conflict, and without a firm groundwork for postwar reconstruction and planning, Britain might win the war but lose the peace of a democratic, egalitarian society.[2]

As a product of the social progressive movement within the American middle class, and an ardent adherent of the New Deal, Winant proved himself more attuned to the economic hopes and aspirations

[1] JGW telegram "For the President", February 17, 1942; Charles G. Bolté to JGW, October 22, 1942.
[2] Kingsley Martin, *Harold Laski (1893-1950): A Biographical Memoir* (New York, Viking Press, 1953), p. 144. A basis for social progress was achieved during the war years when the famous Beveridge Report was endorsed in its major principles in 1943. The family allowance section of the Report was enacted in 1944, but the comprehensive scheme was not adopted until after Labor had won in 1945. A White Paper recommendation to reform the Educational System appeared in 1943, on the basis of which historic legislation was passed in 1944.

of a majority of the British than their own great Prime Minister. At home with Socialists as well as Tories, Winant's inclinations lay with the working men and women who assembled at the Labor Party's annual conference at London's Central Hall in May 1942. As a guest of Clement Attlee, he was deeply moved by the long, effusive applause of delegates following announcement of his presence in the hall. And he appreciated the significance of Laski's resolution, committing the Labor party to oppose "any effort which seeks to preserve the main characteristics of the existing economic order", for he forwarded it to the President and Mrs. Roosevelt.[3]

When the Workers' Educational Association sought a keynote speaker for their annual meeting, its scholarly president, R. H. Tawney, turned to the American Ambassador. The former assured him a warm welcome, and an enthusiastic group which would be genuinely influenced by his words and carry them to a wider audience. "Your heart is, I know, with Labour", insisted Tawney, "and you know too how much it needs to hear the right thing said by the right person".[4]

After Julian Huxley completed a manuscript on the Tennessee Valley Authority, he induced the Ambassador to write a foreword which endeared him further to Laborite friends. Winant recalled that the vested interests in the United States had fought the TVA development with a "bitterness that has seldom been equalled in any controversy involving private property and the public welfare". The problem of intervention by government for the common good, he felt, had always been the concern of statesmanship, and the continuing development of the TVA had marked the advance that science, in combination with the popular will, could evolve out of a coordinated national and local authority. It proved that under wise leadership, democratic government could direct the nation's resources to serve the needs of mankind.[5]

Before 1,300 businessmen, the Envoy insisted that all was not right with a world in which the Great Depression and the two most destructive wars of all time had fallen within the life of a single generation. He maintained that "no man could live by himself alone, nor

[3] *The Star,* May 27, 1942; *Daily Herald,* June 8, 1942; K. Martin, *Harold Laski,* p. 153; JGW to Eleanor Roosevelt, June 3, 1942.
[4] R. H. Tawney to JGW, July 10, 1943; *Manchester Guardian,* September 6, 1943.
[5] J. S. Huxley to JGW, May 20 and 28, 1943; JGW to Huxley, May 26, 1943; Julian Huxley, *TVA: Adventure in Planning* (Surrey, England, The Architectural Press, 1943), p. 6.

could any group in the complex social order of today safely attempt to support itself at the cost and to the detriment of other groups without injury to the general welfare." Winant urged men of industry to accept larger responsibilities, assume far wider vision and support the basic philosophy that must guide democratic nations in the future, one in which "social justice and world peace were inseparable".[6] He constantly criticized the limited goal of military victory in the absence of social reforms essential to a better life. In words which made a significant impression throughout Britain, the Envoy contended that, "It is fatal for a nation to place inspiring political watchwords on the facades of official buildings if to display the same mottoes in factories would promote only cynical laughter."[7]

To Winant, industry performed a social function — its success could not be judged by dividends alone but by services rendered. Workers were entitled to a share in decision-making within economic enterprises as it related to their individual welfare: "To widen the meaning of democracy by extending it from political to economic life is the most urgent task of the coming generation."[8]

In Northern England, meanwhile, a wave of unauthorized strikes by coal miners swept collieries in Durham, Lancashire and Yorkshire, despite the military crisis caused by Rommel's renewed counter-offensive in North Africa and Nazi drives deep inside southeast Russia. The miners struck because the war had burdened them with long hours of labor, comparatively heavy taxation, rationing, and an unfavorable disparity between their earnings and those of workers in other industries. They were galled too by the absence of a national minimum wage for which they had fought some twenty years.[9] After Labor Minister Ernest Bevin and other Socialists had failed to settle the strike, Deputy Prime Minister Attlee turned to Winant for help. In June 1942, the Ambassador accompanied Attlee to the mining town of Durham, where he was warmly greeted by union leaders and a hall-full of delegates representing thousands of striking workers. To these hard-working miners, who had spent much of their lives in the depths of the earth, Winant spoke movingly of the fight against fascism and against those forces which would make this a world of

[6] June 5, 1943 issues of *The Times* and *Manchester Guardian*.
[7] *New York Herald Tribune,* October, 7, 1944; *The Times,* October 7, 1944.
[8] *Ibid.,* copy of address in author's possession; *Our Greatest Harvest, Selected Speeches of John G. Winant* (London, Hodder & Stoughton, 1950), p. 151.
[9] H. Freeman Matthews telegram "To Secstate", April 25, 1942; JGW telegram "To Secstate", May 15, 1942.

"silent peoples". At the same time he insisted that this was a war for social democracy, which had to be won on the economic as well as military fronts, and laborers everywhere had to fight and work, had to man and arm the forces of democracy.

The unity of purpose of our people in the common war effort will be carried over to help us in the common social effort that must follow this war. You, who suffered so deeply in the long depression years, know that we must move on a great social offensive if we are to win the war completely. Anti-Fascism is not a short-term military job. It was bred in poverty and unemployment. To crush fascism at its roots, we must crush depression democracy. We must solemnly resolve that in our future order we will not tolerate the economic evils which breed poverty and war. This is not something that we shelve "for the duration": it is part of the war.[10]

Hailing the gallantry of their fighting men, he lamented the fact that too few Britishers had caught the "enduring courage" of the common men and women — not in the blitzes, but in their day-to-day work. What they wanted was not complicated; with technical knowledge and organizing ability the basic problems of the postwar world could be solved and creation of a "people's democracy" insured. At that time the energies of a war population must be converted to peacetime purposes — to build houses instead of tanks, to produce food for all instead of wartime allies, to make full employment and freedom from want a living reality, and to convert an all-out war effort to an all-out peace effort. The "people's democracy", he concluded, must be kept "wide and vigorous, alive to need, of whatever kind ... always remembering that it is the things of the spirit that in the end prevail — that caring counts, that where there is no vision people perish, ... and believing in the inherent goodness of man we may meet the call of your great Prime Minister and 'stride forward into the unknown with growing confidence.'" [11]

His style and deep emotional appeal evoked a long pause at the conclusion of these remarks. Suddenly the awed group burst into thunderous applause and shouts of "hear, hear". For an hour and a half afterwards, the group sat patiently listening to his "off the record" replies to questions on racial discrimination, Russia, the Monroe Doctrine, and industry's role in America.[12] When there were no more

[10]   Address by JGW at Durham, June 6, 1942. Copy in author's possession. Also, *Manchester Guardian*, June 8, 1942; *Our Greatest Harvest, Selected Speeches of John G. Winant*, pp. 56-59.
[11]   *Ibid.*
[12]   *Daily Express*, June 8, 1942.

questions to be asked he was quickly surrounded by many miners who shook his hand and thanked him for coming and for what he had said. It was Sam Watson, the mine local's treasurer, who voiced general reaction when he told the Ambassador, "We think, sir, that you are a great guy." [13] Never once had Winant referred to the work stoppages, yet the delegates knew that he had come to praise their role in the long, hard conflict and to remind them of their responsibilities in winning the war. Shortly after his departure, the group voted to return to work, and striking miners in Lancashire and Yorkshire followed suit. [14]

Within forty-eight hours, Winant's words swept across the world. The Conservative *Daily Express* greeted its readers with the headline, "Winant Talks, Strike Ends." Labor's *Daily Herald* called it "Gettysburg in Durham!!!" Lamenting the backwardness of the British government in defining the postwar world they hoped to have, *Herald* editors suggested that Winant possessed more vision than Whitehall, and urged that his words "be committed to memory, recited in all the schools, preached about in all the churches so that its implementation is insisted upon by all the free nations". [15]

The *Manchester Guardian* hailed the remarks as "one of the great speeches of the war", its simplicity and earnestness evoking a unique quality of eloquence. His words went far beyond the United Nations and would hearten and sustain the oppressed everywhere, for he had given the phrase "a people's war" new meaning. Having joined the struggle for democracy with a concrete social purpose, at a critical stage in the war, Winant had enlarged its objectives for the common man. [16] A Harvard professor, at that moment an attaché at the American Legation in Stockholm, Sweden, learned from confidential sources that Winant's remarks had reached Germany where he was considered "the hope for reason and justice by the groups who are

---

[13] *Manchester Guardian*, June 8. 1942.
[14] Not long after the Ambassador's achievement in Durham, the Government awarded the miners a national minimum wage, an increase in daily pay, plus an output bonus, and substantially reduced the disparity in earnings between workers in the mine industry and other war industries. Memorandum from Samuel D. Berger to JGW, July 23, 1942.
[15] June 8, 1942 issues of *Daily Express* and *Daily Herald*.
[16] *Manchester Guardian*, June 8, 1942; *The New York Times*, June 7 and 8, 1942; Howard Braucher to JGW, June 11, 1942. In Washington, the Office of War Information included the Durham address in the first publication of statements and speeches "which define or illuminate the developing policy of the United Nations". JGW Collection, Drawer 30, 3-OWI.

beginning to work for a change of regime". The Ambassador was well known to these German groups, primarily because of his years with the ILO, but also because of judgment of his character as revealed by his speeches throughout Britain. The Envoy's years of "hovering over dramatic scenes in the 30's" was bearing fruit.[17]

The turning of the hinge of fate, as Winston Churchill put it, occurred in October 1942, when the initial Allied assault in North Africa developed in Libya, where General Montgomery's British army won a resounding victory. Within ten days after the start of the battle of El Alamein, Axis forces speedily retreated. As the Prime Minister subsequently remarked: "It may almost be said, 'Before Alamein we never had a victory. After Alamein we never had a defeat.'"[18]

On November 8, the first of the Allied invasions occurred in French Morocco and Algeria, when Anglo-American forces under General Eisenhower successfully assaulted the beaches at Casablanca, Oran and Algiers. When Eisenhower discovered the basic loyalty of French military leaders to Marshal Pétain and Admiral Jean Darlan, he quickly reached an agreement with Darlan to end hostilities at Casablanca. This decision to seek the cooperation of Vichyite Darlan and to recognize him as the leader of French military forces cooperating with the United Nations insured political revulsions in Britain and America rarely equalled through the war. Since 1940, the British government and press had vilified Darlan as one of the worst of the quislings and traitors. For weeks thereafter, Winant was placed in the unenviable position of engendering support, or at least sympathetic understanding, of the Darlan agreement among individuals he respected and admired. Military necessity alone forced Eisenhower to make his decision, in an endeavor to save American lives.[19]

Despite Winant's appeals for understanding, friends and allied spokesmen remained profoundly disturbed by what they felt was a perversion of Allied political objectives. In Washington, Roosevelt sought to still the clamor by insisting that the political arrangements in French North Africa were a temporary expedient justified by the

[17] Bruce C. Hopper to JGW, June 18 and 26, 1942.
[18] Winston S. Churchill, *The Hinge of Fate* (Boston, Houghton Mifflin Co., 1950), p. 603.
[19] Dwight D. Eisenhower, *Crusade in Europe* (Garden City, Doubleday and Co., 1948), pp. 103-14; JGW telegram "To the Secretary", November 17, 1942.

stress of battle and would be maintained only until hostilities in Africa drew to a close.[20]

In the midst of this row Ivan Maisky visited Winant on Grosvenor Square and offered the "happy suggestion" that the Allies solve the problem by shooting Darlan. In a more serious vein, the Soviet Envoy noted that the Darlan affair disturbed Moscow for fear that there might be practical reasons in the future for dealing similarly with German generals. When Winant asked Maisky whether he wanted American troops killing Frenchmen or fighting Germans, and if it wasn't more helpful to draw off Nazi air and land forces from the Russian front, the Soviet emissary did not pursue the point.[21]

Winant was exasperated by his defensive position and hurt by telling blows from Harold Laski and others. For almost two years now he had been urging the British working class to continue the fight against Nazism and their quisling spokesmen. It was only a few weeks since he had responded to an honorary degree at Leeds University with the thought that it was not enough "to defeat our enemies on the field of battle. We must discover and correct those conditions in our world which made their reaction possible. . . . The world revolt against civilization might begin again unless we destroyed the roots of cynicism by proving in conduct that we believed in the words for which our world was supposed to stand — justice, freedom, and Christian brotherhood."[22]

A few days after Winant returned to the United States for a much needed rest, Darlan was assassinated in Algiers by a fellow Frenchman.

Throughout 1943, the Axis powers remained on the defensive, as in North Africa, on the Eastern Front, and even in the distant Pacific, the Allies went over to the attack. This became the critical year: for Allied military collaboration, the planning of surrender terms and the occupation of conquered enemy nations, for political principles and issues, and for a world organization to maintain the peace.

With the turn of the military tide, the British no longer required the unique strength and determination of a vibrant Winant who had helped sustain them during trying days. Without an important role to play in diplomatic councils, and no longer called upon to interpret

[20]   *The New York Times,* November 18, 1942.
[21]   JGW telegram "To the Secretary", November 25, 1942.
[22]   *The Times,* October 10, 1942; JGW telegram "To the Secretary", November 25, 1942.

the desires of working men and women for a "people's democracy", the Ambassador weakened under the unending pressures of the Embassy. Greatly in need of rest, he returned home for a few months to look after some minor, though irritating, medical needs at Johns Hopkins Hospital.[23]

Following high level conferences in Washington, Winant returned to London encouraged by public opinion polls which demonstrated greater awareness of world problems, and overwhelming support for postwar collaboration with foreign countries through some international organization to maintain the peace.[24]

During Winant's absence, Britain and her Allies experienced many significant changes. Landings in North Africa and a mild winter had helped sustain morale at an unusually high level in Britain, even though some of the beneficial effects of the North African venture had been obscured by the Darlan affair and by some misgivings over the length of the Tunisian campaign. The initial invasion, followed by the Churchill-Roosevelt declarations at Casablanca, had served to concentrate thought and energies upon offensive action.

In July 1943, the Ambassador learned with mixed feelings that Ivan Maisky would not return to London but remain in Moscow as an Assistant Commissar for Foreign Affairs. Winant had come to view the scholarly Russian envoy as a tactful, well-informed and wise individual. The American interpreted the recall of a western-oriented Russian as a bad omen, one suggesting to him that Stalin was dissatisfied with an Anglo-American policy which had ignored the Soviets in planning for political developments in Italy. Winant's fears seemed substantiated when Maxim Litvinov was likewise recalled from Washington, for Moscow replaced these two friendly Russian diplomats with more disciplined and rigid exponents of Stalin's viewpoints. Winant felt that his government had not sufficiently consulted with the Soviet Union concerning plans for Italy, particularly following Benito Mussolini's downfall. He had urged Roosevelt not to ignore the sensitivity of Moscow, especially when the Soviets made clear their feeling of exclusion from important decisions involving the Allies on European developments. He insisted that these latest switches in London and Washington had tremendous significance

---

[23]   H. L. Chant to author, November 12, 1959. Dr. Chant was Associate Director of Johns Hopkins Hospital.
[24]   *The Times*, March 29, April 5, 1943; H. Freeman Matthews telegram "To Secstate", March 20, 1943; Sherwood, *Roosevelt and Hopkins*, pp. 707-20.

for the future of Allied relations with the Soviet Union, and advocated that Russia be taken into closer counsel on the Italian situation before, not after, decisions were made. The Envoy pointed out to his Chief Executive that, "When the tide turns and the Russian armies are able to advance we might well want to influence their terms of capitulation and occupancy in allied and enemy country." [25]

Warnings from Winant and Eden, concerning a lack of coordination in planning for the Italian surrender, helped lay the groundwork for the Foreign Ministers' meeting in Moscow the following October and tentative agreement for a summit meeting in Iran later that year. In addition, Allied military successes in North Africa, Italy and on the Eastern Front meant that governmental spokesman would have to insure closer collaboration concerning planned assaults against Germany and unsettled political issues.

Beginning in September, Ivan Maisky in Moscow and Eden and Winant in London devoted considerable time planning for a Three Power conference of Foreign Ministers at Moscow, to develop the wartime alliance into a partnership for world security.[26] The delegates made considerable progress at the Conference of Foreign Ministers in October 1943, insuring, among other developments, creation of the European Advisory Commission to study plans for liberated areas, and postwar dismemberment of Germany.[27] This Commission would involve much of the energies of Winant during the remaining months of the European conflict.

On the second Saturday of October 1943, hordes of American bombers flew over Western Germany to inflict terrible damage upon the important center of Münster. This particular raid made a shattering impact upon Winant in London for, within hours, he learned that his twenty-two-year-old son was missing in action. While returning from his thirteenth bombing mission, his Flying Fortress, "Tech Supply", had been attacked by three German fighter planes and the wounded ship finally went down after a rocket-gun blast.[28]

[25] JGW telegrams "For the President and Secretary", July 26, 1943; "To Secstate", July 30, 1943.
[26] Interview with Anthony Eden, July 7 and 8, 1951.
[27] For a detailed picture of the Moscow Conference and decisions involving these and other issues, see: Hull, *Memoirs*, II, 1278-1307; Eduard Beneš, *Memoirs of Dr. Eduard Beneš*, pp. 249-50; Herbert Feis, *Churchill, Roosevelt, Stalin* (Princeton, Princeton University Press, 1957), pp. 191-234; Cordell Hull, *The Moscow Conference* (Washington, U.S. Government Printing Office, 1943), pp. 1-9.
[28] Col. Edgar M. Wittan to JGW, October 24, 1943; interview with John G. Winant, Jr., March 5, 1964.

Shortly after broadcast of the news of the downed "Tech Supply", hundreds of telegrams and letters of sympathy streamed into the London Embassy from every corner of the globe. Robert E. Sherwood cabled, "Everyone who knows you and loves you for what you are and what you stand for prays that you will soon have news that your son is safe and well." A British worker in Spofforth, near Harrogate, wrote the Ambassador, "We, in this little working class home, are thinking about you, and we are PRAYING for your son, too." [29] The days passed into weeks, and still no news, until finally, on the twenty-fifth anniversary of the World War One Armistice, Winant learned that his son was alive, a prisoner of war in Germany. Shortly before the fatally wounded aircraft went into its dive, young John had parachuted safely into German territory. Thereafter, Swiss diplomats in Germany kept the American Envoy informed of the health and movements of his son.

[29] R. E. Sherwood to W. Carroll, for JGW, October 11, 1943; Ted Tempest to JGW, October 12, 1943; H. H. Lehman to JGW, October 12, 1943.

CHAPTER XIV

ASSIGNMENT IN FRUSTRATION

The creation of the European Advisory Commission fulfilled the hopes of Winant and Eden that the Soviet Union would be involved in postwar planning. Yet, from the very beginning of its work in January, 1944, the EAC became a source of frustration and anguish for Winant. Confronted by the sustained initiative of a British representative armed with challenging working papers and the informed, authoritative comments of a competent, determined Russian completely familiar with the British material, Winant found himself shaken and embarrassed, handicapped as he was by inadequate, infrequent directives from Washington and publicly circumvented or ignored by his own government.[1]

Even before the European tide of battle turned in favor of the Allies, a small group of men on both sides of the Atlantic outlined plans for postwar occupation and control of Germany. In 1942, the State Department had gathered a group of distinguished civilians to create the Advisory Committee on Postwar Problems. This committee opposed forcible dismemberment of Germany — a view contrary to that held by the President and Sumner Welles. At Casablanca, the Chief Executive went ahead with the unfortunate policy of "Unconditional Surrender", insistent that Germany be divided into several states.[2]

Soviet Envoy Ivan Maisky and Winant met with Anthony Eden

[1] Interview with Anthony Eden, July 7-8, 1951; William Strang, *Home and Abroad* (London, Andre Deutsch, 1956), p. 208.
[2] United States Department of State, *Postwar Foreign Policy Preparation, 1939-1945* (Washington, U.S. Government Printing Office, 1949), pp. 19, 104, 107, 135-39, 154-55; Winston S. Churchill, *The Grand Alliance* (Boston, Houghton Mifflin Co., 1950), pp. 434-36; Philip E. Mosely, "Dismemberment of Germany: The Allied Negotiations from Yalta to Potsdam", *Foreign Affairs*, April 1950, Vol. 28, p. 488; Ernest F. Penrose, *Economic Planning for the Peace* (Princeton, Princeton University Press, 1953), p. 225; Sherwood, *Roosevelt and Hopkins*, pp. 227, 711; Sumner Welles, *The Time for Decision* (New York, Harper and Brothers, 1944), pp. 336-61.

early in 1943 to discuss the need to work together to destroy Nazi domination and to rehabilitate Europe. Partly as a result of these informal conversations, the idea for a Moscow Conference emerged.[3] When Eden visited the United States in March 1943, he discussed with Harry Hopkins, Cordell Hull, and the President the question of whether the Allies would deal with Germany as a unit after the war, or seek to split her into several independent states. After insisting that Germany be divided, Roosevelt directed Hull to consult with the British and Russians on the question of German and Italian occupation. At Quebec in August 1943, Eden informed Hull that while some members of the British government thought that Germany should be dismembered, he and the Cabinet generally opposed a mandatory plan as impractical.[4]

The Moscow Conference of Foreign Ministers created the European Advisory Commission (EAC) in October 1943 to draft the terms of the German surrender and its administration. The Commission would function as an operational unit to which matters would be referred only after the unanimous consent of the heads of the three governments. At Teheran, the following month, the governments designated their representatives to the EAC: Sir William Strang for Britain, Fedor T. Gusev for the Soviet Union, and Winant for the United States.[5]

In mid-January 1944, the EAC convened for the first time at Lancaster House in London. Gusev, the new Soviet Ambassador to Great Britain, proved a glum, humorless Russian who rarely socialized and, in contrast to his predecessor, Maisky, was limited in his experience in the diplomatic corps and in his world outlook and intellectual capacity. Suspicious of his foreign colleagues, determined to assert himself as their equal, and lacking the confidence or freedom to bequeath responsibility of decision-making to subordinates, he slowed

---

[3] JGW telegram "To the President", January 28, 1945; *Foreign Relations of the United States: The Conferences at Malta and Yalta 1945* (Washington, U.S. Government Printing Office, 1955), p. 130.

[4] Sherwood, *Roosevelt and Hopkins*, pp. 711, 714; Hull, *Memoirs*, II, 1233-34, 1265-66, 1284-85.

[5] Philip E. Mosely, "The Occupation of Germany: New Light on How the Zones Were Drawn", *Foreign Affairs*, July 1950, p. 582n; Hull, *Memoirs*, II, 1284-1305. The Moscow Declarations of November 1, 1943, are available in Hajo Holborn, *American Military Government: Its Organization and Policies* (Washington, Infantry Journal Press, 1947), p. 132. For a survey of the Moscow Conference see Feis, *Churchill, Roosevelt, Stalin*, pp. 206-34; William M. Franklin, "Zonal Boundaries and Access to Berlin", *World Politics*, October 1963, pp. 3-4.

the work of the EAC by insisting that all business be conducted by the heads of delegations. Stubborn and capricious, he often opposed proposals for weeks on end until, suddenly, in the midst of an interminable argument, he would yield with the simple statement, "I have no objection." [6]

Sir William Strang, one of the first "outsiders" in the British Foreign Service, had not graduated from one of the exclusive institutions which traditionally trained diplomats. A man of exceptional ability and strength of character, he had attended London University and eventually became permanent head of the Foreign Office. Strang made use of the advantage of being in London, clearing papers with his Foreign Office and the unified British agencies at inter-departmental meetings where he solicited, collated and reconciled the views of interested departments within a matter of hours, at most days. [7]

Handicapped by what Strang described as a "self-tortured soul" and by his own inarticulateness in large conference gatherings, Winant nevertheless achieved considerable success in gaining the confidence of Soviet spokesmen. The British Foreign Secretary subsequently observed that throughout the war years Winant had won the respect of the Russians because of his intense desire to avert "a third world war ... the theme of his life as the Second World War was coming to a conclusion". [8] In contrast to his colleagues, Winant's role was severely circumscribed by serious divisions in Washington over German policy and the tensions created by departmental rivalries. The State Department neglected for too long to draw upon the advice of German experts and hammer out a unified policy. Consequently, when controversies arose in Washington, the State Department was not prepared to offer guidance and alternatives. Secretary of the Treasury Henry Morgenthau contributed additional confusion with his proposal for the "pastoralization of Germany", as did the President with his indecisiveness. [9]

[6] Interview with Anthony Eden, July 7-8, 1951; Strang, *Home and Abroad*, pp. 206-07.

[7] D. W. Brogan in his review of Strang's *Britain in World Affairs* for *The New York Times*, August 6, 1961, Book Review Section, p. 3; Strang, *Home and Abroad*, p. 203.

[8] Strang, *Home and Abroad*, pp. 206-07; interview with Anthony Eden, July 7-8, 1951.

[9] Philip E. Mosely, "Dismemberment of Germany ...", *Foreign Affairs*, April 1950, pp. 488-89; Mosely, "The Occupation of Germany ...", *Foreign Affairs*, July 1950, p. 584n; Welles, *The Time for Decision*, pp. 336-61; Hull, *Memoirs*, II, 1227-30, 1256; interview with Philip E. Mosely, June 7, 1951; interview with

Upon the suggestion of Roosevelt, authorities in Washington created a Working Security Committee (WSC) composed of State, Navy and War Department representatives. Prior to its creation in mid-December 1943, contact with Winant on postwar Germany had not been systematized, but from its inception, there was no real agreement on the proper functions of the WSC, worsening the confusion.

The State Department projected a comparatively lengthy period of occupation with essential political tasks to be assumed by Allied forces, while Secretary of War Henry L. Stimson and planners in the Civil Affairs Division of the War Department contemplated a "brief punitive spasm" of some two months of military government and a minimum of political responsibilities.[10] The State Department felt that the WSC should recommend surrender terms for enemy European states, together with proposed enforcement machinery. Determined to protect the traditional jurisdictional control of the War Department over postwar occupation of conquered territory, Army representatives insisted that the surrender and recuperation of Germany remained purely military matters, to be decided at the military level. They sought to preserve the autonomy of the British and American Combined Civil Affairs Committee (CAC) — a joint military planning unit — from being displaced by the Working Security Committee, by insisting that the CAC, not the EAC, advise the military leaders as to objectives in Occupied Germany. The Pentagon apparently felt that such classified military questions as zones of occupation in Germany, already under extensive consideration by

---

David Harris, May 24, 1960. Because of friction with Hull, Welles was replaced as Under-Secretary by Edward R. Stettinius, Jr., in September 1943.

[10] Forest C. Pogue, *The Supreme Command* (Washington, Office of the Chief of Military History, Department of the Army, 1954), pp. 75-78; Henry L. Stimson and McGeorge Bundy, *On Active Service in Peace and War* (New York, Harper and Brothers, 1947), pp. 559, 567-68; Penrose, *Economic Planning for the Peace*, pp. 236, 270-71; Walter L. Dorn, "The Debate Over American Occupation Policy in Germany in 1944-1945", *Political Science Quarterly*, LXII, December 1957, p. 487. Dorn worked with documents of the Civil Affairs Division. Also, John L. Snell, *Wartime Origins of the East-West Dilemma Over Germany* (New Orleans, The Hauser Press, 1959), pp. 25-26.

The bulk of information dealing with the WSC was secured from minutes of Working Security Committee meetings, as approved by its participants, found in the Archives of the Historical Division of the State Department. W. S. Minutes 1 to 62, December 21, 1943 to September 18, 1944. Also, Mosely, "The Occupation of Germany", *loc. cit.*, pp. 580-604; Franklin, "Zonal Boundaries and Access to Berlin", *loc. cit.*, p. 15. Mosely represented the State Department on the WSC until June 21, 1944, to be replaced thereafter by David Harris.

the Combined Chiefs of Staff, the President and the Prime Minister — though unknown to the State Department — should not be discussed with civilians unfamiliar with its background. Furthermore, they expected considerable furor from State Department spokesmen should the latter learn, prematurely, that such discussions had been going on outside of the WSC. Unaware that President Roosevelt had been undercutting his own brainchild, distressed State Department representatives pointed out that since Russia was unrepresented on the Combined Civil Affairs Committee, adoption of the War Department's policy of military control and initiative would exclude Russia from postwar decision making, and make it difficult, if not impossible, to insure postwar cooperation among the Allies. The USSR, as a major wartime ally, had to participate in the planning for Germany; otherwise there might be chaos, misunderstanding, and one-sided decisions based on the disposition of military forces at the end of the war.[11]

When State Department delegate Philip Mosely proposed the partition of the Reich into three zones, with Berlin jointly occupied and a delineated corridor joining it to the Western zones, Army officers ingenuously maintained that this problem must be decided by the military. They further insisted that the zones of occupation be determined by the position of the three armies at the conclusion of hostilities. Repelled by the concept that "all or nearly all of Germany should pass under Soviet control", Mosely contended that only with prior agreements on zones of occupation could the Allies possibly avert wartime disunity. Furthermore, without such an agreement the Germans could play off one ally against another and seek a separate peace from the West, while Russia might be tempted to master extensive territory during the dying days of the war in order to insure control over much of postwar Europe.[12]

War Department spokesmen on the WSC were not only of a junior rank but proved reluctant to agree to anything, and usually did little but report back to their superiors. As Mosely subsequently put it: "This system of negotiating at arm's length, under rigid instructions

---

[11]   WS Minutes 1, 2 and 3, December 21, 24 and 27, 1943; Pogue, *The Supreme Command*, pp. 77-78.
[12]   State Department, *Post War Foreign Policy Preparation*, pp. 211-25; Mosely, "The Occupation of Germany", *loc. cit.*, p. 588. By this time, War Department representatives were satisfied to have the barest of minutes kept of the discussions and viewpoints expressed at meetings of the Working Security Committee.

and with the exercise of the 'veto' resembled the procedures of Soviet negotiators in their more intransigeant moods. Under such conditions the pace of work in the Working Security Committee was, of necessity, determined primarily by the outlook of the Civil Affairs Division." [13]

So, when the first meeting of the European Advisory Commission convened, Winant still found himself without specific directives or proposals for a German surrender, while Strang presented twenty-nine detailed British working papers involving military, political and economic questions of major importance, and including a draft surrender instrument and a proposed agreement on zones of occupation. Further advanced than Russia or the United States in postwar planning, German experts in Britain's Foreign Office consistently offered the most sophisticated documents. [14]

Despite a telegram to Hull containing the British working papers, the American Envoy received no comment from Washington for almost two months. He first learned from his military adviser that the Working Security Committee had been considering a paper on control machinery for Germany. Again and again, Winant pleaded with Hull and Washington for directives. "If we take at the outset a negative attitude to the Commission, without having any alternative facilities to propose, I fear that we may cause deep and deplorable discouragement on the British side and indifference on the part of the Russians" and endanger effective Allied cooperation for the immediate postwar period. [15] But Hull could not meet the Ambassador's needs. The WSC had reached an impasse and the State Department remained unprepared, or lacked determination, to break it. Woefully lacking in background for such a task, War Department officers refused, for months, to permit the WSC and, in turn, the EAC to determine zones of occupation for Germany, insisting that it would be useless to set down boundary lines prior to the cessation of hostilities, because the Russians would ignore them anyway and occupy Germany up to the Rhine. Not until March could Winant circulate

[13] WS Minutes 1-4, 7, 8, 13, 14, 33; Mosely, "The Occupation of Germany", loc. cit., p. 585.
[14] WS Minutes 27, February 16, 1944; WS Minutes 34, March 4, 1944; Mosely, "The Occupation of Germany", loc. cit., p. 586; Strang, Home and Abroad, p. 210.
[15] JGW telegrams "To Secstate", January 4, February 12 and 15, 1944; JGW telegram "For Acting Secretary and Mr. Dunn", March 2, 1944.

the American draft on German unconditional surrender, which became the basis of the EAC protocol of July 1944.[16]

The British plan for zonal occupation, not too dissimilar from Mosely's original proposal — unknown to Gusev, Winant and the State Department — had been previously acceded to, in principle, by Roosevelt and his Chiefs of Staff in November 1943. It placed Berlin, a separate joint zone, about 110 miles inside the western boundary of the Soviet area. While having no serious objections to dividing Germany into zones, as suggested by the British, the President insisted that the northwest section, originally assigned to Britain, should be occupied by the United States and extend eastward to include Berlin. When Gusev endorsed the London proposal in February 1944, he did not care how the Allies divided the Western zones, but he did express the hope that they would settle the matter soon.[17] The assignment of the southwestern zone to the United States was rejected for months by Roosevelt and his military advisers because they would have to depend upon transit routes across France to supply the occupation troops, and the Chief Executive feared for the stability of the postwar French Republic. The President preferred to be in the northwest near the ports of Bremen and Hamburg, from which points American troops could be easily transferred from Europe for the war in the Pacific.[18]

Toward the end of February 1944, Army officers on the Working Security Committee suddenly altered their refusal to discuss, let alone present, specific proposals when they displayed a proposed map of postwar Germany. Unbeknown to the State Department, this proposal had been presented by the Joint Chiefs of Staff at the Cairo Conference the previous November, assigning Roosevelt's original huge northwest zone to Washington. No clear demarcation distin-

---

[16] State Department, *Postwar Foreign Policy Preparation*, pp. 211-25; Mosely, "The Occupation of Germany", *loc. cit.*, p. 586; Report submitted by M. W. Boggs, Acting Secretary General, EAC, September 12, 1945, State Department Archives Box 18220.

[17] Winston S. Churchill, *Triumph and Tragedy* (Boston, Houghton Mifflin Co., 1953), p. 508; Philip E. Mosely, *The Kremlin and World Politics* (New York, Vintage Books, 1960), pp. 168-71; *Foreign Relations of the United States: The Conferences at Cairo and Tehran 1943* (Washington, U.S. Government Printing Office, 1961), pp. 253-54, 600-02; *Foreign Relations: The Conferences at Malta and Yalta 1945*, p. 614.

[18] *Foreign Relations: The Conferences at Cairo and Tehran, 1943*, pp. 254-56; Hull, *Memoirs*, II, 1612; Maurice Matloff, *Strategic Planning for Coalition Warfare, 1943-1944* (Washington? 1959), p. 491; Franklin, "Zonal Boundaries and Access to Berlin", *loc. cit.*, pp. 11, 14-15.

guished the eastern from southern zones and no reference was made to the proposed joint occupation of Berlin. Furthermore, this proved a completely unrealistic proposal for Gusev had previously accepted the British plan for the boundary of the Soviet zone and the joint occupation of Berlin. These issues, therefore, were no longer negotiable. Yet War Department spokesmen refused to supply background material for Winant's guidance in substantiating their plan, because they viewed this as a military directive not open to discussion.[19]

State Department spokesmen on the WSC agreed, momentarily, to forward the War Department's proposal to Winant, knowing full well that the American Envoy would make frantic queries to Washington for more articulate instruction. Lacking specific guidance and denied information as to their sponsorship, Winant immediately responded that he could not defend these latest proposals for they ignored state frontiers, transportation and communication lines, and other essential considerations. CAD spokesmen refused to elaborate upon the pencilled lines of occupation zones and the WSC, unable to supply the Ambassador with fuller instructions, remained in a deadlock until early April.[20]

In late March, and still without clarifying directives, American drafts or responses to British working papers, the Ambassador dispatched his advisor, George F. Kennan, to Washington to plead for guidance. Meeting with the President, Kennan underscored the absence of general directives to Winant, and pointed out that the plan for zonal division approved by the Joint Chiefs of Staff ignored the more realistic proposals which the British and Russians had basically agreed upon. Realizing that he had not kept the State Department or Winant abreast of his earlier exploration of occupation zones with London, the President instructed Kennan to ignore the proposal of the Joint Chiefs of Staff and endorsed the British zonal arrangements for the Soviets. He persisted, however, in his desire for the northwest zone. Alerted to this change in policy, Winant immediately advised his colleagues and work resumed in the EAC.[21]

[19] WS Minutes 33 and 34, February 29 and March 4, 1944; Mosely, "The Occupation of Germany", loc. cit., p. 591.
[20] JGW telegram "For Acting Secretary and Mr. Dunn", March 2, 1944; JGW telegram "To the Secretary", March 12, 1944; JGW telegram "For the Secretary", April 3, 1944; Edward R. Stettinius, Jr., telegram "To Secstate", April 14, 1944; Mosely, "The Occupation of Germany", loc. cit., pp. 591-92.
[21] Mosely, "The Occupation of Germany", loc. cit., p. 592; Feis, Churchill, Roosevelt, Stalin, p. 362; unsigned memorandum dated April 5, 1944, found in

Unfortunately, Kennan's meeting with Roosevelt did not remedy the basic problem of insufficient directives which inhibited Winant. The Ambassador was obliged to continue in negotiations with papers inadequately cleared by Washington compelling him to withhold support of definitive positions. Despite insistent requests for guidance between March and October 1944, he received only one policy directive with authoritative clearances. From time to time, Washington barely managed to cable him comments on urgent matters under immediate negotiation.[22] The confusion, frustration and breakdown in communications which enveloped Winant and WSC members was the result of the President's practice, at times, of permitting numerous groups to work on related problems in ignorance of, or at cross purposes to, each other. He would eventually select a solution from among those arrived at by differing groups, sometimes too late and sometimes at great cost to those involved.

Those who contend that Winant was denied broad powers for fear of a "shift in the center of policy-making from Washington to London," that is from America to the British and Russians, overlook the fact that the EAC never concerned itself with the problem of boundaries in Eastern and Central Europe. It operated from the assumption that Germany would be under Allied control within its 1937 boundaries, and it did not consider the conditions under which Allied Commanders would turn over political administration to national authorities. Its arrangements for Germany covered only the first period, that of joint military control, with most of its work related to the Third Reich and Austria.[23]

Within weeks after Kennan's return to London, and still without guidance, a harassed Winant headed for Washington to lay his plight before the Working Security Committee and the Civil Affairs Division. To both he emphasized his major difficulties as stemming from the absence of directives. In the process, he advised War Department spokesmen that he was prepared "... to propose detailed provisions safeguarding American access [to Berlin] by highway, railroad and air", for Gusev had repeatedly assured him that there would be no trouble in arranging for transit through the Soviet zone to

White House files of President Roosevelt at the F. D. Roosevelt Library in Hyde Park, confirms the visit of "George F. Keenan" [sic].

[22] JGW telegram "To Secstate", October 7, 1944.

[23] Dorn, "American Occupation Policy", loc. cit., p. 488. In the case of Austria, EAC agreements foreshadowed the plan for turning over authority to an elected Austrian government, but did not spell this out in detail.

Berlin and that the presence of American and British forces in Berlin "of course" carried with it all necessary facilities of access.[24] A subsequent telegram from the American Embassy in London underscored Gusev's desire, on specific directives from Moscow, to arrange immediately "for transit facilities ... providing US and UK forces and control personnel full access to the Berlin zone across Soviet-occupied territory". Winant, apparently, received no instructions or encouragement from Washington to pursue this Russian proposal. As long as the War Department maintained that agreements with the Soviet Union on transit routes to Berlin were one of those purely "military matter[s]" to be taken care of "at the military level", and "at the proper time", then no predetermined accords could be reached by Winant on this issue. The Ambassador and others would be forced to rationalize that the original British plans had secured from Moscow "recognition of the right of the Western Powers to be in Berlin on a footing of parity with the Russians even though the indications were that the Soviet Army would get there first".[25]

Shortly after Winant failed to convert War Department spokesmen, the military representative of General Eisenhower on the EAC personally appealed to Working Security members for clearance of policy guidance, particularly on control machinery for Germany and Austria. Brigadier General Cornelius W. Wickersham highlighted the "great service" which the Ambassador had performed "day and night in gaining the confidence of Soviet representatives and in securing agreement from the British delegation to fundamental changes in their approach to key issues". Handcuffed though he was in the absence of directives, and confronted with "an intensely suspicious

[24] WS Minutes 39, May 17, 1944; Mosely, "The Occupation of Germany", *loc. cit.*, p. 593.
[25] Gallman telegram "For the Secretary and Undersecretary", November 6, 1944. Waldemar Gallman was Embassy Counsellor. Also, Franklin, "Zonal Boundaries and Access to Berlin", *loc. cit.*, pp. 24-31.

In subsequently apportioning blame upon Winant for the absence of written assurances of free access to Berlin, State Department trouble shooter Robert Murphy overlooks the significance of the late date of his discussions with the Ambassador. He also seems unaware of the frustrating role played by War Department spokesmen on the Working Security Committee. These Army officers maintained that it was impossible, before the cross-channel invasion had begun, and before Allied forces had conquered Germany, to know what railways and highways would be usable when the time came to enter Berlin. Robert Murphy, *Diplomat Among Warriors* (Garden City, N.Y., Doubleday, 1964), pp. 226-33. Also, WS Minutes 1-3, December 21, 24 and 27, 1943; Mosely, *The Kremlin and World Politics*, chap. 6.

and close mouthed Russian", it was Winant's "utter devotion, profound integrity and unbending determination to plan ahead for postwar problems" which helped insure that the EAC, under these circumstances, would be remarkably efficient.[26]

Winant did manage to convince Roosevelt to look into the problem of confused lines of communication to the EAC, and to fundamentally alter the government's policy toward Austria. While the Declaration of Moscow of November 1943 committed the Allies to free Austria and restore her independence, Roosevelt had hesitated to participate in the national control of that nation. He feared isolationism at home, desired immediate redeployment of American forces from Europe to the Pacific theater, and revolted against involvement in Central Europe. He would willingly permit the British to occupy all of Austria.[27] Winant convinced the President to participate in a tripartite control of Austria at the national level, without committing the United States as to the size of the military contingent. The Ambassador announced this concession to the EAC on May 31, immediately after his return from Washington.[28] After Gusev suggested joint occupation of Austria, Winant secured Roosevelt's acceptance of a share in the control of that country, but only with a token force in Vienna. Not until September 1944 did Churchill and Roosevelt agree at the Second Quebec Conference on United States assumption of the southwestern zone in Germany, and on the separate treatment of the Austrian question. When the Soviet delegate to the EAC proposed the division of Austria into tri-partite zones, the American Ambassador finally secured presidential approval for control of the northwestern area. But this, too, he achieved only after months of exhausting meetings in London with an increasingly obstinate Soviet envoy and constant pleading with Washington for directives and confirmation of tentative agreements.[29]

[26]   WS Minutes 45, July 7, 1944.
[27]   An authoritative account of the proceedings of the EAC on Austria is contained in an article by Edgar L. Erickson, "The Zoning of Austria", *The Annals of the American Academy of Political and Social Science* (January, 1950), pp. 106-13. For additional information see M. Balfour and J. Mair, *Four Power Control in Germany and Austria* (London, Oxford University, 1956), pp. 269-94.
[28]   JGW telegram "For the Secretary and Mr. Dunn", June 17, 1944.
[29]   JGW telegrams "To Secstate", August 1, 1944; "For the Secretary and Assistant Secretary Dunn", January 2, 1945; "To the Secretary", March 19, 22, April 5, 15, July 4 and August 28, 1945; "For Mr. Matthews", April 23, 1945; "For Acting Secretary and Dunn", June 27, 1945. See Balfour and Mair, *Four Power Control in Germany and Austria*, p. 288; Erickson, "The Zoning of Austria", *loc. cit.*, p. 109; Department of State, *Bulletin*, XIII, 1945, 221-22.

In June 1944, Philip E. Mosely became the key State Department adviser to the Ambassador, immeasurably strengthening Winant. A master of Russian history and politics, patient, with excellent com· mand of language and diplomatic skill, Mosely proved the equal of Gusev and his counsellors.[30] The problem of planning for postwar Germany, however, remained an impossible task, for despite progress on draft surrender terms, Winant labored on without instructions. In August, he urged the President to formulate an economic policy toward Germany and Austria. Reminding Roosevelt of the great need for material aid to help repair vast destruction in Russia, and with the bulk of German industry in the western zones, the Ambassador proposed a reparations policy which would "satisfy a part of the Soviet demands without involving an undue burden for the United States." He warned the President that without a detailed accord in advance on reparation, "the proposed system for the joint control in Germany would break down. Rivalry for control over Germany . . . would follow".[31]

After Anglo-American success in establishing a Second Front in France, the President could have begun to cope with some of the postwar problems. Instead, he capriciously adopted, rejected and then modified Morgenthau's pastoralization plan, insuring that, for six months thereafter, the United States would indulge "in a policy of 'no policy' toward Germany".[32] As Philip Mosely implied, some years after the war, Roosevelt may not have been certain that he had the authority to commit the nation on matters traditionally settled in treaties of peace. In addition, he worried about a revival of isolationism after the war and negative reaction by citizens of foreign origin to any attempt on his part to conclude, in advance, concrete boundary and related issues of conquered nations. Distraught by Morgenthau's forceful intervention in postwar German questions, Winant justifiably concluded that the ensuing row would hamper consolidation of gains in the EAC. Not until Roosevelt returned from Yalta in February 1945, could Winant impress upon him the dangers in postponing policy for Germany.[33] It was too late.

[30] JGW telegram "To Secstate", August 1, 1944; Strang, *Home and Abroad,* p. 211; Franklin, "Zonal Boundaries and Access to Berlin", *loc. cit.,* pp. 30-31.
[31] Penrose, *Economic Planning for the Peace,* p. 233; JGW telegram "To the Secretary for the President", August 19, 1944; Mosely, "The Occupation of Germany", *loc. cit.,* p. 597.
[32] Mosely, "The Occupation of Germany", *loc. cit.,* p. 596.
[33] Henry Morgenthau, Jr., *Germany Is Our Problem* (New York, Harper and

At the Second Quebec Conference in September of 1944, the President did not make effective use of knowledgeable advisers and German experts, and thus the document on Germany proved a disaster, for it accepted Morgenthau's major premises. Eden rushed to Quebec to denounce the Morgenthau plan, and strong opposition from London and Washington subsequently led to a repudiation of the proposal. With Allied troops inside Germany before the end of September, with General Eisenhower urgently requesting policy directives for a Third Reich he soon expected to control, and with the German government and military veering toward collapse, Roosevelt recoiled from the Morgenthau fiasco by advising his Secretary of State that he disliked "making detailed plans for a country which we do not yet occupy". Furthermore, he did not want the question of dismemberment taken up in the EAC which, he felt, was "on a tertiary and not even secondary level . . .".[34] Unable to devote to this subject the concentration of thought it rightly deserved, Roosevelt would improvise inadequate and conflicting solutions.

In London, meanwhile, the Ambassador found it increasingly difficult to reach satisfactory agreements with stubborn, confident and procrastinating Soviet spokesmen. Having seen enough of Soviet machinations in Bulgaria and elsewhere in Eastern Europe to know that written, specific agreements had to be concluded beforehand, Winant alerted General Eisenhower to "the difficulties [he] would encounter when [he] started working with Russian leaders".[35]

Following his disenchantment with the Morgenthau plan, the President appeared to surrender any hope of influencing conditions in the Russian occupied sector of Germany. He, thereafter, adopted a policy of postponement which made it difficult, if not impossible, to challenge postwar Russian initiative in certain fields. He also approved a special Cabinet Committee's interim directive to General Eisenhower, a compromise of irreconcilable viewpoints but largely

Brothers, 1945), frontispieces, and pp. 23 and 50; Stimson and Bundy, *On Active Service in Peace and War*, p. 571; Hull, *Memoirs*, II, 1605; Penrose, *Economic Planning for the Peace*, pp. 243-48; Mosely, *The Kremlin and World Politics*, pp. 158-59.

[34] Morgenthau in the *New York Post*, November 28-29, 1947; Churchill, *Triumph and Tragedy*, p. 157; Stimson and Bundy, *On Active Service in Peace and War*, pp. 576-77, 580-81; Hull, *Memoirs*, II, 1610, 1619-22; Penrose, *Economic Planning for the Peace*, p. 255; State Department, *Postwar Foreign Policy Preparation*, p. 347; President to Secretary of State, October 20, 1944, *Foreign Relations: Conferences at Malta and Yalta*, pp. 158-59.

[35] Interview with Dwight D. Eisenhower, August 8, 1951.

a Treasury document, which forbade the American Commander from doing anything to rehabilitate or maintain the German economy. Whereas Winant and the State Department sought the repeal or major modification of this impractical, punitive document, known as J.C.S. 1067, the War Department joined Morgenthau in accepting it and preventing any material policy alterations. As a sympathetic student of the military afterward explained, "So long as Mr. Morgenthau had the ear of the President no other directive was obtainable and an immediate directive, indeed any directive, was a necessity required by the military situation, a circumstance which the State Department, thinking largely in political terms, was inclined to forget." Rejecting the urgent need for a long-range occupation policy, the President's decisions put a stop even to informal discussions between Winant and the British on postwar planning for Germany.[36]

Unhappy with the failure of Washington to ratify the EAC zonal agreement of the previous November, Winant conferred at length with Harry Hopkins as the latter passed through London in January 1945, on his way to the Yalta Conference. As in his telegrams to the President, Winant pressed for confirmation of the protocol. With American forces barely entering the Rhineland, while the Russians were already on the Oder River some 45 miles from Berlin, Winant feared that the Red Army "might reach the border of their zone and then keep on going" unless there was a firm prior commitment concerning the zones of occupation. Within days, Hopkins, Stettinius and Eden secured approval from the Combined Chiefs of Staff, authorizing Winant to endorse the document. The Soviets immediately followed suit and the Three Power agreement on zones of occupation in Germany was finally in force.[37]

A distraught Winant, having learned that he would not accompany the President to Yalta, wired him in despair about this decision "to

---

[36] Dorn, "The Debate Over American Occupation Policy in Germany in 1944-1945", loc. cit., pp. 488, 491, 494-95, 498-99; Hull, Memoirs, II, 1605, 1607-09; Penrose, Economic Planning for the Peace, pp. 259-74; Foreign Relations: Conferences at Malta and Yalta, pp. 174, 291; Churchill, Triumph and Tragedy, pp. 258-59; New Statesman and Nation, XXIX, January 27, 1945, p. 51; Mosely, "The Occupation of Germany", loc. cit., p. 596.

[37] Edward R. Stettinius, Jr., Roosevelt and the Russians: the Yalta Conference (Garden City, N.Y., Doubleday, 1949), p. 56; JGW telegrams "For the Secretary", December 14, 1944; "To the President", January 10 and February 7, 1945; Foreign Relations: Conferences at Malta and Yalta, pp. 118-21, 201, 498; Report submitted by M. W. Boggs, Acting Secretary General, EAC, September 12, 1945. Box 18220, Historical Division, State Department.

exclude me from the conference . . .". Gusev would be at Stalin's side, advising him on EAC discussions and decisions, while Anthony Eden, close friend of Winant and immediate superior to Strang, would be with Churchill. But no one intimately familiar with the labors of the EAC and the nuances of the Russian mind would be available to the President.[38] Despite Winant's reaction, his presence at Yalta would have made little difference, for Roosevelt had been his own Secretary of State for years, and furthermore, did not permit the State Department, let alone an Ambassador, to influence his determination of German policy.

En route to Yalta, Roosevelt received a lengthy telegram from Winant warning him of potential conflict among participating occupation powers if they did not agree on control and planning prior to German surrender. The Ambassador's experiences in hard dealing with Gusev for over a year had demonstrated that it would be "easier to get agreement prior to occupation than after occupation". Equally important, from a moral point of view, Winant recalled that the United States had insisted in the Surrender Instrument that the signatory powers were "acting in the interests of the United Nations", which, he felt "we will fail to discharge unless we get agreement, for example, on freezing of property until equitable arrangements can be made to protect the rights of our other allies to restitution and reparation".[39]

Unfortunately, the President placed too much confidence in his own ability to grapple with international problems on a man-to-man basis. At Yalta, as at the Cairo Conference, he neglected to surround himself with "authoritative and keen-minded experts" on German affairs. The Big Three postponed final consideration of reparations and sought to dispose of dismemberment by creating a Committee of Eden, Gusev and Winant to "study the procedure for the dismemberment of Germany", a venture doomed to failure because Committee members remained without instructions from their governments and without proposals to discuss. Earlier, Stalin, Churchill and Roosevelt had agreed that their three governments "will take such steps, including the complete disarmament, demilitarization and the dismemberment of Germany as they deem requisite for future

---

[38] *Foreign Relations: Conferences at Malta and Yalta*, p. 958. The President sought to make amends to Winant by inviting his Envoy to join him in Egypt, after the conference. F. D. Roosevelt to JGW, February 11, 1945.
[39] *Ibid.*, pp. 132-33.

peace and security". Unfortunately, after Stalin agreed to admit France to share in the occupation and control of Germany through the EAC, there was no move to include France in the new, secret Committee on Dismemberment, which overlapped in membership the European Advisory Commission. Thus, France was not officially notified of Allied support for dismemberment at Yalta, making for serious difficulties during the dying days of the war.[40]

In late March, a few days after Gusev made clear that the Soviet Union did not have a firm view on dismemberment, the President advised Winant that "I think our attitude should be one of study and postponement of final decision". With the attention of Allied leaders riveted on the rushing events in a collapsing Germany, the question of dismemberment had to await the end of hostilities when, according to Mosely, the bargaining powers of Great Britain and the United States would be further weakened by the death of Roosevelt and the tremendous success of the Red Army.[41] In the meantime, Winant had had to contend with increasingly stubborn and unco-operative Russians. Gusev's negative attitude finally moved Winant to advise Stettinius that if the Soviets persisted in their refusal to cooperate in the economic planning for postwar Germany, then it was the responsibility of the other Allies to proceed with their own proposals.[42]

With German armies capitulating in Italy and in northwest Europe during the first days of May and total surrender expected momentarily, Winant suddenly discovered that General Eisenhower at Supreme Headquarters (SHAEF) had not received the EAC Instrument of Surrender from the Combined Chiefs of Staff in Washington and, furthermore, had not been authorized to sign the document. Telephoning the State Department during the night of May 4, the

[40]   Sumner Welles, Seven Decisions that Shaped History (New York, Harper & Bros., 1950), p. 216; Foreign Relations: Conferences at Malta and Yalta, pp. 132, 655-59, 700-09, 921-22, 936-37, 969-71, 978-79; Stettinius, Roosevelt and the Russians, p. 138; Snell, Dilemma Over Germany, pp. 139-68; W. Strang to JGW, March 9, 1945; Mosely, "Dismemberment of Germany", loc. cit., pp. 493-98; United States Department of State, The Axis in Defeat, A Collection of Documents on American Policy Towards Germany and Japan (Washington, U.S. Government Printing Office, n.d.), pp. 8-9.

[41]   F. T. Gusev to Anthony Eden, March 26, 1945. Copy found in Drawer 28 of Winant Coll.; JGW telegram "For the Secretary, Assistant Secretary Dunn and Mr. Matthews", March 29, 1945; Mosely, "Dismemberment of Germany", loc. cit., pp. 493-98.

[42]   JGW telegrams "To Secstate", March 3 and April 17, 1945; Stettinius, Roosevelt and the Russians, pp. 311-16.

Ambassador learned that texts of the Surrender Instrument were available in London and could be flown immediately to SHAEF. But there could be no final decision as to the propriety of the document until the Soviets, in accordance with the understandings reached at Yalta, permitted Britain and the United States to officially advise the new French representative to add the word "dismemberment". However, the Russians were no longer interested for, within days, Stalin would denounce dismemberment.

EAC representatives, meanwhile, had been working on a Declaration on the Defeat of Germany to be used in the absence of a German government to sign the Surrender Instrument. If they resorted to the Surrender Instrument, then the question of dismemberment would not arise as the draft preamble contained a clause which gave the victorious Allies the right to "determine the boundaries of Germany or any part thereof and the status of Germany or of any area at present being part of German territory". Before concluding his telephone conversation with a State Department spokesman, Winant urged that the Secretary of War and the Combined Chiefs of Staff wire immediately the necessary authorization to SHAEF to sign the Surrender Instrument.[43]

The next day the American Envoy learned that SHAEF had been negotiating independently with Churchill for substitution of an entirely new text for the EAC instrument which provided only for a military surrender in the field and which "omitted all mention of the assumption by the four Allies of supreme power over Germany". Realizing that the Third Reich was smashed and incapable of effective resistance, and concluding that a quick surrender would save many lives, SHAEF spokesmen sought a brief, simple document of surrender.[44] These military spokesmen, however, ignored vital political considerations: a purely military surrender in the field would cost the Allies an opportunity to secure German acknowledgment of unconditional political surrender, and place in jeopardy the supreme authority which the Allies had agreed to exercise over Germany. In addition, an exclusively military surrender would oblige the Allies to adhere to the Geneva and Hague Conventions, requiring them to

---

[43] From the stenographic record of Winant's telephone conversation with H. Freeman Matthews on May 4, 1945. Winant Coll.; Undated Secret Memorandum, Committee on Dismemberment, Winant Coll.; Mosely, "Dismemberment of Germany", *loc. cit.*, pp. 494-96.

[44] *Ibid.*; JGW telegram "For the Acting Secretary and Mr. Matthews", May 5, 1945.

maintain the laws and institutions of the Nazi regime, prevent the Allies from trying and punishing political war criminals and deprive the victors of the right to exercise full control over a defeated Germany. Furthermore, the SHAEF document, in contrast to the EAC Surrender Instrument, would not be a quadripartite proposal, thereby endangering Allied unity at the very cessation of hostilities, and after months of trying negotiations among Russian, British and American representatives.[45]

During the late hours of May 5, Winant spoke with Winston Churchill, and then by telephone with General Walter Bedell Smith at SHAEF Headquarters, underscoring the dangers in the briefer Instrument. Through Winant's insistence, the Prime Minister and the General facilitated the addition of Article 4 to the Surrender Instrument — signed at Rheims on May 7 and at Berlin the following day — an article worded in such a manner as to leave the way open for subsequent imposition on Germany of the terms contained in the EAC Instrument or in the Declaration based on the Instrument. Article 4 became the basis on which the Four Powers issued the Declaration on Germany on June 5, 1945, and assumed supreme authority to control and administer that state.[46]

Some twenty-four hours after Germany's unconditional surrender, and without prior consultation with his Allies, Stalin denounced dismemberment. The term "dismemberment" was excluded from the military instrument of surrender and the Declaration issued on June 5, and formally signed in Berlin by the four Allied Commanders-in-Chief. While the heads of state did not discuss dismemberment at the Potsdam Conference, a dismembered Germany became a reality on the battlefields by the time the war had ended.[47]

---

[45] JGW telegram "For the Acting Secretary and Matthews", May 10, 1945; Mosely, "Dismemberment of Germany", loc. cit., p. 496.

[46] JGW telegram "For the Acting Secretary and Matthews", May 10, 1945; Mosely, "Dismemberment of Germany", loc. cit., p. 497. Article 4 of the brief Instrument of Surrender, whereby a collapsing Germany surrendered unconditionally, provided that "This act of military surrender is without prejudice to, and will be superseded by any general instrument of surrender imposed by, or on behalf of the United Nations and applicable to Germany and the German armed forces as a whole." Germany Surrenders Unconditionally, National Archives Publication No. 46-4 (Washington, U.S. Government Printing Office, 1945), pp. 9-10, 32-33.

[47] Department of State, Bulletin, XII, pp. 1051-55; The Axis in Defeat, Department of State Publication 2423, p. 71; Mosely, "Dismemberment of Germany", loc. cit., p. 498; JGW telegrams "For the Acting Secretary and Matthews",

On August 2, 1945, the European Advisory Commission terminated with a tri-partite conference in Berlin. The Allied Control Council would carry on the functions of the Commission in the battered capital of the German Reich. During their nineteen months of deliberations, EAC members had approved twelve formal agreements and referred them for ratification to their respective governments. The British member of the EAC insisted, a decade later, that "Never before nor since have agreements of such volume or importance been reached with the Soviet Government." [48]

The assignment in frustration was at an end. After four years in which his energies and endurance had been taxed to the danger point, Winant was now obliged to face a new world and a new way of life. His primary work in Great Britain was completed. At home, meanwhile, the mantle of political leadership had fallen from the hands of Roosevelt. Harry S. Truman would grow into the presidency, while Winant faced the bleak prospect of dealing with a Chief Executive unfamiliar with his background and unappreciative of his role on the American progressive scene.

May 10, 1945; "To Secstate", May 12, 1945; James F. Byrnes, *Speaking Frankly* (New York, Harper & Bros., 1947), p. 26; *Foreign Relations of the United States: The Conference of Berlin, 1945*, II, 522; Harry S. Truman, *Memoirs*, I, *Year of Decisions* (Garden City, N.Y., Doubleday, 1955), p. 300; Lionel Kochan, *The Struggle for Germany, 1914-1945* (Edinburgh, Edinburgh University, 1963), pp. 91-96.

[48] Report by M. W. Boggs, Acting Secretary General, EAC, September 12, 1945. Box 18220, State Department, Historical Office Files; Strang, *Home and Abroad*, p. 208. Some of the agreements signed by the Commission included: Unconditional Surrender of Germany, Declaration Regarding the Defeat of Germany and the Assumption of Supreme Authority with Respect to Germany, Zones of Occupation in Germany and the Administration of Greater Berlin, Control Machinery in Germany, Occupation and Control of Austria, Control Machinery in Austria, Zones of Occupation in Austria and Administration of City of Vienna, Armistice with Bulgaria.

CHAPTER XV

"TIME ... TO GO HOME"

Winant's last years in London proved lonely and debilitating. With little social life, vacation or relaxation, the strain of responsibilities upon his tattered nerves often provoked explosive responses to slight provocations. In early Spring of 1945, he suffered for weeks with the flu. And then came the tragic news from Warm Springs, Georgia on April 12.[1]

A few weeks earlier, while seeking a belated Christmas present for the Chief Executive, Winant had discovered George Washington's walking stick which the first President had given to Jerome Bonaparte. On this remarkably well preserved piece of wood could be seen thirteen notched stars. With this gift to Roosevelt, Winant sent extracts from the great Rectorial Address of Sir James M. Barrie to the students of St. Andrews, in which the Scottish dramatist and novelist maintained that he could not provide them with a staff for their journey in the world that lay before them but perhaps he could tell them a little about it, "how to use it and lose it and find it again, and cling to it more than ever. You shall cut it", he said, "as is ordained, every one of you for himself, and its name is Courage".[2]

It was nighttime in England when Winant learned of the Chief Executive's death. Already weak from illness, this staggering blow left him unable to walk for hours. The Ambassador spent the rest of the night trying to visualize a world without Roosevelt.[3] In the 1936 campaign, this maverick Republican had forfeited any hopes for the G.O.P. Presidential nomination. "The Republicans won't have me", he said on more than one occasion. "I'm read out of that party. I'm Roosevelt's man. If Roosevelt want me to do anything I'll do it. That's my political future." Roosevelt's death, therefore, seemed the end of the road for Winant. Could he continue to contemplate ap-

[1] Maurine Mulliner to author, July 6, 1963; JGW to Ross T. McIntire, March 3, 1945; JGW telegram "For the Secretary", March 19, 1945.
[2] JGW to Franklin D. Roosevelt, March 4, 1945; F. D. Roosevelt to JGW, March 16, 1945.
[3] Interview with Orol Mears, July 30, 1952.

pointment to significant administrative positions at home or abroad?
Following the traditional practise, Winant submitted his resignation
to the new President, but it was rejected.[4]

Thousands of telegrams and letters of sympathy swamped the
Embassy of London, the greatest numbers sent by "the common
people of England". The Ambassador advised Mrs. Roosevelt, "We
are trying to make grateful acknowledgments. People really cared
here." Britain paid tribute to Roosevelt's memory when the King,
Queen and 3,000 others jammed every available space inside historic
St. Paul's. Additional thousands stood patiently in silence in surrounding streets. Winant read the lesson from the seventh chapter of
Revelation in the dimness of the Cathedral, his stark figure outlined
by thin rays of light near the lectern. The last post sounded, and
after it Reveille, blown from the gallery over the great west door of
St. Paul's by buglers of the Royal Marines. The silent crowds dispersed.[5]

As the American 7th Army reached the Nazi center of Nuremberg,
Hitler issued his last directive to armies on the Eastern Front: "he
who gives order of retreat . . . is to be shot on the spot." Within
seventy-two hours American forces entered Czechoslovakia, occupied
Magdeburg, and fought their way into Dusseldorf. Like thousands
of other parents of prisoners of war in Germany, Winant waited with
trying patience for news of his son. The previous October the German
High Command had ordered the transfer of at least eight important
POW's to Colditz, including the Queen's nephew, a relative of Winston Churchill, young Winant, and Polish General Bor-Komorowski
of Warsaw fame. As Allied forces closed in, these POW's were transferred to Weiden, then to Laufen near Salzburg, and finally to the
Schongau area in the Tyrol, where the collapsing German government lost contact with the group. By late April, the Ambassador
scanned the daily press for news of his son, as events moved too
rapidly for detailed information to be sent back through regular
channels. To his wife in the States, the Envoy could only urge that

[4] JGW to Constance Winant, May 9, 1945; JGW to Harold J. Laski, May 10,
1945; Maurine Mulliner diary, entries for July 15, September 24, 1945 and
January 2, 1946; interview with Grace Hogarth, July 10, 1951; interview with
Jacob Beam, July 26, 1951. Miss Mulliner arrived in London in July 1945 to
become Winant's personal assistant in the Embassy.
[5] JGW telegram "To Secstate", April 21, 1945; Harold J. Laski to JGW, April
14, 1945; Eleanor Roosevelt to JGW, April 18, 1945; George M. Trevelyan to
JGW, May 7, 1945; The Times, April 18, 1945.

she be "brave . . . patient and believing".[6] Seeking to suppress fears for the safety of his son at the hands of fanatical Nazis, he concentrated on the problems of imminent surrender and on the United Nations Conference in San Francisco. Within days after Italian partisans shot Benito Mussolini, Hitler committed suicide in a bunker of the Reich Chancellery. German Headquarters in Italy agreed to unconditional surrender and hostilities ceased on the Italian front at noon on May 2. General Jodl finally signed the instrument of surrender for all Germany in the morning hours on May 7.

Four days earlier, the General in charge of the prominent group of POW's in the Tyrol took matters into his own hands and arranged for the safe transfer of his prisoners to Switzerland. As soon as the convoy crossed the frontier, a news flash reached the Ambassador in London and, within hours, young Winant flew directly to England. The anxious father found his son forty pounds lighter and weary to the point of exhaustion. Lord Beaverbrook expressed the gratefulness of a nation when he wrote, "That your anxiety for him should have been removed in the hour of triumph to which you have so greatly contributed, will be cause for rejoicing among all your friends in this country. And that means the whole British people."[7]

Within two days, young John and his father greeted the Prime Minister who had come to personally express the gratitude of the British. The end of the European conflict, however, proved of momentary relief, for the Ambassador still had to face the worrisome problem of another son fighting in the Pacific.

Winant hoped to leave for the States shortly after V-E Day, but he had to delay his departure for five months. While he continued to devote considerable time to the German issue, and to difficulties with the Soviet Union, the urgency of worldwide conflict was gone. One night, within weeks after conclusion of European hostilities, he came storming into his newly rented house on Aldford Street. Without bothering to go to his bedroom, and ignoring a waiting associate in the den, the Envoy ripped off his evening dress jacket, his black tie and stiff white shirt, threw them on the couch and exploded:

---

[6] JGW to Constance Winant, April 19, 20 and 21, 1945. Out in the Pacific, Rivington was part of the Marine elements which landed on Okinawa.

[7] Information secured from German General Berger, captured at Berchtesgaden on May 8, 1945. His statement is found in the Historical Division of the State Department, Box F-802, 18220; *The New York Times,* May 7, 1945; JGW to Constance Winant, May 9, 1945; Max Beaverbrook to JGW, May 10, 1945.

"When I have to wear formal attire to a dinner gathering in England then my work is completed and it is time for John Winant to go home." Home, however, remained in the future, for, though his interests lay with the UNO being born in San Francisco, he found himself utterly involved though completely bored with postwar details such as shipping G.I. brides across the Atlantic.

Sometime after plans had developed for creation of a United Nations Organization, Winant advised Roosevelt that he would like to become its Secretary General. This challenging appointment would not only satisfy his innermost desires to serve the public but would enable him to carry out, on a grand scale, his work as Governor, Social Security Chairman, ILO Director and Ambassador. Apparently assured by Roosevelt that he would do everything possible to secure him this post, Winant was unprepared for the crushing events which followed. After Roosevelt's death, he was overwhelmed by moroseness and despondency. Refusing to accept reality, his mental state worsened when he learned that the projected selection of the United States as the headquarters site for the UN would mean a non-American as Secretary General. In addition, he had not solved personal financial problems which plagued him throughout the Ambassadorship. Displaying signs of despair, he began to speak frequently of suicide.[8]

As General Douglas MacArthur announced the liberation of the Philippines on July 5, 1945, the voters of Great Britain shocked Winant and others when they gave the Laborites a landslide victory in Parliamentary elections. The turning out of Churchill did not mean any dramatic break in British foreign policy at the ongoing Potsdam Conference, though it did accentuate Winant's feeling of having familiar pillars torn away.[9] When the Potsdam Conference resumed in late July, Winant became increasingly embittered for he was left in London while his political adviser on the EAC, Philip Mosely, along with Strang and Gusev, attended the meetings. Truman had rejected the suggestion of his personal emissary, Joseph E. Davies,

[8] Interview with Thomas C. Blaisdell, November 12, 1959, who was present during the Ambassador's outburst. Also, Maurine Mulliner diary, entries for August 6, September 9, 18, 19, 21, 24, October 1, 5, 31, 1945, January 2 and 31, 1946; Stettinius telegram "To Secstate", September 5 and October 1, 1945; *The Times*, December 12, 1945.
[9] JGW telegrams, "To the President", May 24, 1945; "To the Acting Secretary of State", June 16, 1945; "For the Secretary", July 8, 1945; Strang, *Home and Abroad*, p. 203.

that he invite Winant. The Ambassador's subsequent meeting with the President aboard the USS *Augusta* at anchor in Plymouth Roads apparently did not go off well, for the Envoy returned to London with an obvious feeling of alienation. The following morning, pacing up and down his Embassy office, he suddenly blurted out: "I have no life".[10]

Early one July morning in 1945, the first atomic bomb exploded in a desolate desert area near Alamagordo, New Mexico. Although Stalin was advised of this development during the Potsdam Conference, the world first learned of this awesome weapon after it dropped on Hiroshima the following month. That same night in August, Winant returned to the Aldford Street house with his personal Embassy assistant to hear a recorded radio announcement by Winston Churchill concerning the bomb. From the start of cooperative endeavors between the British and Americans in the development of this weapon, the Ambassador had been intimately involved in the exchange of plans and personnel. When the former Prime Minister concluded his remarks on the significance of the "A" bomb, the Envoy turned to his colleague and remarked, "I've told you most things, but I never mentioned this, did I?" [11]

On midnight of August 14, Attlee and Truman announced that Japan had surrendered unconditionally. Within moments, Winant wired Eleanor Roosevelt, "My love to you and forever I shall be grateful to him and to you." [12]

A week later, the Ambassador arrived in rainswept Portland, in southern England, pale and shaken after a rough plane flight from London. A silent crowd stood bareheaded as the band of the 1st Battalion of the Dorset Regiment played the Star Spangled Banner, and then across the harbor echoed the words of "O God Our Help in Ages Past". The major portion of the American Assault force had embarked from this site during the twenty-four hours preceding D-day, and the townspeople had selected Winant to unveil the tablet

[10] Supplemental report of Joseph E. Davies to President Truman on his Conferences with Foreign Minister Anthony Eden, June 12, 1945, as found in *Foreign Relations: The Conference of Berlin*, I, 81. Also, Maurine Mulliner diary, entries for July 31, August 2 and 30, 1945.

[11] Maurine Mulliner diary, entry for August 6, 1945; Richard G. Hewlett and Oscar E. Anderson, Jr., *The New World, 1939-1946* (University Park, Pa., Pennsylvania State University Press, 1962), pp. 268, 286, 287, 331-33.

[12] JGW to Eleanor Roosevelt, August 14, 1945.

commemorating this event because, as the Town Council put it, he was "... beloved and respected by this nation...".[13]

Taking advantage of this radio broadcast, he alerted listeners to the fact that the vast destruction and death caused by two missiles dropped on Hiroshima and Nagasaki meant that the world now lived under the sword of Damocles. Mankind had finally learned how to destroy life on this planet, for it had uncovered the last secret of nature and the power of destruction had become absolute. If man survived he would have to master a moral secret before he could use this dynamic power for good; to "learn how to live together in friendship". No other problem seemed as important, for failing on this issue, mankind failed everywhere. The wartime concept of mutual aid, of putting everything into a common pool, had to be carried into the future, for only with this spirit of dedication could the world be saved. It meant changing customs, guarding tongues, passions and habits; it meant acting as if the welfare of a neighboring nation was as important as the welfare of your own. "It is almost impossible — but so was D-Day. If that could be done, anything can be done if we really care." [14]

Winant gave increasing thought to the implications of the A-bomb. Convinced that the atomic bomb could not remain an exclusive American secret, Winant felt it would be dangerous to give the American people a false sense of power by letting them believe that scientific research in nuclear physics could be carried on without eventual disclosure. Instead, he endorsed international agreements providing for prompt and detailed exchanges of scientific knowledge in the field of atomic energy, for he believed that the more extensive the knowledge for scientists throughout the world, and the more nations involved in the research, the more difficult it would become for any nation to isolate its own scientists and to conceal their work.[15]

A rare, happy interval for the Ambassador occurred during Christmas 1945, when his personal assistant, who understood him well,

[13] A. N. Tattersall, Portland Urban District Council, to JGW, June 16, 1945.
[14] Speech of the American Ambassador at the unveiling of the Memorial Tablet to the U.S. Forces. Portland, Dorset — August 22, 1945. In author's possession.
[15] *New York Herald Tribune*, October 11, 1945; Ed. C. Betts to JGW, October 12, 1945 extracts of which follow: "Walter Lippmann, in his 11 October 1945 column in the *New York Herald Tribune*, ... has stated with admirable clarity the issues at stake arising out of the atomic secret. ...

His views are so interestingly parallel to your own, as discussed by us recently, this article is passed along for the satisfaction you may have in it."

arranged a party with his closest associates on the Embassy staff. Alerted in advance, the Envoy hung small gifts on a lovely decorated tree, along with a jingle for each of his assistants. He played Santa Claus, in unusually gay spirits and with full knowledge that he would not be in London for another Noël. From this party, he hurried directly toward Chichester to spend the rest of the holiday with the Edens at their country place.[16]

The first months of 1946 proved extremely busy for the Ambassador, as he worked closely with the United States delegation to the first General Assembly of the United Nations meeting in London. With the subsequent creation of the Economic and Social Council (ECOSOC), President Truman, at the behest of Senator Robert F. Wagner and others, designated Winant as America's representative. This presidential recognition seemed to lift him from his depression. The eighteen-member ECOSOC met frequently through mid-February, accomplising the unspectacular but important organizational tasks. The American Delegation, meanwhile, received a barrage of briefing messages and directives, including a preliminary "top secret" document of twenty-three single-spaced pages which delineated the United States position on every major issue on the agenda. These were supplemented daily by a stream of messages and memoranda from Washington. How different from the European Advisory Commission! [17]

Heated and acrimonious debate did develop over the definition of "refugees" and "displaced persons", and the responsibilities of the Committee established to deal with this problem. While State Department spokesmen expressed satisfaction with the accomplishments of this session, delegates were sobered by the basic differences which erupted between the Russian and Western blocs. Winant now realized that the task ahead would not be easy, and that skill and patience would be needed to break deadlocks in order to insure

---

[16] Maurine Mulliner to author, July 6, 1963.
[17] James F. Byrnes to Secretary of State, January 11, 1946; Acheson to Byrnes, January 11, 1946; *The New York Times,* January 13 and 24, 1946; Maurine Mulliner diary, entries for January 2, 3, 13, 26 and 31, 1946. Miss Mulliner wrote a confidential note to her former employer and close friend, Senator Robert F. Wagner, urging him to suggest to President Truman the merit of a permanent appointment of Winant to ECOSOC. Also, "Questions on the Agenda of the Economic and Social Council", USES/2a. Undated; USES/20, January 29, 1946; USES/22, January 30, 1946; USGA/Ia/SHCom/40, February 7, 1946; USES/43, February 14, 1946; USES/46, February 15, 1946; USES/47, February 15, 1946. All in Winant Coll.

positive accomplishments; the cold war had come to the U.N.[18]

Within days after ECOSOC adjourned in March, Winant flew to Washington amid rumors of his imminent resignation as Ambassador. Although President Truman first informed newsmen that the Envoy had returned for consultation, within a fortnight the latter advised White House reporters that he would relinquish his London post. He had gone to Britain "to do a war job", and that was now "pretty well done". Within days, the President hastily appointed W. Averell Harriman as his successor, and the retiring Ambassador as permanent United States Representative to ECOSOC.[19]

British newspapers, meanwhile, lamented the departure of Winant. A leading Conservative journal ranked him "as one of the greatest Ambassadors", because of his wisdom, humanity and sincerity. A Liberal daily bade farewell with the knowledge that Britain has "lost an Ambassador whose deep sincerity touched the heart of the British democracy". A Labor newspaper suggested that no two Ambassadors, so different as Joseph P. Kennedy and Winant could ever be imagined. Kennedy lacked faith in democracy and Britain, while Winant believed in, and inspired, Britishers, by walking the streets of London during air raids and sharing their dangers and rations. The learned editor of the *New Statesman and Nation* maintained that almost everyone in Britain knew his name, respected him as a "Great American" and as one of the best friends Britain ever had. His appointment, at a critical time for Britain, "was one of the most popular and sensible things that Mr. Roosevelt ever did". The *Manchester Guardian* recalled that the retiring Emissary "stood for democratic America, not plutocratic America, ... and had the liberal approach that appealed to the British mind".[20]

From a small community outside London, an "ordinary citizen" spoke of the "reality" of the Ambassador's friendship for her country; a "tower of strength" through "heartbreaking years". R. H. Tawney

[18] UN ECOSOC Documents E/27-31, adopted February 16 and 18, 1946; Department of State, *The Economic and Social Council of the United Nations* (Washington, U.S. Government Printing Office Publication 2600, 1946), pp. 1-74; memorandum from Alger Hiss to James F. Byrnes, January 18, 1946; *The New York Times*, February 12, 1946; *The Times*, February 12, 1946; JGW to James F. Byrnes, February 19, 1946.
[19] *The Times*, March 18 and 25, 1946; *The New York Times*, March 24, 1946.
[20] *Evening Standard*, March 19, 1946; *Sunday Express*, March 24, 1946; *News Chronicle*, March 25, 1946; *The New York Times*, April 2, 1946; *The People*, April 28, 1946; *New Statesman and Nation*, March 30, 1946; *Manchester Guarddian*, March 26, 1946.

would always remember the wonderful hours spent with Winant which had "been among the few bright of a sometimes gloomy period".[21]

During their month's stay in London, closing shop, the Ambassador and Mrs. Winant were feted at a series of dinners. At the government's farewell at Lancaster House, members of the Labor and Coalition Cabinets heard urbane Anthony Eden describe the event as sorrowful and triumphant — sorrowful because they had met to say farewell to a great Ambassador and to a loyal friend; triumphant because Winant could look back upon an Embassy which had few parallels and which was nowhere surpassed in the recorded history of their two peoples.

He came to us in a dark hour in that winter of '40-41; while always 100 per cent American, watchful and mindful of his country's interests, . . . we knew him at once for a friend. From the first, he had our confidence . . . . There is no man on this earth with whom I had rather work in such an ordeal, in so searching a testing time, as John Gilbert Winant. Nothing but the highest standard of service would ever satisfy him — he worked much too hard — if he had had his way, he'd have worked the Foreign Secretary of this country much too hard also. Patience and humor, modesty and integrity, . . . above all, a passionate devotion to the task at hand. These things we grew to expect of him. No man was ever more thorough — nothing but the best would do.[22]

Two nights later, at the Mansion House, Churchill recalled that the Envoy had "been with us always, ready to smooth away difficulties and put the American point of view with force and clarity and argue the case with the utmost vigour, and always giving us that feeling, impossible to resist, how gladly he would give his life to see the good cause triumph. He is a friend of Britain, but he is more than a friend of Britain — he is a friend of justice, freedom, and truth." [23]

As Winant boarded the plane at Hurn Airport on May 4, 1946, he turned to surrounding newspapermen and remarked, "I arrived in the thick of the storm and I'm leaving it in sunshine".[24]

In July, 1946, fifteen months after the death of Roosevelt, Congress finally met in joint session to pay tribute to the late President. Winant

[21] Phyllis Huxtable to JGW, April 23, 1946; R. H. Tawney to JGW, April 26, 1946.
[22] Taken from printed transcript of radio addresses at "Farewell dinner to Mr. J. G. Winant at Lancaster House", April 23, 1946, in author's possession.
[23] *The Times,* April 26, 1946.
[24] *The New York Times,* May 5, 1946.

gave the only address of the day, which, typically, he completed minutes before he left his hotel. He recalled Eleanor Roosevelt's suggestions that, in view of the unusual delay of the memorial, he should note that as time passed the perspective of what a man lived by was probably more important than the actual things he did. New situations necessitated new answers and no one could apply the same theories or exact methods. "The background of a man's thinking and acting is at all times a living thing", Mrs. Roosevelt had written. She hoped that Winant would in some way touch upon this thought for "it might help a lot of progressives who are feeling rather lost and friendless at the present time".[25]

Winant noted to the assembled dignitaries that the final estimate of the late President would be made years later, by men who would judge them all, not only the Chief Executive. Turning to Lincoln, the former Ambassador recalled his Annual Message to Congress in December 1862, in which the Civil War leader remarked: "We cannot escape history. We of this Congress and this administration will be remembered in spite of ourselves. No personal significance, or insignificance, can spare one or another of us. The fiery trial through which we pass, will light us down, in honor or dishonor, to the latest generation."

In a voice that cracked, he recalled that many in the room had assumed responsibility at Roosevelt's urgings, sat in council with him, or had watched him in "the great trial which was his life". A man who did not believe in abstractions but in free human beings, he loved mankind and won the confidence of people throughout the world.

He was brave. There is no main in this room — not those who saw him in the weakest moments of a frightful illness — not those who saw him in the most terrible moments of the war — there is not one of us who can say that he saw Franklin Roosevelt afraid.

. . . .

At a time when it was intellectually unpopular and politically dangerous to face the facts, he faced them. Neither the initial indifference of many among our people upon whose understanding he must have counted, nor a campaign of personal vilification in certain sections of our press rarely equalled in any country, deterred him. He carried the distasteful burden of an unpopular awakening and brought the people, not of his own country only, but of the democratic world, to see their danger while yet there was

[25] Eleanor Roosevelt to JGW, June 25, 1946; Maurine Mulliner diary, entry for July 1, 1946.

time — how little time — to save themselves and save the world they lived in.[26]

Winant recalled that Roosevelt's leadership had altered history in two great crises — he restored and strengthened the confidence of the American people in 1933, and saved Great Britain in 1940 by his courage and decisive action. He dared to hope, in the darkest years of the depression, and during the blackest years of the war, in new worlds of peace. In his concluding words, he maintained that, "Whatever verdict history writes down; this much we know who knew him — that he was a man! God give us heart and will to take this nation as he left it — not only powerful, not only rich, but young and hopeful and confident and believing and strong — God give us heart and will to take this nation forward as he meant to take it to a new, more daring future, a new world of peace." [27]

---

[26] July 2, 1946 issues of *The New York Times, New York Herald Tribune,* and *Evening Star* of Washington, D.C.; mimeographed copy of address by Winant, issued by the United States Delegation to the United Nations on July 1, 1946, in author's possession. Also, Roy P. Basler (ed.), *The Collected Works of Abraham Lincoln* (New Brunswick, Rutgers University, 1953), p. 537.
[27] *Ibid.*

CHAPTER XVI

"THROUGH HARDSHIP TO THE STARS"

Upon his return to the United States in May 1946, Winant parried reporter's questions concerning the discouraging results of the Paris Conference of Foreign Ministers. Privately, he felt that the coordination and good will of the war years had disappeared; in the turbulent aftermath of the conflict the pressures from without that had united the people had vanished along with trust and mutual respect.[1]

Two months earlier, Winston Churchill had captured headlines as he made a triumphal tour of the States. After receiving an honorary degree from Westminster College in Fulton, Missouri, he threw the nation into heated debate when he called for a military association of the United States and Great Britain to stem the tide of Russian expansionism, and to oppose appeasement. The "Iron Curtain" which had gradually descended upon the European continent, separating Russian-dominated Europe from the Western democracies, was not what Churchill had fought for during the war.[2]

While joining in the tribute to his wartime comrade, Winant disapproved of a British-American alliance to counterbalance Russian control and expansion. He viewed Anglo-American endeavors as embracing "cooperation to secure peace and prosperity on a world-wide basis — not collaboration for selfish purposes", and insisted that Churchill's proposed alliance would do more harm than good, for it would lead to suspicion and antagonism in other countries. He preferred "a world-wide application of the idea of mutual aid — a universal good neighbor policy", through the United Nations.[3]

The disputes which raged through four weeks of the Second Session of the Economic and Social Council at Hunter College illustrated the cleavages emerging in the parent organization. Consuming the greatest amount of time, and stimulating the most intense emotional

[1] *The New York Times*, May 6, 1946; JGW to Lt. Gen. A. C. Wedemeyer, May 30, 1946.
[2] *The New York Times*, March 6, 13 and 16, 1946.
[3] *Ibid.*, March 31, 1946.

fervor, was the 215-page report of the Special Committee on Refugees and Displaced Persons. The Soviet bloc unsuccessfully sought to deny to the International Refugee Organization authority to care for political dissidents outside their countries of origin. This position, together with other amendments seeking to restrict the authority of the new Organization, were rejected by a Council majority at the behest of American and British delegates.[4]

Despite attempts at optimism in his report to the State Department, Winant could not refute the conclusions of a perceptive observer who insisted that during the previous eleven months the United Nations had not, in the words of the first article of the Charter, done much to "develop friendly relations among nations"; nor had it served as a "center for harmonizing the actions of nations". It had not done much to develop among the Big Five the unity on which the charter rested, nor had it been able to induce an agreement among these five on the meaning of the Charter. Nevertheless, the UN had helped to clarify the issues that divided Russia and the United States by providing a sounding board for their differences. It had started on a wide range of constructive work, and it remained the best immediate hope for preventing or repelling aggression. It was generally agreed that if attempts were made to write the Charter in May 1946 instead of June 1945, it "would have been destroyed by the suspicion engendered among the great powers since the end of the war".[5]

Spending four weeks on organizational problems at a time when human misery was so widespread and human need so pressing had been a difficult and at times discouraging discipline for Winant. Those close to him knew that he was unhappy and discouraged by the endless talk and slow progress of ECOSOC. Wherever he looked he found the world a troubled place. As he wrote to Ernest Bevin, it seemed so hard to get working on the constructive side in fields in which the Allied victors could be doing things together to ameliorate life for the underprivileged.[6]

[4] ECOSOC documents, Second Session, E/38, 50, 55, 56, 73, 74, 79, 80, 86-89, 92; *The New York Times,* June 1-22, 1946; Department of State, *The Economic and Social Council of the United Nations.* Report to the Secretary of State by the Honorable John G. Winant, U.S. Representative on the Council, July 15, 1946, p. 19. Hereafter cited as Winant, *Economic and Social Council.*
[5] James Reston in *The New York Times,* June 26, 1946; Winant, *Economic and Social Council,* pp. 1-19.
[6] JGW to Ernest Bevin, June 8, 1946; interviews with Maurine Mulliner, May 16, 1951, December 7, 1959, June 12, 1960; and with Thatcher Winslow, May 16, 1951.

At the Third Session of ECOSOC in September, the issue of shipping on the Danube engendered the greatest bitterness between the Soviet bloc and the United States, and stimulated Winant's decision to resign. By the end of the war, Yugoslav and Czechoslovak barges on the Upper Danube had fallen into the hands of United States military forces. Both countries requested the return of their barges, but to no avail. Confronted by the refusal of Soviet military authorities to restore free navigation on the Danube, Washington held on to the barges, contending that their disposition was only a small part of a broader problem. After fruitless negotiations, the Yugoslav and Czechoslovak Delegations requested ECOSOC to recommend that the United States restore their vessels.[7]

Having vigorously supported every move to strengthen the crisis-ridden economy in Europe, Winant was forced to the conclusion that an injustice was being done the Yugoslavs. Washington was using their barges as a leverage to settle a dispute with the Soviet Union. Inwardly he rebelled against a stream of policy directives emanating from others in the State Department which required him to defend untenable positions in the Council. Nevertheless, after enumerating the many occasions when his country unsuccessfully sought to insure free navigation on the Danube, Winant introduced an alternative resolution which recommended the convening in Vienna of a conference on Danube navigation.[8]

The Russian Delegate immediately launched a vigorous assault upon Winant. He accused the American of presenting an ultimatum and of "direct intervention in the internal affairs of countries which are directly concerned in Danubian shipping." The Soviet spokesman insisted that there was free navigation on the part of the Danube controlled by the Russian military, but cited Article 107 of the UN Charter as sufficient authority to warrant the Soviets in maintaining, without interference from the UN, such control over the Danube as they felt desirable.[9]

An unhappy Winant attempted to refute the charges of the Soviet Delegate when he explained that the United States was holding the barges "as an offset to American property which has been seized or nationalized and for which no compensation arrangements have yet

---

[7] ECOSOC documents, Third Session, E/97, 121, 193, 194.
[8] *The New York Times,* September 28, 1946; ECOSOC document, Third Session, E/192.
[9] *The New York Times,* September 28, 1946.

been made". His country fully intended restitution when the U.S.S.R. permitted unrestricted movement of vessels on the Danube. His remarks completed, Winant placed his elbows on the table in front of him and, with his head in his hands, moaned loud enough for surrounding advisors to hear him lament the "terrible remarks he had just made".[10] While delegates rejected the Yugoslav and Czechoslovak resolutions, 4 to 8, 6 abstentions indicated the weakness of the American position. Winant had failed to convince a majority that the United States had not resorted to threats or technicalities to deprive member States of their property. They adopted the American resolution 8 to 5, with 5 abstentions.[11]

Winant felt the need for decisive action to revive war-shattered economies and to raise the pitiful standards of millions of underprivileged, yet he found himself increasingly entrapped in enunciating positions he opposed. He was particularly distraught by his powerlessness, his lack of flexibility or independence of expression which obliged him to voice the sentiments of those in Washington with whom he found himself increasingly in opposition. Confrontations with State Department spokesmen had failed to budge them. Worried, furthermore, that his personal differences with official directives might result in behavior prejudicial to his country's policy objectives, Winant submitted his final resignation as a public servant. After ten years of foreign service he was again a private citizen.[12]

Relieved of his stultifying responsibilities to the State Department, the former Envoy should have been gay and carefree. Instead, the next months were harrowing ones for Winant. He was under pressure to a publisher to complete the first of a series of books on the Ambassadorship and to repay some of the debts he had accumulated over the years. Not only did he find writing a trying experience, but he was totally unprepared to pick up life as a private citizen. Fifteen years of intense and stimulating public service had kept him at a

[10] *Ibid.*; interview with Thatcher Winslow, May 16, 1951, an adviser to Winant at this session of ECOSOC.
[11] ECOSOC documents, Third Session, E/240; and E/101, 102, 104, 108-114, 117-120, 124, 126-128, 134, 135, 138, 148, 153, 160-162, 164, 166, 169-171, 176, 184, 203 and 243.
[12] JGW to Harry S. Truman, December 19, 1946; James F. Byrnes to JGW, December 21, 1946; Truman to JGW, January 2, 1947; *The New York Times*, January 3, 1947; interview with Thatcher Winslow, May 16, 1951, and with Lewis Lorwin, December 17, 1959.

high emotional pitch; he could not adjust himself to a lower-keyed routine of life.[13]

Unfortunately, no member of his family and few of his friends realized the depths of his despair. Winant's writing, proceeding at an excruciatingly slow pace, remained a tortuous struggle. A skilled assistant might have eased the pressure and made the future less foreboding. As a result, he no longer looked forward to his memoirs. Besides, his had never been the mental makeup for a diligent, persevering scholar. He was much too restless a soul, with a burning fire which could only be controlled and constructively channeled by active involvement in planning and directing for the social welfare of the nation and the world. Unfortunately, no such prospect came his way during the remaining months of his life. Close friends and associates mistakenly afforded him a peace and quiet which tended to suffocate and then obliterate his good judgement.[14]

Winston Churchill once vividly described the emotional impact of withdrawal from public life by an involved official.

The change from the intense executive activities of each day's work at the Admiralty to the narrowly measured duties of a counsellor left me gasping. Like a sea beast fished up from the depths, or a diver too suddenly hoisted, my veins threatened to burst from the fall in pressure. I had great anxiety and no means of relieving it; I had vehement convictions and small power to give effect to them. I had to watch the unhappy casting away of great opportunities, and the feeble execution of plans which I had launched and in which I heartily believed. I had long hours of utterly unwanted leisure in which to contemplate the frightful unfolding of the war. At a moment when every fiber of my being was inflamed to action, I was forced to remain a spectator of the tragedy, placed cruelly in a front seat.[15]

His nerves shattered, the tensions and anxieties no longer submerged by the excitement of a key public office, Winant fell into a deepening depression. Where he was formerly incisive and entertaining in the presence of a handful of people, he could not now transpose this manner to the written page. Fearful of affronting wartime friends and colleagues, his writing became far less vivid than his conversational portrayals; when informally entertaining an English newspaper

[13] Henry A. Laughlin to JGW, August 10, November 1, 1945, August 1 and 20, 1946; W. P. Watt to JGW, September 20, 1945; J. Bernard Teulon to JGW, January 20 and July 12, 1947; JGW to William J. Donovan, October 27, 1947; interview with Grace Hogarth, July 10, 1951.
[14] Entries in diary of Maurine Mulliner, December 7 and 21, 1946; interview with Grace Hogarth, July 10, 1951.
[15] *Washington Post*, April 14, 1949.

friend, he could recount an endless stream of fascinating stories involving Maisky, Gusev, Churchill and Eden, but the humorous and meaningful events would not find their way into his first and only book.

Prior to his resignation, Winant had spent an uncomfortable summer in Britain laboriously dictating his book. Although his secretarial assistant knew no shorthand, she had little difficulty with his excruciatingly slow pace, as he grumbled to himself before softly issuing a sentence or two. He hoped that his memoirs might regain him national renown and ease the imposing financial debt of some three-quarters of a million dollars. During this unhappy summer, the one-time teetotaler began to drink heavily. On more than one occasion he remarked, "I can't look myself in the mirror".[16]

Nervous and depressed, he required constant encouragement as he gradually realized that his work would not be the literary landmark he had originally projected. He needed family and friends nearby, to strengthen him, renew his confidence and assuage his restlessness. His feelings of insecurity plagued him anew as he mistakenly concluded that friends ignored him. Instead they left him alone for they feared to disturb his writing.[17] Mrs. Winant continued busy with her social activities; daughter Constance was in Lima, Peru with a gay, charming two-year-old boy who had never met his grandfather; young John was a student at Oxford, England, planning to marry his Swiss sweetheart in July; Rivington, the youngest, was back at Princeton seeking to adjust himself after three eventful years with the Marines in the Pacific. Returning to the theme of suicide, Winant felt it would be better if he killed himself, thus solving the many problems which seemed to grow more imposing with the passing weeks. He replied to his secretary's charge of cowardice with the comment that there was a right time and a wrong time for taking one's life. He would pick the right time.[18]

---

[16] Interview with Grace Hogarth, July 10, 1951. The amount of indebtedness was determined after reviewing Winant's financial records at the Roosevelt Library.

[17] Interviews with Eileen Mason, July 2, 1951; and with Grace Hogarth, July 10, 1951; Katherine S. Thompson to JGW, June 6 (1946 or 1947); Wallace Carroll to JGW, March 1, 1947; Katherine S. Thompson to author, June 2, 1960. Miss Mason and Mrs. Hogarth took Winant's dictation of the book in London and Concord, while Mrs. Thompson and Carroll did some editorial work on the manuscript.

[18] Interviews with Grace Hogarth, July 10, 1951; and with Maurine Mulliner, December 7, 1959 and June 12, 1960.

On New Year's Day 1947, King George announced the award of the honorary Order of Merit to Winant. Returning to London in mid-January to renew work on his book, the former Envoy journeyed to Buckingham Palace to receive the insignia. Upon entering the room where the monarch awaited him, the two shy men greeted each other as they had done six years before upon a windswept railway platform near Windsor Castle. Accepting the proffered box, the American murmured his thanks and absentmindedly slipped it into his pocket. Realizing that there should be something more to this ceremony, the King asked: "Don't you want to look at it?" Winant thereupon withdrew the package, handed it to Britain's royal head who opened it and displayed the award. At this moment the Queen entered the room greeting the guest with the remark: "You deserved it more than anyone." [19]

Reluctant to call upon friends for fear he might be intruding upon their lives, a morose Winant eagerly accepted an invitation from the Herbert Agars to spend an evening at the theatre. Afterwards, as the three wandered into the London streets, they were quickly surrounded by crowds emerging from other shows. Many recognized the tall figure who recalled for them memorable, smoke-filled mornings when an entire city came up out of shelters after a long night of brutal bombing to find a weary Winant walking fearlessly among them. A number of theatregoers pushed toward him to touch his coat gently and say, "Good evening, Mr. Winant". His caring had been felt and understood in Britain. In America, he was all but forgotten.[20]

By mid-February, the former Ambassador was back in the United States to fulfill an imposing obligation as Chairman of the Fourteenth Annual Brotherhood Week — to enlist "a million of our citizens . . . consciously to practise brotherhood in all relations which they sustain to one another". The crosscountry speaking schedule would have exhausted a vigorous young man. When he debarked from the plane in Dallas, Texas, the start of his itinerary, he found Arthur Coyle among the welcoming committee. The latter was shocked by his friend's appearance and nervous behavior. Early the next morning, when Coyle awakened his friend in the hotel room, Winant hurried to a dresser drawer from which he withdrew a small bottle of liquor and gulped down its contents. He explained that he needed this to

[19] *Manchester Guardian,* January 1, 1947; undated memo taken by Maurine Mulliner, as recalled by Winant. Also, *Washington Post,* January 17, 1947.
[20] Interview with Herbert Agar, July 11, 1951.

start off the morning. Coyle's pleas to cancel the trip and fly home for rest and medical attention fell on deaf ears. A fortnight later, a wilted Winant concluded the tour and collapsed in his Park Avenue apartment.[21]

Through the Spring months he gradually regained strength. Early in June, immediately after reading Secretary of State George C. Marshall's commencement address at Harvard University, which set the guideposts for the Marshall Plan to aid Europe, Winant dashed off an enthusiastic note. The Secretary's remarks, he felt, had "brought out in clear relief the contrast that we should always draw between our aims and what appears to be the present Russian policy — the contrast between unity and recovery on the one hand, and disunity and misery on the other." After his depressing experiences as United States Representative to ECOSOC, Winant was delighted with this turn of events and with President Truman's desire to avoid the pitfall of conditioning American aid. In his judgement, this was "the best speech on foreign relations since the war's end".[22]

Within days, Winant finally managed to complete work on the first volume of his manuscript. After a quick trip to Geneva to attend his eldest son's wedding, he returned to Concord to begin work on the second. Day after day, as he paced up and down the long, book-lined library, skirting piles of notes and wartime cables, he found it increasingly taxing to assemble his thoughts. Quickly tiring, he would select a Ruskin volume and read extracts to his British secretary, or gaze for hours upon the soft rolling hills which spread out from his home. When the pressure and tension became unbearable, he would escape down the road to the beautiful campus of St. Paul's School, to the memories of teaching days when he felt appreciated and needed. Turning slowly back toward home with heavy steps, he was forced to confront the reality of his writing chore. As a beautiful Indian summer came and departed, leaving the surrounding country-side in a wondrous blaze of colors, Winant frequently spoke of illness and fatigue as mental exhaustion and melancholia enveloped him.[23]

21 *The New York Times*, January 8, 1947; *Washington Post*, February 18, 1947; interview with Arthur J. Coyle, March 19, 1952.
22 JGW to George C. Marshall, June 7, 1947. Shortly before his death, Winant consented to become a member of the executive body of the Committee for the Marshall Plan to Aid Europe.
23 Interview with Eileen Mason, July 2, 1951; interview with Orol Mears, July 24-31, 1952; JGW to A. M. Schlesinger, Jr., October 30, 1947; Maurine Mulliner diary, entry for September 14, 1947; interviews on July 23, 1953, with Drs. James W. Jameson and C. H. Parsons of Concord. Dr. Jameson had been the family

On November 3, 1947, Winant arose at noon, but did not dress. Aimless and distant, he managed to inform his financial secretary that a copy of his book, *Letter From Grosvenor Square* would be bound that day and rushed to Concord in time to be picked up at the Post Office by 7:45 p.m. He gave instructions for a plane reservation to New York the following day, because he wanted to show the book to his wife and take care of some business errands.[24] Orol Mears brought dinner to his bedroom; the tray she removed soon afterward was untouched. Winant rose from the bed, left his chamber and wandered down the quiet hallway to young John's former room. From its window, lights could be seen twinkling on the rolling hills he loved so much; darkness had engulfed the shadows which earlier hovered about leafless trees. Years before Winant had said, "To the tiny valley I owe the sense of peace and to the rolling hills a sense of time."

Into a black Belgian automatic he inserted three bullets. Slowly he knelt on the floor, steadied himself with his left elbow on the chair and held the pistol against his right temple. In the living room below, Orol Mears heard a loud crash. Within a half hour, John Gilbert Winant was dead. *Letter from Grosvenor Square* was waiting for him at the post office, but he would never see it.[25]

---

doctor until the postwar years, while Dr. Parsons had been the last one to examine Winant while he was alive and functioning.

[24]   Interview with J. Bernard Teulon, July 23, 1953.

[25]   "Investigation of the death of John Gilbert Winant, 58 years old, of 274 Pleasant Street, Concord, New Hampshire. Investigation conducted by County Solicitor Raymond K. Perkins, Deputy Chief J. Edward Silva, Inspector Mark D. Casey, and Patrolman Daniel Abbot of the Concord Police Department." Also included were statements to the police by Orol Mears and Eileen Mason on November 3, 1947. Carbon copies of these reports are in the author's possession. Also, November 5, 1947 issues of *The Times*, *The New York Times*, and *Boston Post*; interviews with James Langley, August 11, 1952; with Frances Perkins, December 15, 1959; with John R. McLane, July 6-7, 1960; Maurine Mulliner to author, July 6, 1963.

BIBLIOGRAPHY

PRIMARY SOURCES

Robert P. Bass Papers, Baker Library, Dartmouth College, Hanover, New Hampshire.
> All of the correspondence cited in this volume as relating to Bass is to be found in this unusually lucrative, and ideally, arranged collection. During his productive and involved lifetime, which spans the first half of the twentieth century, Bass assembled tens of thousands of pieces of correspondence, memoranda, governmental reports and surveys, which give an invaluable insight into political, social and economic forces in New Hampshire as well as the nation.

Roger W. Drury, son of St. Paul's School Rector, Samuel S. Drury.
> Mr. Drury supplied copies of key correspondence between Winant and his close friend, Dr. Drury.

International Labor Organization, Washington, D.C.
> *Verbatim Record* of ILO Conferences, and *Minutes* of Governing Body Meetings (Private), during Winant's association with the Organization.

George H. Moses Archives, New Hampshire Historical Society, Concord, New Hampshire.
> A censored collection of former Senator Moses' letters, which is not unusually lucrative.

Diary and Memoranda of Maurine Mulliner.
> Miss Mulliner was a key staff member of the Social Security Board under Winant, and a personal secretary-adviser during his latter days in London and with the Economic and Social Council of the United Nations. She also made available Winant correspondence and records of the early days of the Economic and Social Council.

National Archives, Washington, D.C.
> Official records of Winant's Aero Squadron units during World War I, and unpublished manuscripts and material relating to the Air Service. Also, diplomatic correspondence between Washington and Geneva relating to the International Labor Organization, 1935-1940.

Oral History Office Collection, Special Collections Library, Columbia University, New York.
> Contains tape recorded interviews of a number of former friends and associates of Winant, such as Frances Perkins and Henry A. Wallace.

Franklin D. Roosevelt, Official File. F. D. Roosevelt Library, Hyde Park, New York.
    Correspondence of President Franklin D. Roosevelt.

Chester H. Rowell Papers, Bancroft Library, University of California at Berkeley.
    A former California progressive and newspaper publisher, Rowell records Winant's personal proposal to avert World War II at the last moment.

St. Paul's School Files, Concord, New Hampshire.
    Authorities made available survey reports by university researchers, school records, newspapers, and correspondence relating to Winant as student and schoolmaster.

State Department, Historical Office Files, Washington, D.C.
    Minutes of the 62 meetings of the interdepartmental Working Security Committee meeting in Washington, and diplomatic correspondence with Geneva and the London Embassy, while Winant was attached to the ILO and as U.S. Ambassador to Britain.

John G. Winant Collection, Franklin D. Roosevelt Library, Hyde Park, New York.
    Here is the key source of information concerning Winant. It contains thousands of pieces of correspondence, memoranda, official reports, legislative bills, campaign posters and leaflets, photographs, reprints of speeches, press releases and newspaper clippings involving Winant since his days as a legislator in 1917. This collection was supplemented by hundreds of invaluable letters, official reports, and diplomatic correspondence given the writer by friends and associates of Winant, which will soon become part of the collection at the Roosevelt Library.

John G. Winant, Diplomatic telegrams from London to President Roosevelt, Cordell Hull, Harry Hopkins, and others, 1940-1945.
    Copies of a few thousand of the more important diplomatic telegrams sent by Ambassador Winant from London, which he had reproduced in preparation for his projected memoirs on his London assignment. They are presently in the possession of the writer.

John G. Winant, Letters to his mother.
    Over 100 informative letters written by Winant while a student at St. Paul's and Princeton, as schoolmaster, and as pilot in France during World War I. They are on loan from Mr. Winant's children and from Mrs. Carol Riegelman Lubin.

INTERVIEWS

Theodore Achilles — Embassy staff member under Ambassador Winant in London.

Herbert Agar — political historian and Embassy staff member under Ambassador Winant.

Arthur J. Altmeyer — one of three members of the Social Security Board and Winant's successor as Chairman.

Clement R. Attlee — British Labor Party leader and Deputy Prime Minister in wartime coalition cabinet.

Albert S. Baker — political reporter for the *Concord Daily Monitor* during Winant's governorship.

Frank Bane — experienced state and federal administrator who played a key role in creating the social security organization under Winant.

Robert Perkins Bass — progressive Republican governor of New Hampshire, 1911-12, and vital force behind Winant's political victory in 1924.

Jacob Beam — Embassy staff member under Ambassador Winant.

Robert P. Bingham — legal counsel to Governor Winant, and subsequent Democratic candidate for Governor.

Thomas C. Blaisdell — American staff member of the International Labor Organization under Winant.

Wallace Carroll — newsman and Embassy staff member under Ambassador Winant.

Winston S. Churchill — British wartime Prime Minister.

John Corson — Assistant Executive Director, Social Security Board.

Arthur J. Coyle — close, wartime comrade and manager of Winant's oil wells in Texas.

Virginia Crawley — writer and Embassy staff member in London.

Dr. Spenser Douglas — classmate at Princeton college.

Anthony Eden — British Foreign Secretary during World War II and close, personal friend.

Dwight D. Eisenhower — Supreme Allied Commander in Europe during World War II.

P. Sargent Florence — British economics professor and adviser to Ambassador Winant.

William J. Ford — an unemployed youth hired by Governor Winant during the depression, and one of many sustained by Winant as a college student.

Felix Frankfurter — an interested observer of Governor Winant as Harvard University law professor and as a member of the United States Supreme Court.

Carter Goodrich — Columbia University professor, U.S. Labor Commissioner in Geneva, and Chairman of the ILO Governing Body.

Mary Healy Harley — young, idealistic secretary to Winant in Concord, Washington and Geneva.

David Harris — Stanford University professor and State Department representative on Working Security Committee in Washington.

Earl S. Hewitt — Deputy Secretary of State under Governor Winant.

Grace Hogarth — took Winant's dictation in London for his book, *Letter From Grosvenor Square.*

Ernest M. Hopkins — president of Dartmouth College when Winant was active in New Hampshire politics.

Edgar P. Hunter — New Hampshire state legislator who worked closely with Governor Winant and directed work relief programs.

Robert Jackson — state chairman of the New Hampshire Democratic party.

Dr. James W. Jameson — Winant's family physician in New Hampshire.

C. Wilfred Jenks — ILO international law adviser to Winant.

Ethel M. Johnson — Director of New Hampshire's Minimum Wage Labor Board; wartime head of the Washington office of the ILO.

De Witt C. Jones — permanent vice president of Winant's Princeton Class of 1913.

James M. Langley — publisher and co-owner of the *Concord Daily Monitor* with Winant.

Lewis Lorwin — American ILO staff advisor on economic affairs.

Carol Riegelman Lubin — American secretary to Winant during early ILO days and frequent correspondent.

John R. McLane — lawyer-son of a former New Hampshire governor, one-time legal counsel to Winant, and close friend of Bass.

Kingsley Martin — British author and editor of the *New Statesman and Nation.*

Eileen Mason — Embassy librarian and secretary to Ambassador Winant.

Orol Mears — shy English woman hired by Governor Winant as housekeeper, who remained with him until his death.

Charles C. Monie — schoolmaster at St. Paul's School.

Philip E. Mosely — Columbia University Professor; State Department representative on Working Security Committee in Washington; chief aide to Ambassador Winant on the European Advisory Commission.

Maurine Mulliner — working colleague and personal friend since social security days.

Dudley Orr — son of an early business and political associate in New Hampshire, and personally involved in a gubernatorial campaign.

John Pearson — a New Hampshire friend, subsequently appointed head of the Boston Regional Office of the Social Security Board.

Frances Perkins — President Franklin D. Roosevelt's Secretary of Labor and close working associate with Winant during Social Security and ILO days.

Edward J. Phelan — key ILO staff member since its origin; Deputy Director under Winant; Acting Director following Winant's departure.

Dr. James J. Powers — lone Democratic member of New Hampshire's Executive Council, 1931-32.

Clarence E. Rexford — schoolmaster at St. Paul's when Winant was a Princeton student.

Henri Reymond — key ILO staff member in Geneva.

Eleanor Roosevelt — wife of President Franklin D. Roosevelt.

T. T. Scott — headed Winant's Cabinet in the ILO.

Henry P. Seidemann — Brookings Institution staff member who undertook a number of surveys of New Hampshire.

Geoffrey S. Smith — a student of Winant at St. Paul's, who subsequently played an important role in his financial affairs.

Jack Tate — assistant general counsel, Social Security Board.

R. H. Tawney — British historian and frequent visitor to Ambassador Winant's London apartment.

J. Bernard Teulon — Winant's financial secretary in Concord.

Mrs. Constance R. Winant (now Mrs. Eppley) — the widow of Winant.

Frederick Winant, Jr. — younger brother of John Gilbert.

Thatcher Winslow — American aide to Winant on the Economic and Social Council of the United Nations Organization.

INDEX

STUDIES IN AMERICAN HISTORY

1. HEINZ K. MEIER: *The United States and Switzerland in the Nineteenth Century.* 1963. 208 pp. Cloth.   Glds. 18.—

2. JACK AUTREY DABBS: *The French Army in Mexico, 1861-1867.* A study in Military Government. 1963. 340 pp., 10 plates, map. Cloth.   Glds. 30.—

3. DAVID H. MAKINSON: *Barbados. A study of North-American— West Indian Relations, 1739-1789.* 1964. 142 pp., 6 plates. Cloth.   Glds. 22.—

4. ODIE B. FAULK: *The Last Years of Spanish Texas, 1778-1821.* 1964. 156 pp. Cloth.   Glds. 20.—

5. WILLIAM RAYMOND SMITH: *History as Argument: Three Patriot Historians of the American Revolution.* 1966. 207 pp. Cloth.   Glds. 26.—

6. MAXWELL H. BLOOMFIELD: *Alarms and Diversions: The American Mind Through American Magazines, 1900-1914.* 1967. 174 pp.   Glds. 24.—

MOUTON · PUBLISHERS · THE HAGUE

DATE DUE

DEC 0 8 2015	
4/26/22	

GAYLORD   PRINTED IN U.S.A.